Crafting Rural Japan

This book discusses the place of creative village policy in the revitalisation of rural Japan, highlighting how rural Japan is moving from a state of regional extinction to regional rejuvenation.

Using the case study of Tamba Sasayama in Hyogo Prefecture, where collective initiatives by local government and the role of the local traditional potters are invested in fostering an aura of creativity in the region, the book examines the complex social relations and the intertwining values of different actors to illustrate how a growing outlook on creativity, rurality, and rural creativity requires a renewed perspective on and of rural Japan.

Based on extensive field research, this book will be a valuable resource for students and scholars of Japanese studies, rural studies, and anthropology.

Shilla Lee is a Departmental Lecturer in Japanese Social Anthropology at the Nissan Institute of Japanese Studies at Oxford.

Japan Anthropology Workshop Series

Series editor: Joy Hendry
Oxford Brookes University

Women Managers in Neoliberal Japan
Gender, Precarious Labour and Everyday Lives
Swee-Lin Ho

Global Coffee and Cultural Change in Modern Japan
Helena Grinshpun

Inside a Japanese Sharehouse
Caitlin Meagher

Mental Health and Social Withdrawal in Contemporary Japan
Nicolas Tajan

Japanese Diaspora and Migration Reconsidered
Yvonne Siemann

Revitalization and Internal Colonialism in Rural Japan
Timo Thelen

Scandal in Japan
Transgression, Performance and Ritual
Igor Prusa

Crafting Rural Japan
Traditional Potters and Rural Creativity in Regional Revitalization
Shilla Lee

For a full list of available titles please visit: www.routledge.com/Japan-Anthropology-Workshop-Series/book-series/SE0627

Crafting Rural Japan

Traditional Potters and Rural Creativity in Regional Revitalization

Shilla Lee

Routledge
Taylor & Francis Group
LONDON AND NEW YORK

First published 2025
by Routledge
4 Park Square, Milton Park, Abingdon, Oxon OX14 4RN

and by Routledge
605 Third Avenue, New York, NY 10158

Routledge is an imprint of the Taylor & Francis Group, an informa business

British Library Cataloguing-in-Publication Data
A catalogue record for this book is available from the British Library

ISBN: 978-1-032-35367-8 (hbk)
ISBN: 978-1-032-35369-2 (pbk)
ISBN: 978-1-003-32654-0 (ebk)

DOI: 10.4324/9781003326540

Typeset in Times New Roman
by SPi Technologies India Pvt Ltd (Straive)

Contents

Illustrations

Figures

Maps

Tables

Acknowledgements

This book is the result of the efforts of many people I met in Tamba Sasayama. The more I think about their hospitality, the more grateful I am. They were kind and patient with my first attempts at a thick description. I am grateful to them for letting me be and for letting me in.

Out of respect for their privacy, I will not list the actual names of the ones I owe my debt in the field. They will be able to recognise the codename. First of all, I would like to express my deepest gratitude to W. He welcomed me into every corner of his everyday life, at his workshop and home, despite the fact that I was a complete stranger to him. I learned a lot from his decades-long career as a Tamba potter. But above all, I came to respect him for the sheer generosity of his spirit. Without X's hospitality in the early stages of my fieldwork, the year in Tamba Sasayama would not have been as fruitful as it turned out to be. He has done more than anyone else to promote his hometown, and I hope more people will notice his unheralded efforts. Y, a dear friend only a few dozen years older than me, introduced me to the village life of a female potter living in the hills outside Tachikui. Although fascinating and inspiring, many of her stories remain unwritten in this book. It is my hope that one day I will have the opportunity to meet her again. Finally, without Z's generosity, I would not have been able to experience the diversity of Tamba Sasayama. I owe him a lifetime of memories for taking me to countless ceramics exhibitions and tea ceremonies.

I cannot list them all, but there were many other wonderful people in Tamba Sasayama who kindly took the time to chat with me, including the City Hall staff, friends from the Wednesday pottery class, members of the Concierge Group, the staff of *Tamba tachikui tōjiki kyōdō kumiai*, and all the other potters I met.

I would like to thank my host institution, Doshisha University, where I stayed as a research associate during the fieldwork. I would like to thank Gregory Poole for always being supportive of my studies. Bruce White allowed me to share my preliminary findings with his undergraduate students, and Hiroi Akihiro helped with the logistical details of my visit.

I must acknowledge my friends who, despite not understanding what I was doing, helped with my research. Yoon and Adee miraculously arranged an appointment with a used car dealer to help me get a decent Toyota at an affordable price. I must also express my gratitude to the car for taking me to Tamba Sasayama's most remote areas. To see it end up in a junkyard was heartbreaking. I am also fortunate to have a wonderful colleague from my former workplace, Minkyung, who allowed me to join her group from Busan to attend the UCCN annual conference in 2017.

The research project is part of the 4th IMPRS ANARCHIE programme at the Max Planck Institute for Social Anthropology in Halle, Germany. I had the most supportive supervisor, Christoph Brumann, who read every letter and dot of my early drafts and provided the most practical and thoughtful comments. I am genuinely grateful to him for patiently guiding me to the very last page of my doctoral dissertation. I gained invaluable feedback from the Wednesday departmental seminar led by Chris Hann. The administrative team at the Institute provided me with the best possible environment to conduct my research. I thank Jutta Tuner for the maps used in early versions of this book. Brian Moeran provided insightful feedback on my initial research ideas. My closest allies have been my colleagues. They have been a blessing and perhaps what has ultimately remained as the fruit of my doctoral studies. Anu Krishna, Nikola Stefanovski, Sofia Lopatina, Adrià Moreno Gil, Milana Čergić, Ruben Davtyan, Pablo Ampuero Ruiz, Adrian Wesołowski, Julius Roch, Frank Rochow, Lisa Kröger, Carlo Diesterbeck, Floramante John Ponce, and Bada Choi. How could I have spent the time in Halle without them? I am glad to have been surrounded by such a jolly group of people. I will always remember Sascha's generosity. Sandra made the best soup out of leftovers.

I spent a magical year at the Sainsbury Institute for the Study of Japanese Arts and Cultures in Norwich, UK, working on this book. It was a privilege to dwell in the beautiful brick building next to Norwich Cathedral. I want to thank everyone, including Simon Kaner, Akira Hirano, Eugenia Bogdanova-Kummer, Ryoko Matsuba, Alison Miller, Kaoru Sakurai, Olivia Butler, Denisa Edwards, Phoebe Young, and many others who came across.

Support and love came from afar, but it was never short. I am grateful to my closest friend, Soyoung, for always being there when I needed a heartfelt conversation. Nari sent me cheerful messages, and her inspiring works always reminded me of my almost forgotten passions back in Busan. Yong was by my side throughout the entire journey of this book and has been the one I could lean on. And my family. At the bottom of all the work and mess I have created has been their warm understanding of what I do.

I was motivated to turn my doctoral dissertation into a book, in part, by the feeling that remained in me after my young and daring attempts to meddle in the "everyday lives" of others. The fieldwork was challenging, but not as tricky as the sense of debt that grew the longer I owed my intellectual adventure to the people I met. Anthropology is an odd discipline.

Technical Remarks

I use the modified Hepburn system for the romanisation of Japanese terms. Japanese names are written in the order of family name followed by given name. The names of my interlocutors are pseudonyms, except for the officially known figures such as politicians. I also modified certain aspects of individuals to prevent exposing their identities. A referendum during my fieldwork changed the municipality's name from Sasayama to Tamba Sasayama, as of May 2019. I use "Tamba Sasayama" to refer to the municipal district and "Sasayama" to refer to the central town areas near Sasayama Castle and Tamba Sasayama City Hall. For local government reports published before the name change, I reference them as sources of Sasayama City Hall. I use "Tamba" instead of "Tanba" based on the conclusion of a Concierge meeting where the Tourism Division decided on the former as the official transliteration (21 January 2019). During fieldwork, I found it challenging to use a recorder; hence, most of my interviews were hand-written.

Introduction

With the new normal life under the pandemic, YouTube has become a crucial channel through which we learn about distant places. An interesting feature is the live CCTV streams of cities around the world. The most popular video in Japan is the Shibuya Crossing in Tokyo. Being one of the world's most popular scramble crossings, it represents the cityscape of Japan that we find familiar from popular films, animations, and music. In the tight shot of the crosswalk with tall rectangular buildings in the background, large TV screens show commercial advertisements, and neon signs brighten the street 24 hours. Flocks of pedestrians are exhibited day and night. There is an endless influx of people, taxis, and bicycles.

While the city's vibrancy is captured effortlessly in the live-streaming cameras, distant places require attentive observation to sense their liveliness. *Inland Sea* (2018), a documentary film set in the coastal village of Ushimado in Oku district, Okayama Prefecture, is a visual record of a rapidly ageing and declining community.[1] Although the film does not use deliberate shots or interviews to depict an emptying town, there is a sense of loneliness and void in the background. Serenity and stillness are dominant throughout the film. Kumiko, a central protagonist, is an elderly woman in her eighties who offers a tour to the innermost areas of the town. Despite her cheerful personality, one cannot shake the impression that her daily lives must be monotonous like the film's black-and-white pictures. If the bustling crossroads and bright neon signs stage the post-war prosperity, the calm of the rural landscape seemed to reflect its backstage.

Scholarly interests in Japanese society no longer linger on the vitality of the post-war economic growth, examining the unique socio-cultural traits of the corporate culture or expanding middle class. They have shifted to social calamities of the post-1990s economic stagnation, realigning the regional focus to provincial areas of starkly ageing and declining population, which has, in fact, been a problem accruing over time with Japan's rise as the economic rival to the United States. Public concerns about the sustainability of peripheral regions have existed since at least the 1960s, through the discourse of *kaso chiiki* (too-sparsely populated region) that refers to an increasing outflow of rural residents to urban areas and *genkai shūraku* (marginal settlement) that

DOI: 10.4324/9781003326540-1

deals with the rapid ageing of the rural population (Lützeler et al. 2020: 1–2). The most recently popularised discourse that continues the debates about regional sustainability is *chihō shōmetsu*, literally meaning regional extinction, which derives from the 2014 Masuda Report that claim half of the nation's municipalities being at risk of disappearing within this century due to population drainage from provincial to metropolitan area. The documentary film, in this perspective, is not a simple panoramic view of a village life, just like the early village studies that tried to capture the holistic structure of local communities (Ryang 2004: 81–87); instead, it is a metaphoric reflection of a place neglected and left behind the development of a society mired by the ideology of growth.

However, concurrent with the sense of enervation prevalent in the distanced communities of seashores and inlands is an ongoing attempt to re-evaluate the very conditions of these areas. After rounds of the "lost decade" (*ushinawareta jūnen*), the disparity in the socio-economic conditions of the core – Tokyo and the metropoles – and the periphery – the rest – have become less stark, at least in the public imaginary. Amidst concerns about the economic and demographic circumstances that threaten regional sustainability is a widespread optimism from across institutions and media that depict provincial regions under a new light. The special issue of *Forbes* Japan, published in May 2019, a month that marked the beginning of the Reiwa era, covered over 30 pages of interviews of young entrepreneurs starting new businesses in provincial areas and highlighted key points that make the rural environment appealing. *Yohaku* (emptiness), a concept that conventionally denotes a negative conception of rural space as vacant and in lack of social activities, was reinterpreted in a positive tone, paired with the concept of *potensharu* (potential). There have also been scholarly endeavours to uphold a renewed perspective on declining peripheries, for instance, the Hope Studies (*kibōgaku*), led by Genda Yūji of the University of Tokyo's Institute of Social Science. The research group investigated how hope can be retrieved despite the dominant "sense of stagnation" from economic deflation, rising unemployment, ageing population, and decreasing rate of advancement to higher education, emblematic of the post-bubble era (Genda 2017: 103). Counter-intuitively, the fieldwork was set in a declining town community of Kamaishi in Iwate Prefecture, an area later hit by the March 11 earthquake and tsunami. Rather than dwelling on the chaotic situations in the region, the study showed how interpersonal connections could generate hope and foster community movements for regional revitalisation.

The spirit of community revival that Genda saw in Kamaishi was not particular to the town's social atmosphere at the point of his visit, but a lasting observation made from across Japan. A similar attempt to subvert the popular conceptions of rural lifestyle took place under the restricted social conditions of the COVID-19 pandemic. Yasutoshi Nishimura, the then minister of economic revitalisation, claimed that the high infection rate is "a good opportunity to promote regional revitalisation", as it would turn people's attention to less-populated areas outside of Tokyo.[2] Numerous news sources discussed the trend of "Corona Shift" and its influence on the Tokyoite's intolerance for condensed spaces where they consider "swap[ping] metropolitan life for the countryside".[3]

This reflects a particular spatial configuration of the hope discourse that preoccupies contemporary Japanese society. Kleist and Jansen argue that the discourse of hope emerges amidst "a widespread sense of crisis and a heightened sense of lack of political and ideological direction" (Kleist and Jansen 2016: 374; see also Miyazaki 2004). Hope has been the keyword that encapsulates the recent scholarly works of Japan's post-bubble social panorama, of which Genda's work (2017) is only one of many examples (Allison 2014; Furuichi 2017). In the introduction to a special issue published in *Contemporary Japan* in 2016, titled *Introduction: Reorienting Hopes*, Kavedžija delineates the widespread sense of enervation by the notion of hope. Citing the work of Japanese novelist Murakami Ryū, *The Exodus of a Country of Hope* (*Kibō no kuni no ekusodasu*, 2000), and the theoretical contribution on hope by Miyazaki Hirokazu, *The Method of Hope: Anthropology, Philosophy, and Fijian Knowledge* (2004), considered seminal works on the theme of hope in Japan (Allison 2014, 2015; Genda 2017; Leheny 2018), she defines the general sentimental tractions of contemporary Japanese society under economic and demographic crisis as "hopelessness", which in her definition, refers to the lack of social relation (see also Allison 2014). Hope has become one of the key rubrics that captures the struggles of everyday life amidst the widening social stratification, disintegration of communities, socio-environmental aftermath of the Fukushima nuclear disaster, and many more of Japan in its sobriety of the post-war economic prosperity.

While the discourse of hopelessness pervades the urban backdrop, the locus where hope is sought and believed to exist in its nascent form is situated in distant places. In Allison's analysis of the precarity of "post-post-war Japan", she refers to "the breakdown or liquidisation of the relationship between human time and capitalist value" as the fundamental cause to the prevailing sense of disconnectedness (Allison 2014: 118). The anxiety of being alone and socially isolated stretches throughout one's life course, and the wish to be cared for and remembered leads to the development of various public and private programmes that support one's social life and even life after death (Allison 2023). As she notes, contemporary Japanese society is marked by the sense of hopelessness and the struggles to regain: "For, if hope is the vision of the future in a state of becoming, I see signs of not only hopelessness but also of people struggling to make Japan a place where fewer will fall prey to precarious lives" (2014:18). The hope-scape of contemporary Japan, which focuses on the experience of hopelessness (i.e., *hikikomori* and homelessness), is located explicitly in urban sites such as net cafés, capsule hotels and city parks, implying a fundamental link between the sense of precarity and urban lifestyles.

This abstract quality of hope, discussed as in deficit within the urban landscape, becomes an object of analysis that can be grasped and studied in its wealth through its reference to peripheral space, or more specifically, to the "rural" peripheries. (Klien 2020; Love 2014). Allison (2014), towards the end of her monograph, shifts the focus of her analysis to areas directly affected by the disasters of the March 11th earthquake and tsunami. Watching young volunteers shovelling mud in devastated towns, she ponders whether a new form of belonging or connection might emerge in a country that has been described as a *muen shakai* (no relationship society). Resonating with Leheny comments on Genda's Hope Studies project, "hope suddenly seemed dependent on the periphery's ability to rebuild" (Leheny 2018: 182). His remark implies an important bedrock of Japan's current sentimental topography: an intimate relationship between the revitalisation of the national future and that of peripheral regions, or even of dependence of the former to the latter.[4] The Fukushima nuclear disaster has certainly raised awareness of this particular hope-scape of Japan. Despite the fact that post-war economic progress has amplified regional inequalities to an extent that "extinction" (*shōmetsu*) has become a buzzword that describe the fringes of metropoles, the policymakers, researchers, and grassroots activists are nonetheless invested in discovering the seed for a new future path from the rural peripheries (see Love 2014: 98). The agenda of Regional Revitalisation (*Chihō sōsei*), or the Local Abenomics, which the Abe administration put forward as one of the fundamental tasks for Japan's economic recovery, reflects the hopeful visions placed in the deeds of declining communities.

This book embarks on an ethnographic journey against the backdrop of this dynamic shift in public perceptions of rural peripheries. It seeks to add diversity to the prevailing discourse of hope in Japan, which frequently fixates on urban landscapes of hopelessness as the definitive discourse of the post-growth Japanese society. By examining how the rural space is envisioned as the potential ground for revitalised national, regional, and individual aspirations, my intention is to initiate a discussion that positions rural experiences as the main trajectory for comprehending a society grappling with the challenges of demographic and economic uncertainties. While rural locale and its internal issues have dominantly been seen as the residues of the urban-led developments, this book situates it as the main stage of societal changes. Perhaps one might question why "rural" periphery instead of other denominations such as "local" (see Ganseforth and Jentzsch 2022). I agree that under technological and transportational advancements, the boundary between urban and rural space is disintegrating. However, the term "local" can also restrict our understanding of the geopolitical disparity in a highly urbanised society like Japan. Although there are concepts such as "peri-urban" or "rurban" that denote the complexities of defining urban or rural, we cannot deny the material and symbolic quality of rurality that has served as a categorical basis for public spatial imaginaries. For example, Dilley et al. show how the motivation for young urbanites to move to depopulated (*kaso*) areas is not only a desire to escape the urban lifestyle, but also to settle down with a "rustic way of life" (Dilley et al. 2022: 7). It is difficult to conclude from his findings whether it was the "push" factor (i.e., urban precarity) or the "pull" factor (i.e., rural attractiveness) that caused them to relocate, but it seems clear that their ideas of peripheral destinations were specific and, in this case, rural.

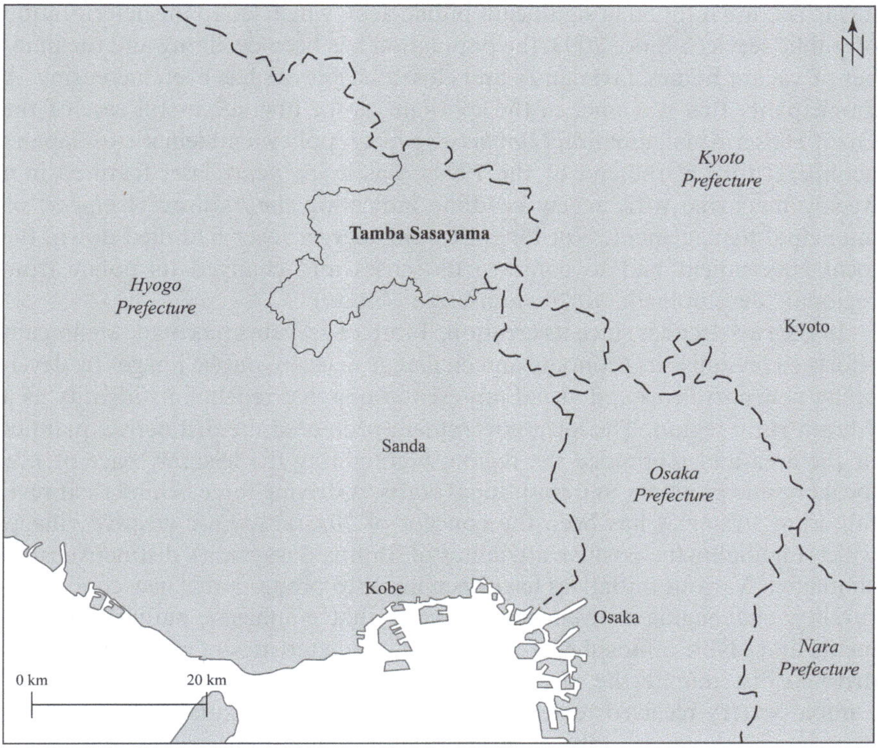

Map 0.1 Tamba Sasayama and Kansai regions.

Tamba Sasayama's case prompts us to explore the various initiatives that respond to the broader societal discourse of hope envisioned in the rural peripheries. The regional history of this modest municipality, from merger to revitalisation, is as much a reflection of the dynamic social changes in post-1990s Japan as it is of urban or industrial centres. The only difference is that it generates a collective sense of optimism that might seem naïve in the context of the latter.

Tamba Sasayama stands as one of many provincial municipalities confronting the challenges of dwindling and declining population and economic stagnation, with quintessential traits of Japan's rural areas, such as sprawling rice fields, a quaint city centre adorned with unpretentious shops, and unassuming customs like traditional folk dances, organic farming, and wild boar delicacies (Sasayama City Hall 2016; Kim 2016). The current district, located in Hyogo Prefecture, has a population of around 40,000 and was formed in 1999 by the amalgamation of four neighbouring towns. The initiative was primarily driven by the need to improve public services under the declining population and economic stagnation. However, the post-merger investments in public infrastructure resulted in significant public debt, which led to the deterioration of public services. Since 2003, the population has been declining and the number of vacant homes, farmlands, and closed businesses has been increasing. A municipality that was once in the spotlight as the first successful case of the Great Heisei Amalgamation (*Dai heisei gappei*) policy, emblematic of Japan's neoliberal turn at the end of the 1990s, was a few years later featured in a weekly magazine with a new headline indicating the "failure" (*shippai*) of municipal management. Not long after the merger fever had died down, the local government had to come to its senses and changed its policy from regional "development" to "revitalisation" (*saisei*).

In the two decades since its creation, Tamba Sasayama has made significant efforts to revitalise its economy and challenge negative public images by developing new narratives and visual representations that redefine its identity as a vibrant rural region. The local government promoted the distinctive qualities of the area and rebranded the region, highlighting the leisurely pace of life, local organic products, and traditional crafts. A driving force behind their revitalisation strategies has been the concept of *sōzō nōson*, or creative village, which highlights the positive attributes of Tamba Sasayama's distinctive rural character.[5] Various initiatives have been made to promote this new concept of rurality, challenging conventional notions that emphasise natural environments and idyllic atmospheres as defining characteristics of rural life. In this drive to disseminate the idea of rural creativity, the local craft culture of Tamba pottery received renewed attention. Its inherent qualities were being negotiated between its adherence to tradition and folkloric roots and a sense of creativity (*sōzōsei*), a much more universal value that appreciates craftsmanship as the cradle of human creativity.

The various scales of local responses and practices of rural hope are not so much concerned with material changes such as the introduction of digital technologies or investment in new industries, but with the internal struggles of native residents to redefine what it means to be "rural". Through their experiences of defining and redefining the new ideals of "rurality", this book attempts to reflect the transitional phase of post-growth Japanese society from a rural perspective. The value of this approach, as I will argue in detail below, is that it allows us to critically examine the gravity of societal hopes directed towards the rural periphery based on the lived experiences of local people rather than on the conceptual discussions of rural idealisation. The chapters explore different narratives and practices that create new rural representations in response to the growing appeal of the rural lifestyle to young urbanites seeking new hope in the rural periphery. In a society that is predominantly imagined as urban, shifting the spatial perspective on the problems of post-growth Japanese society from urban precarity to rural hope is itself an act of re-narration of current social problems from an alternative angle. To do this, we first need to understand how the rural discourses have changed within Japan's larger societal transitions from the post-war period.

From post-war, post-bubble to post-growth rurality

In his reflection on Japan's modernisation processes, Harootunian states that "the construction of memory thus became one of [modernism's] most principal and enduring forms of cognition" (Harootunian 2000: 25). The "symbolic vacuum" (Befu 1992: 43) created by the defeat of the Asia-Pacific war, as well as western cultural norms that pervaded Japanese private lives, contributed to the gradual loss of a sense of "being Japanese" (Befu 1984: 66; see also Ivy 1995). Increased production of local heritage (Ehrentraut 1995) and the popularity of *Nihonjinron* (theory of Japanese national character) during the post-war years demonstrate the public desire to reclaim lost Japanese culture (Sugimoto 1999).

Furusato, which translates as hometown, old village, or native place, is a spatial configuration of these public interests. Although the term has different connotations depending on the contexts (Robertson 1988: 484; Solomon 2017: 14–23), it is often understood as a discussion of remote communities as a repository of nostalgic sentiments and pre-modern ways of life (Dusinberre 2013: 48–52, see also Moon 2002: 240–41; Graburn 1983). Rural space is endowed with "affective capacity" (Robertson 1998: 115), signifying unadulterated traditions and a heartland for people who yearn for lost values "dis-membered by defeat in war, and more recently, by the uncertainties of an international economy" (Robertson 1988: 514; see also Harootunian 2008; Ivy 1995: 70–71). Rural Japan appealed not only for its picturesque images of thatched-roof houses or a natural backdrop contrasting with the bustling metropolis, but also for "the good life, wholesomeness, and moral values" (Creighton 1997: 242). As Robertson notes, "imagination of the past [was] the construction of the future" (1988: 513). *Furusato* is still a powerful rhetoric used in commercial products, such as travel packages, food products, and regional policies (Dilley et al. 2022; Love 2007; McMorran 2014; Moon 2002; Reiher 2020).

However, the recent social climate calls a renewed understanding of the dominant *furusato* discourse. There is an emerging debate about how Japan is approaching the end of modern expansion and undergoing a "post-growth" (Chiavacci and Hommerich 2017), "post high growth" (Chiavacci et al. 2020) or "post-postwar" (Allison 2014) transitions, with the emergence of a new zeitgeist to replace the lingering ideology of growth. The economic turmoil of the early 1990s has been continued for decades. Concerns about Japan's demographic future have replaced the myth of growth and the fascination with the Japanese corporate model. The government's efforts to combat the pessimistic outlook initially appeared to be working, as evidenced by the structural reforms of the Koizumi administration in 2001–2006 and the Abenomics of the Abe administration in 2012–2020. However, the sense of optimism generated by such radical neoliberal measures was short-lived. Social inequalities, such as the urban and rural divide, the rise of part-time employment, and the persistence of traditional gender ideologies that denigrate the role of women, have only continued, or even deepened. The "lost decade" no longer holds the critical edge in the discussions of contemporary Japanese society, as it has become the status quo of this century. Economic stagnation is not a liminal phase, but a permanent condition that epitomises Japan in the contemporary world. Analyses of depopulation and other indicators of social inequality suggest that Japan faces the risks and uncertainties of the second modernity (Chiavacci and Hommerich 2017: 297). As a result, people are becoming less ambitious about their careers or life trajectory, or, as Gagné puts it, "risk averse" (Gagné 2020: 458) and "defensive, clinging to tatters of the previous system" (2020: 474).

The post-bubble instability is making the moderate middle-class life course increasingly difficult to pursue and is recalibrating people's life goals and values. According to Mathews, young people in Japan today prefer a simple lifestyle – "*heibon no shiawase* (ordinary happiness)" – to the conventional urban life of "the old *sararīman/sengyō shufu* model family" (2017: 237; see also Klien 2020).[6] Those willing to take the risk of living independently and pursuing individual happiness are looking for alternative ways of life. One notable phenomenon is the physical relocation of one's livelihood to an entirely new environment where one can rebuild one's life courses – lifestyle migration (see Kato 2015; Kawashima 2021; Kweon 2011; Ono 2015; Suzuki 2015). Consciously rejecting traditional life priorities such as household (*ie*) inheritance or economic achievement, they see "self-exploration" (Suzuki 2015: 235; see also Ono 2015: 614–15) as the new goal of their lives.

While previous discussions of individuals seeking to change their life trajectories have focused on transnational migration, more recent conversations have highlighted domestic examples of this phenomenon, such as people moving to rural areas in search of a more purposeful existence (Dilley et al. 2022; Klien 2016, 2019, 2020; Lewerich 2020; Obikwelu et al. 2017; Reiher 2020; Rosenberger 2017; Takeda 2020: 196). Takeda notes that urban-to-rural migrants come from a variety of backgrounds, including part-time workers, musicians, and activists, but they all share an experience of living at the "outliers of typical modern group structures" (2020: 209; cf. Klien 2020: 179). They see the countryside as a place where they can create a new or healthier way of life, with far more autonomy and freedom than they would have in the city. According to Manzenreiter et al., the phenomenon is a "marker and critique of efficiency goals and over-optimization of the neoliberal self" (2020: 299). Rural peripheries become "unexpected sites of hope in a nation mired in downturns" (Love 2014: 95). Drawing on small-scale grassroots activities led by rural residents, Love shows how "idealized visions of rural community solidarity" provide the ground for a group of academics, activists, and government officials to discuss the "post-growth" Japan (2014: 98).[7] Matanle (2020) also shows how post-growth changes are experienced in everyday rural life, looking at a community on a remote island that promotes well-being, environmental friendliness, and cultural diversity.

According to Klien, this urban-to-rural migration is a sign of Japan's post-growth transition, reflected in the re-conceptualisation of the rural-urban dichotomy of rural backwardness and urban progress (Klien 2020). The nostalgic charm of the countryside, as seen evident in the *furusato* discourse, loses its appeal as its relational counterpart of the urban cityscape no longer embodies Japan's economic prosperity or modern development, but precariousness of capitalist lifestyle (Allison 2014). Under the liquidisation of urban lifestyle, which increasingly represent unstable part-time workers rather than salaried employees guaranteed a lifetime employment, the gaze towards the distant villages reflects not only the fear of losing Japanenseness under the affluence of consumer culture, but also the desire to escape a sense of alienation from the neoliberal orders of life. The rural landscape, supposedly remote and detached, is re-imagined, from the "nostalgia-laden images of rustic life" to the "progressive [arena] for dynamic venture entrepreneurs, IT experts, and high-quality craftsmanship" (Klien 2020: 75). Rural space, once admired for its romantic ambience or idyllic images of nature, is now attracting outsiders as a "ground for experiment" (2020: 10): "the low living cost, available space, and social capital … offer creative individuals an environment to try out their ideas in the form of projects, business start-ups, and other experimental forms" (2020: 10). Such trends may require a further scrutiny in terms of their general impact on wider social and ethnic strata, but they nevertheless reflect the new social imaginaries reflected in rural space.[8] Similarly, there have been attempts to reassess the long-held notion of rural space as the periphery of mainstream (urban) society (Traphagan 2018, 2020; Manzenreiter et al. 2020). Traphagan suggests using "neo-rural" to capture "something distinctive about lifeways at the periphery as compared to urban areas" (2018: 162), and Manzenreiter et al. show that studies of a new rural sociality should be about "reconfiguration rather than decline or stagnation of rural areas" (2020: 5) and suggest using "rurality" as an analytical term to avoid simplistic urban-rural relationship and "conjure … meshes of different textures … which is creating a much more complex pattern" (2020: 12).

In addition, the state and local governments are making conscious effort to reshape rural representation in ways that respond to the growing desire for an emancipation from the urban grid of competition and conspicuous consumption. They have incorporated these needs into their public programmes. The Regional Revitalisation (*Chihō sosei*) initiative of 2015 and the Community Cooperative Support (*Chiiki okoshi kyōryokutai*) programme of 2009 are examples of policies that explicitly aim to revive the dwindling rural workforces by mobilising the dispirited young urbanites in the city. The hope of times is increasingly seen to lie in the rural landscape, within the framework of a highly urbanised society. The search for a new national trajectory takes place against a rural backdrop.

Fluctuating notions of rurality reflect the broader shift of values in a society where stagnation has become the status quo. The new rurality discourse is a product of the specific socio-economic climate of the post-1990s in which the economic miracles of the previous generation have become a bitter memory of the past. The public image of rural space and lifestyle is being re-imagined against the backdrop of a widespread sense of precarity. If enervation is the dominant sentiment of the urban view of the post-growth social issues, vitalisation or "re"-vitalisation is the dominant keyword of the rural perspective. However, it is important to examine the implications of changing rurality from the experience of rural natives in order to avoid another discourse of rurality based on rural idealism.

Rurality as a focus over locus

The official definition of "rural" in the OECD country note for Japan is that "rural areas refer to all non-urban areas" (OECD Country Note 2020: 1). Rural social issues are less discussed in the context of ruralisation than in the context of urbanisation. We tend to think of the urban space as the locus of the divergent social values of contemporary society, while the rural space is latecomer adapting to urban-led changes. Rural actors are rarely seen as the executors of their own social problems, but as scapegoats of urban planners. As scholars have argued, the shift in research focus from rural to urban areas underlies our tendency to see (post)modern problems as inherently urban (Creed and Ching 1997: 6–12; see also Chio 2017a; MacClancy 2015).

In rural geography, discussions of rurality are concerned with the symbolic aspects of rural space. Cloke notes that while the so-called cultural turn has been criticised for "deflect[ing] rural studies away from its fundamental core of concern for socio-economic changes", its intellectual tide provides valuable insights and opens up possibilities for discussing issues outside established topics such as "reconceptualizations of nature-society relations", "rural experience and imagination", "symbolic texts of rural cultures", and "mobilities and fluidities (rather than the fixities)" (Cloke 2006: 23). Murdoch and Pratt (1993: 423) also advocate postmodernist writings for "explor[ing] how rurality is constructed and deployed in a variety of contexts" rather than "trying to pin down a definition of rurality or the rural". In this context, Halfacree proposes a new method that looks at "rurality-in-discursive-motion" to understand the process of how rural space is created (Halfacree 2006: 47). Given the emerging discourses of the post-productivist countryside, it is becoming increasingly important to grasp the complexity of rural space where there are multiple actors and narratives.

This book argues that critical discussions of rurality need to be reinvigorated as it has more to offer. The growing conflation of urban and rural space is precisely why rurality deserves attention (Cloke 2006: 19). It offers a vantage point from which to discuss the blurred boundaries of a rural space undergoing change, with increased population mobility and the dominance of urban values (Halfacree 2006: 56). Mormont, for example, identifies a particular aspect of rural space that has become a refuge from urban misery, with an increasing number of individuals, groups, and institutions identifying it as "a model of an alternative society inspiring a social project that challenges contemporary social and economic ill" (Mormont 1987: 18). The construction of nature parks in rural Belgium demonstrates how the rural world can represent an alternative way of life: "a more convivial form of sociability than in the city, different work relationships and a different relationship with nature" (1987: 11). Another prominent example is the recent boom in organic farming practices in urban areas where rural values are objectified and valorised as a distinct lifestyle (Cody 2018; Ding et al. 2018; Klein 2009). As Woods notes, "'rural' continue[s] to have a very clear and powerful meaning for many people" (Woods 2011: 8).

The challenge, however, is to capture the changing values of rurality without dismissing the locally specific ways in which they are perceived in everyday languages and practices. Woods suggests borrowing the analytical framework of anthropology (e.g., Ingold 2004) to examine how "rural experiences are felt, sensed, intuited through bodily actions and performances" and to bridge discourses of rurality and everyday social practices (Woods 2010: 835; see also Edensor 2006; Carolan 2008). While I agree that anthropology's methodological approach of engaging directly with the locals and the landscape, on foot (Ingold 2004) or otherwise, is crucial to the study of rurality as an experienced reality, this has to be accompanied by a clarification of the notion of rurality within its disciplinary context.

The study of rural societies has historically been the "default focus" (Koh et al. 2021: 296) of anthropologists, in part due to the discipline's mandate to study distant and unfamiliar places. According to Sorge and Padwe (2015), village is a spatial category that is closely linked to the methodological history of anthropology. As a conceptual and spatial boundary, village has often been treated as a way to capture the holistic perspective of human life and social structure. Similarly, the dominance of village studies in the early post-war anthropology in Japan owed more to the dominant disciplinary trend of the time to search for the cultural and structural essence of Japanese society in traditional communities than to an interest in revealing the social or ethnic diversity of village societies (Ryang 2004: 81–87). This explains why village studies were quickly denounced in the face of emerging discourses on globalisation and multi-sited approaches (see Marcus 1995).

There is a crucial distinction to be made between the traditional anthropological study of village society and the study of social and cultural implications of rural space through an anthropological lens. In this book, rural social issues are discussed as a web of discourses, images, and temporalisations of the rural, rather than as a method to study a distant community in a rustic and pastoral setting. While village has a strong connotation of an isolated community with homogenised values and social structures, rural society is a broader analytical framework that addresses not only village contexts, but also contemporary societal issues as seen through rural trajectories. To clarify conceptually, I distinguish the study *in* and *of* a rural space. Counter-intuitively, I borrow Hannerz's insight in his critical account of urban anthropology. In his book *Exploring the City: Inquiries Toward an Urban Anthropology* (1980), he critiques the loose conceptual understandings of urban space in existing works and states that to bring anthropological perspectives and methods to a city is not enough as urban anthropology: there must be a "ponder[ing] over what is urban in urban anthropology, and what is anthropological about it" (1980: 3).

> ...all cities are multi-domain social structures; our position here is that an anthropology which attempts to be *of* the city rather than merely *in* the city should try to deal systematically with precisely this fact. To do justice to both the differentiation and the coherence of the urban social structure, in other words, we should investigate the forms and degrees of interrelationship among roles, not only within but also – in fact, particularly – among domains
>
> (Hannerz 1980: 106)

His conceptualisation of the urban is less about the urban space as a "locus" than as a thematic "focus" of an anthropological inquiry (Hannerz 1980: 3–4).[9] Different forms of social relations and practices, as well as their geographical characteristics, should be taken into account in our understanding of the urban.

Rural space can be studied using the same logic. By adopting a perspective of *focus over locus*, rural anthropology can extend the academic study of rural issues beyond a village space, challenging dominant perceptions that see rural issues as "whatever [that] is leftover after the urban has been identified" (Vasantkumar 2017: 370; see also Creed and Ching 1997: 4–5). Recent scholarship on rural societies has emphasised the need to explore the complexities of rural social issues, intertwined with broader social themes. As MacClancy notes, "[j]ust because cities concentrate people who continue to produce new and unexpected forms of social organization does not mean rurality becomes the emptying home of a tired traditionalism" (2015: 2). Looking at local activities that demonstrate the "refusal of 'the rural' to vanish" (2017b:361), Chio proposes to "[take] the rural seriously" (2017b: 362) in order to unravel the "multiple discourses and desires concentrated around the idea of the rural in the contemporary world" (2017a: 420). In support of her approach, Stasch suggests studying the rural space as a "relational entity" that has links with other kinds of particular forms and values, "not just between villages and cities as spaces, but between larger social, economic and ideological formations interlocked with those spaces" (Stasch 2017: 443; see also Stasch 2010: 53–55).

I contend that to study rurality is to interrogate the perception and experience of contemporary social issues from a rural perspective. Following Chio's suggestion to examine "rural" (as much as "urban") as a category of "experienced realities" (Chio 2017b: 362), I observe the intricacies and dynamics of changing rural values as they are expressed and perceived in the everyday contexts. In doing so, I highlight the complex and multifaceted nature of rural societies, as opposed to a homogenous village society; in particular, how "the coexistence of multiple orders is often lived by rural persons in the form of ambivalent, contradictory emotional structures of simultaneous desire and repulsion, or pleasurable participation and painful deprivation, in relation to other spaces or the coexisting alternatives of their own space" (Stasch 2017: 448). For instance, Chio's study of the ethnic tourism industry in a rural village in Guizhou Province, China, shows how conflicting ideas of rurality shape the local lives and aspirations (Chio 2017b). Villagers project a traditional rural lifestyle onto urban visitors, highlighting the perceived backwardness of their community with the aim, ironically, of transitioning to a more modern way of life. They believe that the most effective means of achieving this goal is to abandon the modern aspects of village life and embrace and promote its backwardness, or as Stasch comments, by "seek[ing] economic and moral betterment, a kind of progress, through the romance of rural rusticity" (Stasch 2017: 452).

When societal hopes for a better future are increasingly projected through the rural space, studies *of* rural society, rather than *in* rural society, are needed. Tamba Sasayama's regional revitalisation efforts and the promotion of the new hybrid concept of rurality offer a nuanced context for this attempt. The stories in the chapters shed light on different practices and perceptions of Japan's post-growth transition, from the ways in which people's lives and dwellings are intertwined with the new concept of rurality – rural creativity – an idea that implies neither complacency nor a complete abandonment of established values associated with the countryside. As Stasch notes, "we are never studying just a space, but a spatial form as a mediation of wider arrays of human structures" (Stasch 2017: 433).

Regional revitalisation as regional re-conceptualisation

How then can we capture the locals' experiences as they go about their lives within these dynamic changes in rural discourses? How are the abstract qualities of space transformed into matters of place? To capture the changing perceptions and experiences of rurality, I look at the process of regional revitalisation for two reasons: methodological and analytical. Methodologically, the recent surge of revitalisation movements across the country, encompassing both institutional and grassroots efforts, provides an appropriate framework for investigation. It sets the boundaries within which one can observe the growing anticipation of the restoration of national hope from the peripheries. Analytically, the process of regional revitalisation involves more than the rebuilding of physical infrastructure; it also involves the reshaping of local perceptions and identities. By examining this process, I aim to shed light on the broader implications and motivations behind the rise of new rurality.

Public discourses on regional revitalisation have mushroomed since the late 1970s and even more so in the 1990s, with growing concerns about regional economic disparities and rural depopulation. The extent to which it has taken hold can be seen from the variety of terms used to describe it. Depending on the size of a community, it has been implemented at various scales, from *machi*, which refers to a town, to *mura* (village), *toshi* (city), *chiiki* (area), and other regional designations. The action of *saisei*, meaning revitalisation, has also been replaced by others such as *zukuri* (making), *okoshi* (rising), *kasseika* (invigorating), and *shinkō* (promoting).

Scholars have pointed out how dominant the self-help ideology is in the post-war regional revitalisation movement. Moon cites the 1980s and the creation of the Third Comprehensive National Development Plan as the beginning of official narratives that emphasise the role of autonomous and self-reliant residents in revitalising their hometowns (1977–1983) (Moon 2002: 223; see also Knight 1994: 646). This contemporary trend of self-help ideology in regional revitalisation has been criticised as a neoliberal strategy that seeks to transfer the state's responsibility for maintaining a basic standard of living to local governments and individuals (Dilley et al. 2017; Love 2010, see also Mathews 2017). Others argue that the growing number of regional revitalisation initiatives is the result of party politics. Sasaki notes that since at least from the mid-1950s, the Liberal Democratic Party (LDP) has been "recycl[ing]" the old revitalisation policies and reinventing them in new terms to appeal to rural voters (Sasaki 2015; see also Rausch 2016).[10]

Looking at the everyday lives of rural residents, however, we can see that local efforts at regional revitalisation are not only driven by state policies or economic and political interests, but also by a desire to restore community solidarity and identity (Matanle 2020: 223; Moon 2002: 229). Various forms and types of grassroots activities have played an important role in the development of local tourism, with research findings highlighting cases involving traditional crafts (Han 1995; Hwang 2016), heritage projects (Ehrentraut 1993; Ertl 2007; Foster 2011), performances and festivals (Rausch 2008; Robertson 1987), natural resources (McMorran 2008, 2014; Moon 1986), and local foods (Knight 1994; Love 2007).

Although many community-led initiatives are taking place at the grassroots level, it is important to recognise that these efforts often prioritise conforming to wider public views on the area, rather than the specific needs and aspirations of the residents themselves. In other words, there are power imbalances in the ideas and methods that drive local efforts for regional revitalisation. Robertson's claim that provincial areas are "imagined communities" is a good starting point for considering this issue (Robertson 1988: 513). According to Moon, there is a distinctive feature of the *muraokoshi* (village revitalisation) initiatives that have taken place since the late 1970s:

> … the representation [of rural society and culture] is often based upon certain selected images of rural life rather than its reality. What is attempted in many *muraokoshi* (village revitalization) movements … amounts to a reconstruction of the countryside in a way that matches this imagery.
>
> (2002: 241)

When we examine regional revitalisation, we discuss not only of how rural social systems or infrastructures have improved, but also of how an area is viewed and shaped in the public imagination, based on public discourses. The physical environments of rural communities continue to be significantly shaped by metropolitan expectations and experiences (Creighton 1995: 468; see also Brumann and Cox 2009: 8). In terms of *whose* imagination, the urban-rural framework creates certain spatial expectations that influence the local identity and regional policies. Although Kelly argues for the need to change our analytical framework of rural society from "agrarian" to "regional" (Kelly 1990: 211), he notes that "[t]here are no agrarian countrysides in contemporary Japan, except in the (senti)mental imagery of *furusato* motifs" (1990: 224). Despite the rise of public transport and digital technology blurring the line between the urban and rural space, certain imaginary dimensions are still fixed on the urban-rural spectrum. Rather than eliminating the dichotomy in the public understanding of Japan's geopolitical structure, we need to trace its transition along the shift in public sentiment. Although Moon's analysis focuses on the sentimental and traditional aspects of rural space, namely the *furusato* discourse, her views are relevant to the contemporary discourses that ascribe different values and meanings to the rural landscape.

Tamba Sasayama's regional revitalisation strategy is also a process of constructing unique images of the region in conjunction with the broader social discourse that shapes the values of rural space. As I have mentioned earlier, in the changing social climate where urban precarity prevails, there is a particular aspiration for rural qualities that can provide an alternative lifestyle. Tamba Sasayama's strategy of promoting rural creativity is also inextricably linked to external notions and expectations of an ideal rural life. The concept of *sōzō nōson* is a response to the growing search for alternative lifestyle and the increasing demand for culturally dynamic and creative rural places, inviting new ways of thinking about the general rural livelihood. Consider its linguistic components: *nōson* (village), a repository of tradition and nostalgia, is combined with *sōzō* (creative), which reverses conventional notions of rural time and mobility as past-oriented. In the campaign for this new rural value, Tamba pottery has been promoted as the key cultural emblem that exemplifies the essence of *rural* creativity, denoting both the traditional and inventive facets of creative activities.[11] On the one hand, it boasts the reputation as one of Japan's Six Ancient Kiln (*rokkoyō*) sites and one of the key folk craft items that featured in Yanagi Muneyoshi's *mingei* philosophy.[12] On the other hand, craft is an embodiment of human creative expression. There have been various philosophical reflections not only on the tactile sensation of working with hands, but also on the experiential features of its cooperative processes, spontaneous practices and creative imagination that come into play (O'Connor 2005; Sennett 2008; Marchand 2008). Through the concept of *sōzō nōson*, the local craft culture is imbued with a hybrid value of rurality, embodying the complex intertwining of rural values that neither completely undermines nor relies on traditional preferences for rural space. Tamba pottery is valued not only for its long history and traditions, but also for its creativity in the making of tradition. By providing tourists and visitors with hands-on experiences through promotional events, the potters create an atmosphere of vitality in the region.

The quest for regional revitalisation is thus inherently intertwined with the embodiment of the imaginative facets of rural space, which reflect wider societal concerns. Rather than succumbing to a narrative that oscillates between regional despair and hope, Tamba Sasayama's story sheds light on the nuanced realities of rural existence, at a time when the pursuit of regional revitalisation has become a shared mantra. Rurality, in this context, is the conceptual cornerstone through which we can understand how the diverse visions, aspirations, and concerns of a post-growth society are manifested against the dynamic rural landscape.

Out in the field

Struggling to find a direct contact for my research in Tamba Sasayama, I stumbled upon information that the Busan UNESCO Creative City of Film team, partly led by my old colleagues, would be attending the UNESCO Creative City Network in Krakow and Katowice, Poland, in June 2018, where representatives from the Tamba Sasayama UNESCO Creative City of Crafts and Folk Arts were also joining. After successful communication via email, I was unofficially hired as an interpreter for the Busan team and followed their official schedule. On the second day of my arrival at the conference, I finally had a chance to hear the presentation on Tamba Sasayama's regional revitalisation initiatives and the idea of a creative village, which I later identified as the campaign for *sōzō nōson* (creative village).[13] Networking at the party led to an exchange of business card with an official from Tamba Sasayama, marking the beginning of my fieldwork.

Only a few months after I arrived in Tamba Sasayama, public debates erupted about changing the name of the region, which by then was Sasayama. It was fascinating to witness the passionate debates, which introduced me to the dynamic social fabric of a quiet rural area. During this vibrant period, I wandered around, tracing different kinds of local social networks. The City Hall officials were enthusiastic about my research from the start, arranging an official meeting with the mayor and interviewing local journalists shortly after my arrival in Tamba Sasayama. My presence in the area quickly spread across the region through newspaper headlines, making it easier for me to start conversations with the locals. To gain insight into the meaning of *sōzō nōson* and its implications as a public slogan, I attended local government meetings as an observer and accompanied officials on business trips throughout the municipality and beyond. Casual conversations in informal settings in local restaurants and cafés were valuable opportunities to learn about the personal aspirations of officials in regional revitalisation initiatives. I also took on various odd jobs at the City Hall, including interpreting for foreign visitors and being a member of a group discussing strategies for attracting foreign tourists. This allowed me to develop a close relationship with the local government officials and gain practical knowledge of their inner workings.

Establishing rapport with the officials was relatively straightforward but establishing contact with the potters proved challenging. Firstly, they lived in a remote village that was not easily accessible from the central town area where I was residing. Relying on public transport was not enough, so I had to take the risk of buying a second-hand car and practically driving for the first time in my life on the road that runs on opposite side of South Korea. Even then, socialising with the potters was not easy. I later realised that they were unsure whether I was an independent researcher or someone hired by the local government to carry out surveys on them. It was only when I began to explore the village on my own, knocking on the workshop doors and making doorway (*genkan*) speeches about my genuine interest in Tamba pottery, that they began to relax their guard. Gossip played a crucial role in this process. The potters' community was so close-knit that news travelled fast. By the time I visited the last few potters on my list, some of them had already heard of my arrival and were anticipating my visit. In all, there were about sixty-five independent workshops in Tachikui, and I visited all of them except for those that were temporarily closed.

Participation in the social activities of the potters depended heavily on my close relationships with a few potters. Although I was introduced to several potters by local government officials, it was difficult to break the ice in formal settings. Instead, the potters I became closest to were those with whom I had a personal relationship. For example, my friendship with Shōhei, a middle-aged potter under whom I later became his informal assistant, began with an unexpected chance to visit his workshop. A week after bumping into a small group of potters renovating signs in Tachikui, I ran into one of the potters on the street, who happened to be Shōhei. When I spotted him from a distance, I waved to him with a big smile, which he later told me he thought was strange because I was being overly friendly. However, he thought I was a nice kid (*ii ko*). Perhaps noticing how much I was sweating under the scorching September sun, he invited me into his workshop for a cup of cold tea. As I later discovered, our long conversation that afternoon was unusual for his busy schedule. The following week I attended his private pottery class with his older friends. A few months later, he asked me to help him produce and distribute his pottery. Thanks to his generosity, I was able to attend formal and informal meetings of the Tamba Tachikui Pottery Cooperatives (*Tamba tachikui tōjiki kyōdō kumiai*, hereafter *kumiai*), where I learned about the social and political relationships among the potters. Their social gatherings were often impromptu, making it difficult to attend without being present in the village 24/7. However, thanks to him, who always texted me in advance, I was able to join them and gain an insight of the community issues. Once I had established a solid relationship with the members of the *kumiai*, I received numerous requests to help them plan public events and conduct surveys among foreign tourists.

During my fieldwork, I conducted semi-formal interviews with a wide range of people, including public officials, potters, young migrants, business representatives, and other residents of Tamba Sasayama. Their perspectives provided valuable insights into the region's social and economic conditions. To create a relaxed environment, I avoided using voice recorders during the interviews. Taking notes in my notebook was more suitable for a natural conversation, being immersed in the moment and capturing the sense of things. It was also a way of reminding others that I was a researcher and that data collection was ongoing. My interactions with people were more like "fluid give-and-take conversations rather than one-sided interrogations" (Kingsbury 2019: 61). I also distributed a survey to the member potters of the *kumiai*, but only during the last month of my fieldwork, when I had established a level of trust with them. To ensure that I received timely responses, I visited each workshop rather than relying on the *kumiai* staff. However, this task proved particularly challenging due to the notoriously high humidity in Japan that summer.

The opportunity to participate in the process of creating a pottery proved to be both engaging and educational. From the initial preparation of the clay to the final stages of firing and selling, the experience provided me with valuable insights into the social lives of Tachikui. I was often asked to elaborate on the potters' skills, physical movements, and their social implications in my analysis of their everyday lives. But the more I learned, the more cautious I became about romanticising their craft. Engaging in archival research was crucial in broadening my understanding of the historical and cultural context of Tamba Sasayama, particularly in relation to Tachikui and the Tamba pottery industry. This involved reviewing local government reports, news articles, and visual sources about the earlier regional policies that shaped the local history of municipal amalgamation. In addition, the archive of the Museum of Ceramic Art, Hyogo, provided a wealth of books, journals, and catalogues on Tamba pottery. The Kobe City Archive proved to be an equally rich source of rare books, offering valuable insights into the history of local industries in Hyogo Prefecture, including the Tamba pottery industry.

My Korean nationality was of personal significance as a researcher during the fieldwork. Political and diplomatic relations between Japan and South Korea were tense during my stay in Tamba Sasayama, with historical disputes being addressed in the media without a fair understanding of each other's perspectives. I often ended up discussing Japan-South Korea relations with my interviewees over a similar question that Han recalled from her fieldwork: "what do you as a Korean think about Japan?" (1995: 216). Initially, I was reluctant to engage in such a conversation and tried to censor personal views so as not to damage my relationships with counterparts. However, I eventually realised that this self-censorship reflected my own preconceptions about Japan. When I spoke openly and confidently about my thoughts, many responded positively and shared honest opinions.

The post-fieldwork phase, the transition from on-site observer to remote spectator, has had an unexpectedly significant impact on my research. Learning about

Tamba Sasayama's UCCN report a few months after my return to the research institute in Germany caused me to reassess my position in the field. I was cited as an example of Tamba Sasayama's scientific collaboration with external researchers. I had not discussed this with the local government officials, and they had even misidentified my affiliation. However, it was a relief to realise that there was a mutual gaze and that they had their own interest in and understanding of my research project, even if it was not entirely accurate. This seemed to show the enigmatic constellation of fieldwork, full of surprises and ambiguities, composed of multiple authors. Nevertheless, the sense of indebtedness to the valuable stories I gained in Tamba Sasayama remains and will probably continue to do so.

Chapter outline

The book documents various aspects of Tamba Sasayama's regional revitalisation movement, including how a new rural value – rural creativity – is perceived and practised in institutional and everyday settings. In the first four chapters (Chapters 1–4) of Part One, I examine how the concept of creativity has become the new headline of Tamba Sasayama's regional revitalisation policy. Chapter 1 outlines the central government's decentralisation policy and the pervasive self-help ideology among local governments. Against this background, I investigate how Tamba Sasayama adopted creativity as the central concept of revitalisation policy and its promotion of *sōzō nōson* by tracing the history of municipal amalgamation and the local debt crisis. In Chapter 2, I provide an ethnographic account of the organisational meetings of the Creative City Network of Japan (CCNJ), a rapidly expanding non-profit organisation that discusses regional revitalisation policy, to demonstrate how institutional discourses are shaped and maintained, and to understand the international and domestic contexts in which rural creativity emerged as a new buzzword in regional revitalisation policy in Japan. I describe the role of external experts in persuading the local government officials and representatives of local organisations to embrace the idea of rural creativity as a central concept of regional revitalisation policy. Despite a communally shared moral discourse and a group ethos at this national meeting, the concept of creativity in the local context of Tamba Sasayama was confusing rather than convincing. Chapter 3 discusses the prevailing sense of ambiguity surrounding the concept among local government officials. I argue that the ambiguity is a structural product of the central government's regional revitalisation policy, which encourages competition between local governments (e.g., *Chihō sōsei*). Following the public officials of the Creative City Section (*sōzō toshi ka*) at City Hall, I show how they strategically manage their confusion over Tamba Sasayama's *sōzō nōson* campaign. Chapter 4 examines the relationships between the key local actors in Tamba Sasayama's revitalisation policy to demonstrate the mismatch between the ideals of the *sōzō nōson* campaign and the local social and cultural contexts. I illustrate my involvement in organising a meeting between the native residents – the potters – and a recent in-migrant to show how the official narrative of the campaign overlooks the practical ways in which people interact, and how regional stereotypes plays a crucial role in facilitating the social interaction between the local actors.

The interlude and the subsequent ethnographic chapters (Chapters 5–7) of Part Two focus on the more concrete aspect of how rural natives perceive the various public projects that promote the image of *sōzō nōson* and its imposed value of creativity. Zooming in on the village context of Tachikui, the site of Tamba pottery production, I describe how the potters have been involved in the regional revitalisation policies and how they experience themselves as key agents of the *sōzō nōson* initiatives. In Chapter 5, I begin by tracing how Tachikui came to be known for its Tamba pottery, taking into account its socio-economic history. The village has received support from the local government because of the central role of Tamba pottery in shaping the creative atmosphere of the region. However, it has also flattened the diversity of village life. Drawing on Ingold's (1993) concept of "taskscape", I examine the many layers of social practices that have developed around the production of Tamba pottery and that have influenced the lives of the potters and villagers.

As the local government's *sōzō nōson* campaign produces visible results, as evidenced by Tamba Sasayama's designation as the UNESCO Creative City Network and Japan Heritage (*Nihon isan*), the potters have become more involved in related projects. On the face of it, they appear to welcome the local government's support for the promotion of Tamba pottery, seeing it as a necessary measure to adapt to the shrinking ceramics market and the anticipated financial challenges of maintaining the clay factory. However, many also expressed dissatisfaction with their relationship with the local government. In Chapter 6, I show how the potters began to question their role in Tamba Sasayama's regional revitalisation policy. In order to fulfil their expected role as creative agents and hold public events, they had to endure lengthy preparations, including holding numerous meetings, preparing materials, and setting up the venues. However, they did not feel that their efforts were recognised by the public officials, who seemed to think that potters would naturally and effortlessly carry on the traditional craft once the right amount of subsidy was given. As the burden of performing traditional crafts was increasing, they were concerned about another aspect. In Chapter 7, using Ardener's (2012) concept of "remoteness", I explore their dissatisfaction with the dominant representation of Tamba pottery as a *mingei* craft in public events and promotional materials organised by the local government. I examine how they respond with individual and group strategies to promote what they consider to be the correct representation of Tamba pottery.

In conclusion, I provide an overview of the book, reflecting on the implications of the findings within the broader social context of the post-war, post-bubble, and the post-growth transitions in Japan. I outline the changing perceptions of the rural space during these phases, arguing that the idealisation of the rural is still ongoing. An examination of new rurality emerging in Tamba Sasayama reveals that the rural space re-imagined as a creative village or other alternative notion of rurality requires further critical engagement in the livelihoods of the local people. Whether the *furusato* or the creative village discourse, they are "rubrics" (Robertson 1988: 505) created based on the imagination of outsiders. I suggest that the focus of the research should rather be on the everyday experiences of locals as they encounter these "rubrics", and to do this we need to develop a concrete understanding of the local social fabric. The epilogue describes my recent visit to Tamba Sasayama. Based on the conversations I had in Tamba Sasayama during my four-day stay in the summer of 2023, it provides an update on the most recent events in Tamba Sasayama and a personal reflection on the seven-year journey.

Notes

1 *Inland Sea* (2018) is an observational documentary of Minatomachi shot in black and white directed by Kazuhiro Soda.

2 https://www.japantimes.co.jp/news/2020/05/28/business/japan-rural-migration-coronavirus/.

3 https://www.dw.com/en/coronavirus-more-japanese-to-swap-urban-life-for-the-countryside/a-53854362. See also "More people moving to rural areas across Japan as new lifestyles emerge due to virus" (The Mainichi, 14 Jun 2020, https://mainichi.jp/english/articles/20200612/p2a/00m/0fe/016000c), "Will the Coronavirus Pandemic boost rural relocation in Japan?" (Tokyo Review, 31 Jul 2020, https://www.tokyoreview.net/2020/07/will-the-coronavirus-pandemic-spruce-up-rural-relocation-in-japan/), and "As Japan moves to revive its countryside, pandemic chases many from cities" (Reuters, 4 Nov 2020, https://www.reuters.com/article/us-japan-economy-migration-idINKBN27K02P).

4 A similar view was shared by Ishiba Shigeru, the former minister in charge of regional revitalisation from 2014 to 2016, that "twenty-first-century Japan will be shaped by the regions" (Klien 2020: 74).

5 Concerning the idea of creativity, Tamba Sasayama's regional revitalisation strategy is referred to by several terms, including *sōzō nōson* (creative village), *nōto sōzō* (rural city development), and *sōzō toshi* (creative city). In this thesis, I use the term *Sōzō nōson* to describe Tamba Sasayama's revitalisation strategy that draws on the aesthetics and creativity of rurality.

6 *Sengyō shufu* refers to a full-time housewife, and the discourse around it has criticised how the post-war ideology of the family has shaped gender roles in which women belong to the domestic realm of housework and childrearing, while men belong to the public realm of work.

7 Love refers to Hiroi Yoshinori's concept of the "spatial axis" – an alternative concept for imagining the development of a society. Rather than having a temporal axis or an idea of social progress as the basis for social development, he suggests that we think about ways of forming a deeper connection with the land we live on and to invest in maturing our understanding of the relationships between nature and human society.

8 Other scholars have drawn a darker side to rural Japan's symbolic transitions. Rosenberger demonstrates that what appears to be an alternative rural way of life is in fact the "neoliberal life's margins" (2017: 27). She describes a case of newly settled organic farmers who think and act like purist agriculturalists, but who are also risk-taking entrepreneurs. Klien (2020) also highlights the differences between the ideal and the reality of living with post-growth values in rural areas. She finds that urban-rural migrants are often under high mental pressure to succeed and are

vulnerable to self-exploitation as they have to make a living in a place disconnected from previous social and economic networks. Her interlocutors are in a "convenient state of permanent limbo", caught between the conventional values of the normative life course they grew up with and the morality they aspire to in rural periphery (2020: 143). She proposes the concept of "moratorium migration", based on the idea of psychoanalyst Okonogi Keigo, *moratorium ningen*, to describe a specific pattern of relocation found among urban-rural migrants: they "arbitrarily [choose] to evade their obligations and responsibilities to society" and cope with "contradictory elements of 'lifestyle' and 'precariat' into a fuzzy grey zone where work, lifestyle, leisure, self-realisation, and precariousness all blend into one" (2020: 26). Furthermore, for young female migrants, gender disparities in rural relocation are inevitable (Traphagan 2017).

9 Hannerz emphasises the difference between what he means by locus, as opposed to focus, when referring to urban anthropology:

> It is another fact of the same realities of research that the field of urban anthropology has been quite widely defined. More often than not it is taken to include all the studies where the city is the locus rather than the focus. Ethnicity and poverty, for example, may occur *in* the city, but they are not by definition phenomena typical of the city. The euphemistic use of 'urban problems' in political rhetoric is no trustworthy guide here. Investigations of urban family life, or the activities of youth gangs, or occupational cultures, need not be much concerned with any intrinsically urban characteristics either. This generous inclusiveness of all sorts of interests, ideas, and findings, together with a relative unconcern for what might be their common denominator, also contributes to the picture of an urban anthropology which seems to lack a coherent, unifying structure of ideas.
>
> (Hannerz 1980: 3–4)

10 Sasaki Nobuo refers to the following LDP's significant regional revitalisation policies in recent decades: The Takeshita Cabinet's 100 Million Yen Grants for Hometown Revitalisation (*Furusato sōsei ichi oku en*) in 1988; the Obuchi Cabinet's Regional Promotion Coupons (*Chiiki shinkōken*) in 1999; the Aso Cabinet's Hometown Tax System (*Furusato nōzei*) in 2008; and the Abe Cabinet's Strategy for Regional Revitalisation (*Chihō sōsei senryaku*) and Grants for Livelihood Support (*Seikatsu shien kōfukin*) (Sasaki 2015).

11 A similar case can be found in the promotion of Mashiko pottery, also known as traditional *mingei* crafts. Morais mentions how its traditional aspects are highlighted with creativity and other modern aspects (2019: 169).

12 *Mingei*, loosely translated as "people's art", refers to folk crafts in Japan. Its political and practical implications are discussed in Chapters 2 and 7.

13 Creative village is the official English translation of *sōzō nōson* used at the Creative City Network of Japan and by the local government of Tamba Sasayama.

Part One

Tamba Sasayama

1 From the Great Heisei Amalgamation to the *Sōzō Nōson* Campaign

Abstract

Tamba Sasayama's public policy over the past 20 years has undergone a radical shift from an economy of scale, based on regional amalgamation policy, to an economy of appearance, based on the promotional campaigns for *sōzō nōson*. In the context of Japan's decentralisation policy and expanding self-help ethos in regional governance, this chapter provides an overview of Tamba Sasayama's regional policy, from establishing an administrative district of *shi* (city) in 1999 to the local government's decision to focus on regional revitalisation. Since the early 2000s, Tamba Sasayama has continued to restore the region's economy and reputation to dispel the unfavourable perceptions deriving from its recent financial troubles following the merger in 1999. In less than a decade since the birth of the new municipal district, the favourable media attention that depicted the region as the first successful case of the Great Heisei Amalgamation (*dai heisei gappei*) policy had shifted the spotlight to the failure of its post-merger development policies. Since tourists and migrant population were crucial to the sustainability of the local economy and population, re-inventing the regional image was as pivotal as re-establishing the financial and administrative system of the local government. As an attempt to promote regional attractiveness (*miryoku hasshin*), the local government has been investing in promoting the positive aspects of the region, particularly the local craft and art scenes. New regional images and narratives were being created.

The first decade (1999–2009): The bigger the better?

Since the late 1990s, Japan's reputation as a "superstable society" has been faltering (Allison 2015: 41). An ageing and declining population, as well as the rising national debt, have had a significant impact on all facets of daily life, from family structures to the labour market. Corporations no longer provided the safety nets of public welfare, and the system of lifetime employment was replaced by temporary and irregular jobs. The idea of a family-like workplace, a key component of Japan's prosperous post-war business model, was now perceived as "unhealthy" (Allison 2015: 41) and constraining the development of individuality. In its place, self-help, or self-responsibility, has emerged as the new ethos.

DOI: 10.4324/9781003326540-3

The post-bubble period saw active decentralisation campaigns (see Song 2015). The central government passed the Decentralisation Promotion Act (*Chihō bunken suishin hō*) in 1995 and the Omnibus Decentralisation Act (*Chihō bunken suishin ikkatsu hō*) in 1999, which became the basis for the general decentralisation initiatives across Japan. This led to the abolition of the Agency Delegated Tasks (*Kikan i'nin jimu*) system in 2000, under which governors and mayors were treated as regional representatives of the central government. Local government obtained greater autonomy and responsibility in a wider range of areas, including public health, education, and social welfare. In addition, the Grand Design for the 21st century (*21 seiki no kokudo no gurando dezain*), formulated in 1998, shifted national land policy from the then One Axis One Pole (*Ikkyoku ichijiku*) system, which focused land development policy on the Tokyo metropolitan area and along the Pacific coastal industrial belt, to Multiple Pole systems (Ogawa 2016: 18–21). This led to a reduction in direct government-led investment in regional infrastructure and development programmes. Local governments now had to make extra efforts to obtain public subsidies. As Ogawa points out, the title of the new land policy explicitly showed the spirit of decentralisation: "promotion of self-help and creation of a region with pride (*jiritsu no sokushin to hokori no moteru chiiki no sōzō*)" (2016: 21).

The nationwide push for the municipal merger of small villages and towns under the Great Heisei Amalgamation (*dai heisei gappei*) policy corresponded to the decentralisation policy as a remedy for local government's heavy reliance on local allocation grants from the central government. It provided blueprints for depopulated regions to improve public services and increase municipal tax revenues by rescaling the administrative boundaries and financial systems (see Elis 2011; Koike 2009; Mabuchi 2001). Increasing the size of municipalities was seen as the ideal strategy to address the ongoing problems of ageing and declining populations. The Great Heisei Amalgamation policy was the third major state-led initiative after the Meiji Amalgamation, which reduced the number of municipalities from 71,314 to 15,859, and the Shōwa Amalgamation in the mid-1950s, which further cut the number of municipalities from 9,868 to 3,472. The Great Heisei Amalgamation resulted in 1,822 municipalities on the map of Japan.

The administrative district of Tamba Sasayama was established in 1999 in the midst of Japan's bubble crisis and neoliberal turn.[1] The aim of the merger was to improve public services that had previously been a significant burden on the towns in the area, including the maintenance of sewage systems, funeral services, and landfills. A single municipal office replaced the individual town offices of Sasayama, Tannan, Nishiki, and Konda, reducing the cost of public administration. Sasayama, also known as Little Kyoto (*shō kyōto*), was chosen as the new central town of the four, housing the Tamba Sasayama City Hall and other major public facilities such as the Concert Hall and the Citizen's Centre (Moriwaki 2008: 84). Tannan, where the Sasayamaguchi station was located, served as the transport hub, and Nishiki, with its vast black bean fields, became the centre of agricultural activity. Konda, famous for its Tamba pottery, was promoted as a tourist destination. New public facilities were built, including a library, a hot spring, a swimming pool, and a waste treatment plant. Tamba Sasayama's merger was heralded in the public media as the first successful case of the Great Heisei Amalgamation policy, and officials from neighbouring municipalities visited to witness it.

Before the Great Heisei Amalgamation, there had been five rounds of merger, with 18 villages (*son*) being reduced to four towns (*chō*). For this sixth merger, at least 90 briefing sessions were held, attracting over 3,000 people from the region.[2] A special magazine on the merger process was also distributed throughout the area. A merger research committee (*gappei kenkyūkai*) was formed in 1996, and a bill was passed the following year to establish a merger council (*gappei kyōgikai*) to decide on the main terms of the merger. According to the five basic clauses (*kihon go kōmoku*) of the merger agreement, the participating towns would be merged on an equal basis, with the towns' assets to be jointly administered, and the new municipality would be called Sasayama. The merger was scheduled for 1st April 1999, with Sasayama town (*chō*) serving as the central location for local government buildings. In addition, in the same year that the prefectural government approved the merger plan, the Municipal Merger Special Measure Law (*Shichōson gappei tokubetsu sochi hō*) was enacted, allowing municipalities with a population of more than 40,000 to obtain the *shi* (city) status and greater autonomy in regional affairs.[3] This was heralded by the town officials as one of the main reasons for the merger.

While the town representatives were eager to push ahead with the plan and create the new Sasayama-*shi*, not all residents supported the idea, especially the town of Konda. It had little incentive to undergo major administrative reform, given its relative economic stability based on the Tamba pottery industry. Residents were also concerned that the merger would dilute regional identity. They identified their cultural roots with the Himeji region while the other three towns were influenced by *kyō-bunka* (Kyoto culture). According to a Tamba potter, one's *tochigara*, meaning the characteristics of the land, determines one's cultural practices and way of life. He insisted that the people of Konda and the other towns could not be grouped together since their basic natures were different. To this day, only Konda residents write 'Konda *chō*' in their official postal addresses.

In a local survey conducted shortly after the merger, three out of four residents expressed dissatisfaction with the outcome. Around 60 per cent said that "conflicts between old towns remain among assembly members and are not settled (*giin no aida de kyū machi kan no tairitsu ga nokotteite, matomaranai*)" and 35 per cent pointed out that "the wishes of the small towns and outlying areas are neglected (*chiisana machi ya shūhen no ikō ga keishi sarete iru*)" (Moriwaki 2008: 84). The first reason reflects Konda residents' opposition to the merger plan, while the second one reflects the experiences of Konda, Tannan, and Nishiki residents who have to travel a longer distance to visit City Hall and other public facilities concentrated in former Sasayama town. Despite

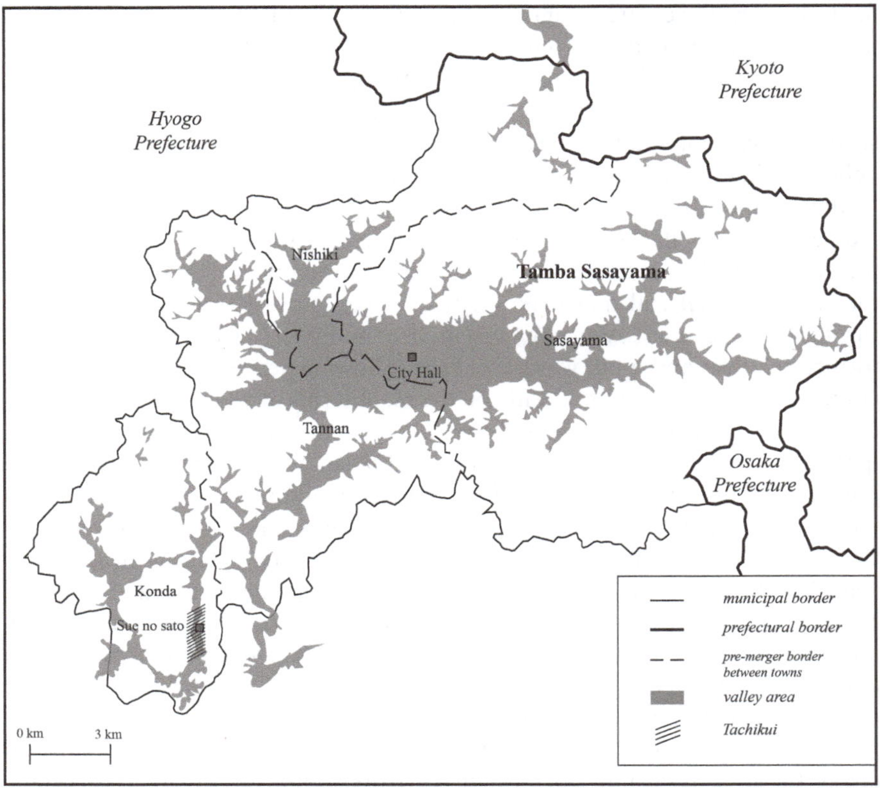

Map 1.1 Tamba Sasayama.

the successful merger of the administrative units, the residents faced difficulties in adjusting their daily rhythms.

Instead of a newfound sense of belonging to the new municipality, what brought them together was a common concern that emerged soon after the merger. New public facilities, roads, water supplies, and museums were being built, bringing visible improvements to the area (Choi 2014: 338). These were largely subsidised by the Special Merger Bonds (*gappei tokureisai*) issued under the Great Heisei Amalgamation plan that were available for merged municipalities. For ten years after the merger, the local government could finance up to 95 per cent of the costs of public initiatives to create new administrative units and public infrastructure. The central government undertook to pay 70 per cent of the bond's principal and interest repayment through the Local Allocation Tax (LAT) (Takaharu 2007: 9). This financial benefit had attracted many of the then economically struggling municipalities to the merger plan, and Tamba Sasayama was also the case. As Choi notes, the generous subsidy led to a construction boom throughout the region, even though some of the newly built buildings were barely occupied (Choi 2014: 338).

However, the extravagant post-amalgamation investments subsidised by Special Merger Bonds would soon expose the area to serious financial risk by turning into a source of massive debt that the local government could not handle. Between 1998 and 2000, Tamba Sasayama's debt increased fivefold, surpassing the combined debt of the four towns before the merger. By 2003, it was double, and in some cases triple, that of other municipalities with comparable populations (Choi 2014: 339). One could criticise the local government's over-ambitious expectation of population increase after the merger, or the local construction boom, much of which was financed by the Special Merger Bonds. However, it would be an oversimplification of the regional context to assume that the local government simply lacked foresight in its post-merger development plans. In fact, it had a solid repayment plan based on the estimates of the LAT grant it would receive. The problem was that they had unforeseen the central financial reform, which would invalidate the original repayment plan itself. There was an unexpected "trap" (Choi 2014:346) in the Special Merger Bonds, which the central government had promised to write off up to 70 per cent with the provision of the LAT grant, regardless of the financial status of the merged city, town, or village. The Trinity Reform (*Sanmi ittai kaikaku*, 2004–2006) implemented by the Koizumi administration (2001–2006) as part of the decentralisation scheme included a comprehensive reform of the regional financial system. The central government's budget for local governments, such as Treasury Disbursement (*kokko shishtsukin*) and the LAT grant, was significantly revised and reduced. This posed new challenges for local governments, which were experiencing depopulation and shrinking tax revenues. In the case of Tamba Sasayama, it is estimated that around 4.47 billion yen disappeared from the original financial plan between 2004 and 2007 (Choi 2014: 346). The combination of central financial reform and the local government's mismanagement of public funds led to the rising costs of public services such as the household water prices which became the highest in Hyogo Prefecture.

In this financial turmoil, the local government had to shift the direction of its regional policy from development to "revitalisation" (*saisei*). Rather than focusing on the growth of the local economy and population, its efforts were redirected towards maintaining, at best, the existing conditions. The Revitalisation Plan (*Saisei keikaku*) was comprised of two major initiatives: first, to reform the administrative and financial systems, and second, to develop a new strategy to restore the region's public image.

The local government formed the Citizen's Council for the Revitalisation of Sasayama (*Sasayama saisei shimin kaigi*) in 2007 and undertook a major fiscal reform. Local government officials had their salaries cut by up to 20 per cent, with the mayor's salary cut to the maximum. The number of City Hall employees was also reduced from 566 to 400. While the reduction in government spending saved the municipality from bankruptcy, the unfavourable images and stories of its financial problems persisted. In 2010, for example, *Bungei Shunjū* published an eight-page article entitled "The Great Heisei

Amalgamation: Sasayama's Failure" (*Heisei no dai gappei: Sasayama no shippai*), which described Tamba Sasayama's amalgamation policy as an outright failure. The magazine, which is widely read in Japan, suggests that negative perceptions of Tamba Sasayama were already widespread in the public mind. I discovered this source while browsing through the Sasayama Library, in a section devoted to government reports and media publications on the 1999 merger. The fact that the library chose to keep it on its shelves seemed to indicate its significant impact on the region. For a municipality increasingly reliant on tourism industry and attracting migrants to the region, negative publicity was a challenge no less significant than financial difficulties. Uplifting stories and images were needed.

The second decade (2009–2019): The more creative the better?

Over the past few years, the idea of conceptualising and promoting creativity as a strategy for regional revitalisation has been gaining traction. According to the 2010 report of the United Nations Conference on Trade and Development (UNCTAD), global trade in creative goods and services remained relatively stable during the economic crisis of 2008. While the financial and economic crisis led to a 12 per cent contraction in international trade, global exports of creative goods and services increased, reaching 592 billion dollars in 2008. This represents an annual growth rate of 14 per cent for six consecutive years since 2002. The report cites this impressive figure as "a confirmation that the creative industries hold great potential for developing countries that seek to diversify their economies and leapfrog into one of the most dynamic sectors of the world economy" (UNCTAD 2010: xxiii).

While the global economy finds hope in the numerical configurations of markets and industries related to creative goods and services, the local economy of Tamba Sasayama finds hope in the re-configuration of the regional representation based on its notions of creativity. In the report of Tamba Sasayama's five-year *Chihō sōsei* (Regional Revitalisation) plan, *sōzō nōson* is proposed as the basic concept (*kihon rinen*) of its regional revitalisation strategy:

> Sasayama is a "creative village" blessed with nature, history, and culture, and yet it is close to the Kyoto-Osaka-Kobe area, making it an easy place to live.... In recent years, Sasayama has attracted attention as a model for regional development, with its recognition as a Japan Heritage Site, membership in the UNESCO Creative Cities Network, and other achievements. It has sought new development while carefully nurturing and passing on its cultural and natural environment, including its agricultural activities, townscape, Dekansho song and Tamba pottery.... Inheriting these ideas, we will protect the rich nature of our hometown (*furusato*) and its landscape, which we are proud of as the original landscape of Japan, and will take pride in the brand of Sasayama as a creative

rural region. We have established the following basic principles to link the happiness of every citizen with the future that can only be achieved in Sasayama.

1 to develop creative industries related to people's daily lives
2 to create a new flow of people by making use of the appeal of Japan Heritage
3 to create a culture of raising children in the affluent environment of the hometown (*furusato*)
4 to create a safe and prosperous lifestyle with one's own hands

(Sasayama City Hall 2016: 16, my translation)

The aim is to create an area where people can live comfortably, "a town that values history, culture, natural environment" based on "農 (*no*)", which means agriculture but also implies the general rural ambience (Sasayama City Hall 2016: 16). In this context, the transformation into a creative village is a matter of epistemological re-configuration, recognising the unrecognised creativity of endogenous resources. The official website introducing the *sōzō nōson* campaign lists the regional events and festivals that are indicative of the region's creativity. Starting with the 400th anniversary of the Sasayama Castle festival in 2011, several events have been held under the *sōzō nōson* banner, such as the Creative Village Forum in 2012, the International Biennale of Gastronomy and Pottery in 2013, a *nō* play at the Kasuga Shrine in 2014, and a Tamba pottery exhibition in Osaka in 2014.[4] The final comment on the website reflects an ideal image of the creative village that the local government aims to promote: "The nostalgic and fresh new lifestyle of Japan is rooted in this quiet provincial area" (*natsukashikute atarashii nippon no kurashi wa, kono tochi ni shizuka ni nezuki tsutsu aru yō da*) (Creative Village n.d., my translation). Rather than relying on economic indicators showing the potential improvement of the local economy through creative goods and services, the creativity implied in Tamba Sasayama's regional revitalisation seemed to emphasise the transformative power of promotional activities such as symposiums and festivals, aimed at re-shaping the public perception from a place burdened by debt to a thriving centre of creativity. The focus seemed to be on the positive nuance of creativity and its ability to change the narrative surrounding the region (Table 1.1).

The most significant achievement in Tamba Sasayama's promotional efforts is its recognition as a UNESCO Creative City of Crafts and Folk Arts in 2015, which highlights Tamba pottery as a symbol of rural creativity and cultural representation in the region. Founded in 2004, the UNESCO Creative City Network (UCCN) is a global organisation that brings together institutions and individuals who support the idea that creativity can be a compass for the social and economic sustainability of regions. Each member city supports local initiatives and events focused on a particular cultural product of the seven clusters of creative industry (crafts and folk arts, media arts, film, design, gastronomy, literature, and music), and UNESCO provides

Table 1.1 Tamba Sasayama's engagement in UNESCO Creative City Network (UCCN) and Creative City Network of Japan (CCNJ)

	UNESCO Creative City Network (UCCN)	*Creative City Network of Japan (CCNJ)*
2009	• The 400th Anniversary of Tamba Sasayama Castle Construction Festival	
2011	• Sasayama City Creative City Network Preparation Committee	
2012	• Creative City Promotion Committee • Creative Rural Workshop • Preservation District for Groups of Historic Buildings	• The first workshop of *sōzō nōson*
2013	• The organising city of the Creative City Network in Japan • International Biennial Pre-Event on Food and Plates • Creative City Promotion Plan	• Organising secretary
2014	• Application for membership in the Crafts and Folk Art cluster • Winner of the Urban Landscape Award • Creative City Symposium • UCCN Chengdu Conference • Visit UCCN Member City (Icheon, South Korea) • Postponement of the UCCN membership	• Organising secretary
2015	• Japan Heritage (*nihon isan*) designation • Visit UCCN Member City (Hangzhou, China) • World Creative City Symposium (Kanazawa) • Visit UCCN Member City (Angarebang, France) • Submitted the application for a UCCN membership in Crafts and Folk Art cluster • International Biennale of Tamba Sasayama Food and Plates • Received the UCCN membership certification	• Organising secretary
2016	• Workshops in Icheon, South Korea • UCCN Conference (Aestelsundo, Sweden)	• Organising secretary
2017	• UCCN Conference (Ang Levan, France) • International Biennale of Tamba Sasayama Food and Plates	• Organising secretary
2018	• Workshop in Icheon, South Korea • Creative City Network Sector Conference	• Organising secretary

Source: Dai ikkai nihon isan sōzō toshi suishin iinkai kaigiroku (Sasayama City Hall 2018).

venues for regular conferences. Kanazawa, the City of Crafts and Folk Arts, became the first Japanese city to become a member of the UCCN in 2005. With the help of the same experts who worked on Kanazawa's application, Tamba Sasayama became Japan's second UNESCO Creative City of Crafts and Folk Arts.

But what exactly is *sōzō nōson* that is behind these initiatives? *Sōzō nōson* is closely related to the concept of *sōzō toshi* (creative city), an idea that gained popularity through the work of Japanese scholar named Sasaki Masayuki, whose writings were influenced by the creative class and the creative city theories of Richard Florida and Charles Landry. According to him, *sōzō toshi* is defined as:

> A city with a rich creative milieu where, based on the unrestricted creative activities of citizen, the creativity of culture and industry flourishes, and at the same time, post-industrial economic systems of innovation and flexibility are established, through which problems of the global environment and regional community are creatively solved.
>
> (Sasaki 2006, my translation)

It emphasises the role of individual citizens in supporting a diverse and thriving cultural and economic environment, and in using their imagination to find creative answers to pressing social and environmental issues on a global scale.

On the other hand, *sōzō nōson* emphasises the creative capacity of individuals living in *rural* areas. The concept was originally conceived as a rural adaptation of the *sōzō toshi* theory at a symposium hosted by the Creative City Network of Japan (CCNJ), an organisation that promotes creativity as a crucial element in regional revitalisation strategies. A group of rural municipalities in the CCNJ had formed a sub-group to discuss the importance of fostering regional creativity outside of urban-centred contexts, of which Tamba Sasayama was an early proponent. With the first *sōzō nōson* workshop held in Tamba Sasayama in 2012, the member municipalities took turns hosting symposiums to solidify the idea. This later led to the publication of a monograph on the *sōzō nōson* theory, co-authored by Sasaki and other academics. In the book, Sasaki defines *sōzō nōson* as:

> A countryside with a rich creative milieu where, based on the autonomy and creativity of the residents, the ecosystem is preserved, local culture is cultivated, new arts, science and technology are adapted, and cyclic local economy is formed in combination with craftsmanship and agroforestry, and through which problems of the global environment and local community are creatively solved.
>
> (Sasaki et al. 2014: 21, my translation)

Juxtaposed, the definitions of *sōzō nōson* and *sōzō toshi* show how they form a complete pair, complimenting what is lacking in urban and rural space, respectively. At the same time, despite their physical and geographical differences, they are treated as equals in terms of their potential to create spatial conditions for creativity. First, they share the common goal of creating a social milieu in which "problems of the global environment and local community (*guro-baruna kankyō mondai ya ro-karuna chiiki shakai no kadai*)" can be solved "creatively (*sōzōteki*)". Secondly, when it comes to the question of 'how', both emphasise the creative ability of individual citizens. According to the definition of *sōzō tōshi*, "the unrestricted creative activities of citizen (*shimin no sōzō katsudō*)" are the answer to a variety of global and local problems. A similar idea is echoed in the definition of *sōzō nōson*, which points to "the autonomy and creativity of the residents (*jūmin no jichi to sōi*)" as the key to solving widespread social problems. In both urban and rural contexts, individual creativity serves as a panacea for regional well-being. Conventional notions of creativity in the Euro-American context assume a fundamental difference in spatial orientation in urban and rural settings. Woods (2012) argues that rural creativity thrives in solitude and quiet, whereas urban creativity thrives in open, densely populated environments where people from different backgrounds can interact and exchange ideas. However, *sōzō nōson* implies that rural space has the same creative qualities as urban space.

However, this hybrid notion of creativity, unconditioned by the social and economic differences between urban and rural areas, has recently raised concerns among scholars. An in-depth analysis of the conceptual history of *sōzō nōson* reveals the lack of coherence in its logical framework, suggesting potential flaws in the underlying principles that form the basis of the idea (Sugiyama 2020: 183). The conceptual design of *sōzō nōson*, based on *sōzō toshi* not only extends the dominance of urban-oriented views (Sugiyama 2020: 161) but also extends the logic of entrepreneurial governance and the market-based approaches to public services to rural social contexts (Kato 2015; Sugiyama 2015: 20, 22; see also Sasajima 2012: 79). As Kato points out, *sōzō nōson* is imbued with the idea of neoliberal agency, as evidenced by its emphasis on the role of the "key person (*kī pāson*)" in the success of rural revitalisation (Kato 2015: 8; cf. Onitsuka and Hoshino 2018: 123). The well-being of a region depends on the ability of individuals to develop creative strategies.

Despite criticism of the idea of *sōzō nōson* for its theoretical inconsistencies and association with neoliberal ideologies, it is valued within Tamba Sasayama's regional revitalisation for its re-conceptualisation of rurality and the projection of a different regional future therein. Tamba pottery shows precisely the way in which an existing social and cultural trope of a rural region is re-framed with new values. Tamba pottery, a cultural symbol of local traditional culture, has been imbued with new values of rural creativity and the potters have received renewed attention from the local government, not only for their traditional knowledge and skills but also for their role in inspiring a new spirit of creativity in the region. As key players in spreading the new slogan, they were involved in the organisation of a series of regional festivals, pottery classes, outdoor sales, and other promotional initiatives with the support of the local government.

These efforts have been accompanied by growing optimism about the region's economic prospects. According to the statistics released by the local government in 2019, the municipality continues to struggle to achieve financial stability: Tamba Sasayama had the highest Real Debt Service Ratio (*Jisshitsu kōsaihi hiritsu*) and the third highest Future Burden Ratio (*Shōrai futan hiritsu*) in Hyogo Prefecture. However, it was reported with an optimistic tone that the situation would improve. Citing the emerging trend of urban-to-rural migration and the increasing number of tourists visiting rural areas, it estimated that by 2027, the Real Debt Service Ratio will be almost half of its 2017 level, and the Future Burden Ratio will be one-third of its 2017 level (Sasayama City Hall, 2019a).

When I conducted my fieldwork in 2018–2019, it seemed that Tamba Sasayama had outgrown the title of failure and had instead gained a reputation as a pioneering municipality promoting the new rurality of rural creativity. Just as when Tamba Sasayama became the first successful case of the Great Heisei Amalgamation, groups of government officials, academics, and business representatives visited to learn about Tamba Sasayama's various revitalisation strategies, such as its designation as a UNESCO Creative City of Crafts and Folk Arts and Japan Heritage. They came from as far as the Kantō and Kyūshū regions and even abroad. As a researcher from a foreign research institute, I might have been one of them, hoping to find something different in the midst of Japan's current demographic and socio-economic crisis.

Conclusion

Since the early 2000s, there seems to be some connection between the emerging neoliberal policies, characterised by the wave of decentralisation, and the increasing emphasis on creativity discourse in public policy. Japan has been one of the early proponents of the "creative turn" (Kong 2014) in East Asia, enriching the academic discourses and public policies with creative theories – creative class (Florida 2003), creative industry (Caves 2002), and creative city (Landry & Bianchini 1997) – that had been dominated by the Euro-American cases. Kanazawa's membership of the UCCN in 2005 heralded a new era in Japan, with creativity as the new slogan and the ethos of regional revitalisation policies. Tamba Sasayama was to follow the path.

Scholars have pointed out how the rise of the creativity discourse in public policy manifests neoliberal values through the way in which state-led development is being replaced by inter-regional competition (Banks and O'Connor 2017; Mould 2018; Peck 2005). The growing role of creativity in regional revitalisation policies coincides with the slogan of the Koizumi administration – "from public to private" (*kan kara min e*) – which advocated the idea of self-responsibility: "an assumption that self-motivated work on the part of rural inhabitants to awaken regional identities will renew the vitality and viability of their home" (Love 2013: 121). As local governments come under increasing pressure to manage regional economies in the face of declining and ageing populations, their dependence on central government subsidies, for which they must compete, is growing. This is leading to various regional initiatives to cultivate internal resources that will differentiate them in their pursuit of public subsidies, tourists' attention, and migrant populations. The key is to have something distinctive, and creativity emerges as a virtue that can give the region a sense of uniqueness. Tamba Sasayama provides a case in which a rural municipality, faced with financial challenges resulting from the drastic fiscal reforms implemented during the neoliberal policies of the Koizumi administration, invents a new discourse of rurality. The concept of *sōzō nōson* reflects how a local government copes with the post-1990s neoliberal policies from a rural perspective.

According to Tsing (2000), in the global accumulation of capital, the aesthetic value, and appearance of regional resources, rather than their physical properties, are the main topics of negotiation. Making clients and investors believe in a region's potential has become a critical economic strategy. A conjuring act makes potential investment sites seem "more dreamlike and sweeter than anything that exists" (Tsing 2000: 120). Carter offers the 2008 Olympics as an example of the economy of appearance, where London used its "ability to host a mega-event" to "claim status as a global city" (Carter 2006: 151). The extravagant Opening Ceremony demonstrated how spectacular performances can represent a city's potential economic strength. In this way, London was presented as a commodity to be "bought and sold, torn down, speculated upon, and fought over" (2006: 152). Tamba Sasayama hopes to become a creative village through community initiatives and festivals, much as the London Olympics helped London achieve its goal of becoming "a global city" (2006: 151). Its local events may be on a smaller scale, but its aim is more audacious: to transform the appearance of failure into the "appearance of success" (Tsing 2000: 141). However, given that the widely praised amalgamation policy received the opposite attention from the media for the financial struggles from unforeseen debts, the *sōzō nōson* campaign requires a thorough examination beyond its outward manifestations of its achievements. Even while it appears to have been effective in producing a favourable public image and developing an appealing atmosphere, there are underlying issues and complexities to be further scrutinised.

Notes

1 The municipality was formerly called Sasayama after one of the merged towns, but in May 2019, it changed its name to Tamba Sasayama after a public referendum of 69.79 per cent turnout. Depending on the context, I will refer to the municipality by its previous (Sasayama, 1999–2019) and present (Tamba Sasayama, 2019–present) names.
2 https://www.city.sasayama.hyogo.jp/city/topgappe.html.
3 It must be noted that *shi*, translated in English as "city", does not necessarily imply urban region, as population threshold is the main criterion of obtaining the status.
4 https://creative-village.jp/project/project05.html.

2 From Bean to Pottery

Abstract

If anyone has heard of Tamba Sasayama, most refer to *Tanba kuromame*, the Tamba black bean. This larger-than-average black bean produced in the region is considered a local delicacy, enjoyed sugar-coated to have as a snack or to go with alcoholic drinks. Another well-known local product is *Tanbayaki*, or Tamba pottery, a traditional craft passed down for centuries in the small village of Tachikui in Konda town. It was heralded as one of the *mingei* craftworks during the folk craft boom in the early 1970s. Combined, these two products form the local culture that bears both the *shoku* (食, food) and *shokki* (食器, tableware) and creates the ideal rural lifestyle around organic food and local craftsmanship. However, when it comes to the idea of creative village, it is mostly the latter that stands out: Tamba pottery has been central to the conceptualisation and promotion of *sōzō nōson*.

This chapter starts with a simple question, why Tamba pottery? With this question in mind, I discuss the institutional context in which Tamba pottery became associated with the new rurality promoted by Tamba Sasayama. This unravels the conceptual underpinning of *sōzō nōson* that is practical rather than theoretical and which is complex and specific to the local context. I first examine the changing value of traditional pottery in the modernisation process of Japan by looking at various ideas that correspond with the ideals of the folk craft movement in Japan, namely the *mingei undō*. Then, based on my observation of the annual meetings at the Creative City Network of Japan (CCNJ) and Japan Heritage Creative City Promotion Assembly (*Nihon isan sōzō toshi suishin kai*), I describe how a moral discourse of traditional craft gains currency among local government officials, providing a rationale for their decision to put forward Tamba pottery instead of Tamba black bean for the designation as the UNESCO Creative City of Crafts and Folk Arts.

DOI: 10.4324/9781003326540-4

Between Tamba pottery and Tamba black bean

It was a humid summer evening, and I finally met Yuya in person in the lobby of the Tamba Sasayama City Hall where half of the lights were turned off. As I waited for him on a leather sofa next to a large, glazed Tamba pottery, he came down the stairs wearing a comfortable semi-casual suit. He could not believe that I had kept my word to fly over to Tamba Sasayama a few months after I had first contacted him to discuss about my research visit to the region. As this was the first official meeting to discuss my research project, we both spoke and behaved in a formal way. Yuya took out his laptop and presented the slides outlining Tamba Sasayama's regional revitalisation policy, explaining key concepts and projects. I took careful notes to make sure that nothing was missed. As he neared the end of the presentation, a janitor asked us to leave as he had to lock up the building. Having nowhere else to go, we packed up and moved to one of Yuya's favourite pubs, known for its use of locally sourced vegetables.

The warm and welcoming atmosphere of the pub was much more conducive to casual conversation than the City Hall lobby. As we sat down over a glass of beer, Yuya inquired about my motivation for choosing Tamba Sasayama as the focus of my research. Like many people I had met, he was curious as to why I was studying a region that lacked distinctive features such as a significant depopulation crisis or unique regional festivals. I explained that I was attracted by Tamba Sasayama's status as a UNESCO Creative City of Crafts and Folk Arts, and the representation of Tamba pottery as a symbol of rural creativity. Yuya then explained that the original plan for the UCCN membership was to apply as a City of Gastronomy with the Tamba black bean as the regional cultural and creative symbol. I thought about how significantly different the representation of the regional image is based on either Tamba pottery or Tamba black bean, and how elusive the notion of rural creativity is that it could be applied to both. He said that an external expert involved in the application process had advised that Tamba Sasayama had a better chance of being designated if it applied for the cluster of Crafts and Folk Art as Tamba pottery was a better representation of rural creativity.

Since that night, I had been preoccupied with two big questions: on what basis was Tamba pottery considered a better representation of rural creativity, and who was the expert that provided the crucial feedback? It was a revealing insight to know that there was conceptual agreement about the kind of rural creativity that the local government wanted to promote, and that there was an external expert who influenced their decision-making processes. By exploring the social context that led local government officials to shift their vision from Tamba black beans to Tamba pottery as the creative symbol of the region, I was able to partially uncover the collective vision that underpinned Tamba Sasayama's efforts to cultivate an image of a creative village.

Why Tamba pottery? Moral geography and the value of craft

Tamba pottery is a well-known local craft in the Kansai region. However, its representation of Tamba Sasayama can be questioned, as its production is limited to a few dozen families living in the village of Tachikui. It was difficult to find Tamba pottery outside of the village, except in restaurants or antique shops where it was deliberately displayed to attract tourists. In contrast, Tamba black beans were produced by a larger number of households across a wider area. They are consumed in a variety of ways, such as in local *kaiseki ryori* (a multi-course haute cuisine), as sweets for tea ceremonies, and as snacks to go with beer. There is no need to visit a souvenir shop to obtain them, as they can be found in any local grocery store. In addition, the producers had more regional authority than the potters. There was a widespread rumour that the recent name change of the municipality from Sasayama to Tamba Sasayama was influenced by the owner of a black bean company who donated a large sum of money to City Hall to promote the Tamba black beans as *the* local brand of the region.

It was not clear what argument had persuaded the officials to withdraw their initial proposal to put forward Tamba black bean as the creative emblem of the region. Was the opinion of an external expert so influential? If so, what made Tamba pottery more valuable and suitable for the UCCN membership? One possible explanation for the decision was the overall economic potential of the craft industry. International institutions such as the UNCTAD and UNESCO have promoted local development initiatives using local products to sustain and revitalise regional economies. The craft industry has been identified as one of the key strategic industries, along with agriculture and arts. However, the economic outlook for Japan's the craft industry is not so favourable: it has been shrinking since the 1990s, contradicting the positive outlook of the 2010 UNCTAD report. The craft market, which peaked in the 1970s and 1980s, has not been the same in recent decades. For example, sales fell by more than half between 1990 and 2006 (Maekawa et al. 2013), and recent reports indicate that gross sales of traditional crafts in Japan have declined since 2008 (Mitsubishi UFJ Research and Consulting 2017). Not only has the prolonged economic recession since the 1990s led to a freeze in public consumption in general, but cheaper imported goods have also replaced handmade products. The lack of promotional strategies to compete in the market and the insufficient role of the Law for the Promotion of Traditional Crafts Industries in preserving the craft industry also contribute to the sceptical outlook (Maekawa et al. 2013). A local government official in Tamba Sasayama once told me that it was difficult to quantify the economic contribution of the Tamba pottery industry to the region. In other words, it was unclear to them what positive impact it had on the local economy. The uncertain economic outlook raised question about the specific aspect of Tamba pottery that Tamba Sasayama highlighted in its application for the UNESCO City of Crafts and Folk Arts designation.

Tamba Sasayama's activities within the network of the Creative City Network of Japan (CCNJ), of which it was a member before applying for UCCN membership reveal the internal context in which charisma, bureaucracy, and moral discourses intertwine to promote Tamba pottery as a representation of rural creativity. Tamba Sasayama was one of the member municipalities of the CCNJ that called for a rural-centred interpretation of the creativity discourse based on the idea of *sōzō nōson*, and it was not only the representatives of rural municipalities who advocated this, but also the academic community. The backbone of the discourse was a creativity "guru" (Peck 2005: 740). Sasaki Masayuki, the scholar who brought about the "creative turn" (Kong 2014) in public policy in Japan, was an adviser to the UCCN, CCNJ and many other public projects related to creativity in Japan. He was one of the key advisers to Kanazawa's designation as Japan's first UNESCO Creative City of Craft and Folk Arts, which served as his central case study for the *sōzō toshi* theory. Tamba Sasayama, on the other hand, a municipality with a population size of about ten times smaller, has been studied as the rural equivalent of Kanazawa's case. For example, the local initiatives for regional revitalisation in Tamba Sasayama appeared as one of the critical case studies in his recent publication on *sōzō nōson* (Sasaki et al. 2015).

Sasaki's earlier works on the *sōzō toshi* theory show his intellectual influence from the Arts and Crafts Movement, in which he identifies creativity as the "spirit of independent freedom that resists authority" (*ken'i ni taikōsuru jiyū to dokuritsu no seishin*) (Sasaki 1997: 209). Drawing on John Ruskin's writings on the virtue of the Gothic craftspeople, he describes the unique styles and atmosphere of the Gothic architecture as a manifestation of the "free flow of ideas" (*jiyūna hassō*) (1997: 209), emphasising the importance of unfettered human creativity.

However, his idea of *sōzō nōson*, although stemmed from a similar interest in human creativity, had an emphasis on the aspect unique to the rural social context and environment. When he was invited to give a talk on *sōzō nōson* during a local government meeting in Tamba Sasayama, he highlighted the thoughts of a Japanese philosopher, Umehara Takeshi.[1] One of the presentation slides included a paragraph on Umehara's ideas about restoring the relationship between human nature:

> … Umehara criticised Western philosophy for its anthropomorphic ideals that place human authority over nature, leading to environmental pollution and natural disasters caused by mass production and consumption. He believed that Japanese culture, with its strong ties to the natural system, offered an alternative way forward for humanity. We need to appreciate the innate creativity within the natural ecosystem rather than the human creativity that the creative city theory purports.
>
> (my translation)

It seemed that he was deliberately addressing Umehara's criticism of the anthropomorphic view of nature in order to address the unique ideas underlying the idea of *sōzō nōson*. While the necessity of creativity for human well-being was an idea proclaimed by both *sōzō nōson* and *sōzō toshi*, the efficacy of human-nature relations in the idea of creativity was something that only the former could emphasise given its intimate connection with the natural environment. His presentation seemed to emphasise that there was something unique about Tamba Sasayama's pursuit of rural creativity, as it addressed a value that the prevailing *sōzō toshi* theory could not convey, namely the centrality of human-nature relations in rural livelihoods and the particular kind of creativity that emerges within. The conceptual foundation and unique appeal of the idea of *sōzō nōson* was the idea of the moral geography of *rural* creativity.

In this context, traditional crafts such as Tamba pottery were valued not only for their potential economic contribution to the area, but also as a source of creativity discourse characteristic of rural regions.[2] The moral qualities of traditional craft have been salient throughout Japan's modernisation processes. Moeran notes that "the destruction of nature" during Japan's rapid urbanisation and industrialisation in the 20th century "has given rise to an aesthetic theory which focuses on nature and the countryside as the epitome of 'beauty'" (1990: 223). Similarly, Creighton argues that "images of a symbolically mediated traditional craft and rural existence address the threat of estrangement by embracing an ideal of communal belongingness that represents … the moral values of Japan" (Creighton 1995: 467). The representation of Tamba pottery in Tamba Sasayama's campaign for rural creativity resonates with this moral discourse, especially when we look at its recent history as one of the key crafts of the folk craft movement.

The early 20th century was marked by rapid industrialisation and westernisation sweeping across Japan. At the same time, there was a sense of loss of traditional Japanese values and ways of life. Yanagi Muneyoshi, inspired by the Arts and Crafts movement, created a Japanese equivalent that shared the widespread sentiment of the time (Kikuchi 1994: 254–5; Moeran 1989).[3] Drawing on his early interests in Buddhist philosophy and English intellectuals such as William Blake and John Ruskin, he developed an aesthetic philosophy of *mingei*, which literally means "people's art" or "folk craft". Concerned about the growing demand for industrial products and the decline of traditional crafts, he sought ways to preserve the unspoiled traditions on the fringes of modernising urban centres. The idea of *mingei* was therefore not only about aesthetics, but also a "moral crusade against a diseased civilisation", echoing Confucius ideas of "goodness and truth" (Jones 2014: 8). As Brandt (2007) notes, the spread of *mingei* ideals was a product of the complex social milieu of the early 20th century: the anxiety of the literati bourgeoisie towards the growing number of the newly educated and wealthy middle class, and the pervasive climate of nationalism under Japanese imperialism. It was in this climate that Yanagi wrote *The Way of Craft* (*Kōgei no michi*) in 1928, an introductory text on *mingei* philosophy. With a keen interest in Buddhist religious philosophy, he saw ordinary crafts as a medium through which he could discover the way of life, or the moral value, that was deprived of Japanese society at the time. For him, only the state of nature, with no preconceived ideas or self-consciousness, could lead to true beauty: to follow the order of nature, which in his view was "'the Other Power' or *Tariki*, the reliance on the grace of Buddha, as opposed to *Jiriki* or the 'Self Power', attaining Enlightenment through self effort" (Kikuchi 1997: 43). In this context, the idea of craftsmanship became closely intertwined with the historically specific moral concepts of the time. The achievement of artistic beauty was a matter of attitude rather than mere outward appearance. Similar ideas can be found in his 1956 monograph on Tamba pottery, *Old Ceramics of Tamba* (*Tamba no gotō*). He describes how the rustic and unpretentious qualities of this local *shokki* (tableware) show the "bottomless beauty of the Other Power" (1956: 25). The unintentional ash glaze that formed on the surface of old jars was held up as an example of the aesthetic achievement of craftspeople who followed the way of nature. Although such moral values were of little relevance to the everyday lives of contemporary potters and were even contested by some as an elite discourse, Tamba pottery remains strongly influenced by the moral idealisation of craft embedded in the *mingei* philosophy, as it was precisely through the folk craft boom that it gained public recognition.

Recent discussions of the craft industry also address the production and consumption of craft as a demonstration of moral consciousness, such as an anti-capitalist lifestyle. Luckman argues that consuming craft products is about "buying into a relationship with a person and a process" (Luckman 2015: 74), where "small, largely home-based handmade businesses are being championed as the answer to industrialisation and unsustainable global value chains – environmentally and in terms of human rights" (2015: 70). Consumers see the direct relationship with the producers of craft – artists or craftspeople – as something "ethical and local" (2015: 72). Miller also shows how producers are aware of the moral implications of their work and use "specific tools, processes, and materials" (Miller 2017: 4). Furthermore, these moral discourses of craft have had a distinct geographical association with the more provincial and rural areas. Craft revival movements throughout history have created "distinctively rural spaces of expression" (Fois et al. 2019: 664; see also Miller 2017), where the moral values of craft were manifest in the display of its affinity with the natural environment. Regional craft scenes often serve as "attractive component of neo-endogenous rural development strategies based on the revitalisation of local 'culture economies'" (Fois et al. 2019: 664). The value of craft is multiplied when it is "imbued with local skills and values and made from local materials which mark them out as different" (Gough and Rigg 2012: 184).

I argue that Tamba pottery exemplifies the inherent value of rural creativity in Tamba Sasayama's campaign for *sōzō nōson*, which encompasses not only the cultural and economic aspects of rural craft, but also certain moral implications. This value emerged from the complex relationship between the craft itself, the moral geography it represented, and the rural space to which it was deeply connected to. In this context, it served as a better representation than the Tamba black bean for its representation of the creativity characteristic of rural space. Promoting rural creativity in terms of the moral superiority of the countryside and through the representation of rural craftsmanship seems to make sense given the trend of urban-rural migration, which reflects a general critique of neoliberal lifestyles (Manzenreiter et al. 2020: 299).

How then did this idea gain traction among local government officials? A national CCNJ conference and a local assembly in Tamba Sasayama show the specific socio-cultural context in which the collective discourse of moral geography is shared among officials and intellectuals in bureaucratic settings.

Bureaucratic formalities and the role of creativity guru

It was early in the morning, around 5:30. I drove to Yuya's house to pick him up and went straight to Sasayamaguchi station to catch a JR train to Osaka station. We were attending the first CCNJ meeting of 2019, which started at 11:00 am at a convention centre near Tokyo. As soon as we got off the crowded commuter train, we dashed to the next platform to catch a Shinkansen train.

There were already lively corridor discussions in the lobby when we arrived at the convention centre. Instead of going straight to the meeting room, Yuya greeted his close colleagues from other municipalities. Soon after, the cheerful atmosphere in the corridors disappeared. As the meeting time approached, the friendly jokes and laughter were put aside and a formal exchange of business cards began.

The room was meticulously organised, with name tags and paper documents prepared. The format of the meeting was simple. The chair made an opening statement followed by a main discussion divided into several topics and a closing message. In attendance to welcome everyone with an opening speech was a renowned scholar at the forefront of the creative turn in public policy in Japan. A central government official from the Agency for Cultural Affairs (*Bunka-chō*) then made brief remarks about current central government policy on regional revitalisation. Representatives from each local government then presented their latest population figures and ongoing regional revitalisation initiatives.

The discussions were strictly formal. A facilitator kept track of the time minute by minute to ensure that the meeting ran on time. Given the limited time to present their current policies, representatives could only provide bullet points and abstract figures rather than specific local contexts. Many of the local projects mentioned were similar, as if there was a standardised guideline for regional revitalisation strategies. Local festivals, educational programmes, and art projects were the most common initiatives. Although the aim of the meeting was to brainstorm creative strategies for regional revitalisation, its formalities seemed to create a barrier to the free flow of ideas. Instead, the scholar's comments at the end seemed to inspire a spirit of creativity in the room. Rather than giving direct feedback, he made a brief but encouraging speech about his philosophies on the meeting's theme. Although craft was not the key local product for all the regions, he referred to the value of creativity based on the story of how the industrial revolution have enabled us to mass produce but devalued the handwork where human creativity lies. Reviving this human creativity in the local cultural production system and tourism could revitalise the local economy. His words were taken with the utmost seriousness and respect, and his influence was felt in the breaks between meetings and in the *konshinkai* (get-togethers), always in the midst of crowds, exchanging business cards and offering advice. I was also advised to bring an omiyage for him, which seemed to serve as a formal introduction to the network.

Such a vision shared by renowned expert had also been of great value in the regional meetings in Tamba Sasayama. Since June 2018, the Creative City Section and the Tourism Division (*kankō bu*) have held the Japan Heritage Creative City Promotion Assembly (*Nihon isan sōzō toshi suishin kai*) with citizen members representing various local organisations. The assembly was less formal than the CCNJ meetings, but also had a fixed order and time constraints. The local government officials began with an opening statement and reviewed the discussions of the previous meeting. Then, in turn, each citizen representative gave their opinion on Tamba Sasayama's regional revitalisation policy, based on the internal contexts of their communities. For example, Toshiaki, one of the key members of the Tamba Tachikui Pottery Cooperative (*Tamba tachikui tōjiki kyōdo kumiai*), spoke critically about the low sales of Tamba pottery over the past four years and how they could be improved by working closely with the local government. Another representative from a neighbourhood organisation discussed residents' discontent concerning a recent festival. The citizen representatives freely shared their thoughts and expectations. The lively discussion, however, was only a prelude to the main task they had come together: drafting the UCCN Monitoring Report that the local government had to submit by the end of the year. As the officials read each page, they invited the audience to ask questions or make comments. If there was silence, the officials turned to the next page.

Halfway through the meeting, an established scholar in the field of regional revitalisation was introduced to the meeting room. After a brief introduction, he stood in front of a large screen displaying his presentation slides and gave a talk summarising the value of the UCCN membership and the ideal directions for Tamba Sasayama's regional revitalisation policy. He explained the theoretical and philosophical background of *sōzō nōson* through various academic references and clarified why it is important to discover new values from rural cultural sources, citing examples of other countries. He then read out the definition of *sōzō nōson* and argued that the concept would become increasingly important in dealing with rural social issues and stressed that Japan would lead its discussions in international forums such as the UCCN conferences. Although he skipped a few slides during the presentation, the handout included other ideas behind *sōzō nōson*, such as quotes from John Ruskin – "cherishing the innate value of nature which gives birth to things around us, and the beautiful landscape allows us to think creatively and artistically" – and a description of an art movement led by *hanno hangei* (half agriculture half art, 半農半芸) farmers of the *Rasukinjin Kyōkai* (People of Ruskin Association).

The presentation was impressive in the depth and richness. However, it was also loaded with highly academic concepts and ideas. Despite the abstract and conceptual nature of his talk, it seemed to be well received by the audience in the room. Conversations with some of the citizens' representatives after the meeting revealed that his ideas were valued not for their logic or philosophical depth but for their optimistic tone. He seemed to have given them the confidence to rethink and reassess Tamba Sasayama's future. His talks were significant in that a renowned expert proposes unconventional ideas of rural creativity and shares hopeful remarks about the prospects of the countryside. When I asked a local government official from another region on her opinion about the scholar's vision, she recited a phrase she claimed to have heard directly from him: "*sōzō nōson no jidai*" (the era of the creative village). She said that the day would soon come.

According to Bortolotto et al., bureaucrats are dedicated to their work "not only because of their training and sense of duty but also because they are committed to certain values and ethics" (Bortolotto et al. 2020: 68). The promotion of Tamba pottery was driven not only by economic prospects but also by its inherent moral and geographical values, which were deeply connected to the conceptual identity of *sōzō nōson* and its distinctive creativity set against the rural environment. Tamba Sasayama's ambition to reshape the public perception of the region was rooted in a hybrid conception of rural space. However, as much as the discourse on the moral values of rural creativity and the representation of Tamba pottery was secured within the bureaucratic formalities and the persuasive, eloquent speeches of experts, another question seemed to remain, as to whether the collective ideas shared by officials and citizens' representatives could extend beyond the bureaucratic sphere.

Conclusion

Sayre and Löwy argue that we are still under the paradigm of Romanticism, in "a cultural protest against modern industrial/capitalist civilization" (Sayre and Löwy 2019: 1). In Japan, the moral connotations of craft that gained popularity in the early 20th century, coupled with the moral geography of the urban-rural dynamics, still carry considerable weight as a narrative for regional revitalisation movements. By tracing the processes by which the concept of *sōzō nōson* gained legitimacy among Tamba Sasayama's local government officials, I demonstrated that Tamba Sasayama's decision to promote Tamba pottery as a symbol of rural creativity was motivated not only by its cultural or economic values, but also by its moral connotations.

However, the idea of *sōzō nōson*, promoted by intellectuals and bureaucrats who supported rural moral values within their comfort zones, had little to do with the social and cultural complexities of the region. This is reminiscent of how *mingei* was promoted by a few "enlightened individuals" (Brandt 2007: 55) who sought to address the social problems of the time. The validity of the moral ideals of rurality and the uniqueness of rural creativity should be questioned outside the formal setting of bureaucratic meetings and without the reliance on inspiring words of an expert. Furthermore, if moral values are the conceptual foundation of *sōzō nōson*, how do local residents understand and perceive them? How do local officials translate the idea of *sōzō nōson* into local social and cultural contexts? The following chapter will address these questions and examine the practical aspects of how Tamba Sasayama's exploration of the new rurality is communicated between local government officials and residents.

Notes

1 Umehara Takeshi was an eminent scholar whose works have dealt with wide-ranging topics concerning the origins of Japanese people and culture. A key figure in the post-war *Nihonjinron* discourse, his early works on Japanese and Ainu culture have been criticised for idealising and essentialising Japan (see Befu 2001, for a comprehensive critique of the post-war *Nihonjinron* discourse).

2 It is important to note that the creativity of the human-nature relationship that Sasaki sought to emphasise in the *sōzō nōson* theory was not entirely new. Both John Ruskin and William Morris recognised the human-nature relationship. Rural space played an important role in the discussion of the moral values of craft: "traditional, especially rural, crafts were at the heart of a democratic approach to creativity" (Luckman 2012: 60). As we know from Morris's classic works – fabrics and wallpapers with patterns of plants and nature – the countryside served as the ideal ground for creativity, "the site of self-actualising labour" (Luckman 2012: 49):

> … the key thrust of the Arts and Crafts Movement in practice was centred on rural creative traditions. Two aspects of this rural focus are particularly notable here: a commitment to regional development via the revival of traditional local handicrafts and skills (including education in new ones) and an attention to the provision of local infrastructure.
>
> (Luckman 2012: 49)

3 In the turmoil of the Industrial Revolution, which transformed all forms of labour into an uncreative, piecemeal, and alienated state, John Ruskin and William Morris "sought to challenge the dehumanising assemblages" (Luckman 2012: 52) by reclaiming human creativity. Ruskin proposed one of the earliest forms of art economics. The task was to distinguish work from labour; the former, the production of human creativity, and the latter, an activity imposed by another. His aim was to preserve both humanity and creativity amidst the unromantic life of repetitive motion, and to produce goods that were both functional and artistically beautiful. A successor to Ruskin's school of thought, Morris also criticised the mass production–consumption system of mechanised industry, which led to the alienation of work. He organised the Arts and Crafts Movement, reintroducing artisanal production and seeking to encourage the creativity of craftspeople.

3 The Ambiguity of Rural Creativity

Abstract

Walking down the streets in the Sasayama Castle town, one can find a statue of a *Dekansho* dancer, kiosks of all sorts of black bean products, and, if lucky, old Tamba potteries displayed by the windows of the Shōwa houses. One can also notice the deliberate displays of these local products in standing banners, posters of local festivals, and placards hanging on walls with UNESCO Creative City and Japan Heritage marks. They decorate the public space of Tamba Sasayama, hinting at the changes that the *sōzō nōson* campaign is bringing to the region. However, to residents' eyes, they are mainly invisible. When I asked questions about the concept of *sōzō nōson* and the related projects, I was often met with an innocent look or indifference. These were the common attitudes among most of the people I met, and in a way, an expected reaction from people busy with their everyday lives.

This chapter examines the prevailing sense of ambiguity surrounding Tamba Sasayama's regional revitalisation policies. I trace the internal context of the local government that had led to the campaign for *sōzō nōson* to elucidate how this somewhat experimental catchphrase was adopted as the slogan for regional revitalisation strategies. In contrast to the sense of optimism shared among bureaucrats, experts, and representatives of local organisations shown in the previous chapter, the municipal-wide trajectory of the campaign shows the limits deriving from the institutional settings of the local government and the shared feeling of confusion and ambiguity.

Ambiguity as a context

It was almost nine o'clock in the morning when I swiftly parked my old Toyota in the communal parking area of Tachikui. Without a moment's delay, I hurriedly made my way to Shōhei's workshop. I had received an invitation to attend a meeting with two local government officials from the Creative City Section, Miu and Yuya. They were visiting Shōhei to discuss about a small booklet designed for elementary and middle school students in Tamba Sasayama, introducing regional products and traditions. Since Tamba pottery

DOI: 10.4324/9781003326540-5

was one of the main cultural representations, it took up two pages of the eight-page booklet. As Miu was overseeing the project, she started the meeting by explaining the concept, aim, and content with a hand-drawn sample design on an A4-sized sheet. The booklet featured a picture of a potter figure discussing Tamba Sasayama's designation as a UNESCO Creative City of Crafts and Folk Arts. One of the reasons Miu and Yuya visited Shōhei was to interview him and fill in the blank word balloon. Miu's first questions were about the definition of Tamba pottery and Shōhei's experience as a potter. He did not hesitate to tell his stories. Then, she asked if he could say something about Tamba Sasayama's designation as a UNESCO Creative City of Crafts and Folk Arts. Shōhei paused for a moment, lost in his own thoughts. Then, he turned to me and asked if I, as a researcher, had anything to add. Since I had nothing to say, I remained silent. Shōhei turned to his right side and asked the Miu what he should say. Now, Miu took her time to think. When she finally broke the silence, her answer sounded more like an excuse than a simple answer. She confessed that she had only started her job in the Creative City Section a few months ago and was still struggling to understand the ongoing projects. I later found out that she had been transferred to her current position from a department that had nothing to do with the promotional campaigns of *sōzō nōson*. She gave a short and vague answer that the whole purpose of the UCCN might have something to do with the use of local products like Tamba pottery "creatively" (*sōzōteki ni*). The conversation was punctuated by frequent pauses, as if silence were an active participant. Nevertheless, we managed to cover all the topics that was planned to discuss.

A few months later, during a public meeting at a citizen centre, a familiar wave of confusion swept through. An elderly gentleman in the audience, who introduced himself as a native resident of Tamba Sasayama, asked a question to the public officials on the stage about the meaning of creative city (*sōzō toshi*). It seemed that he had stumbled across the term in newspapers but had no idea what it meant. Among several City Hall officials present in the room, it was Yuya who took the microphone to respond. At first, he seemed baffled by a straightforward question, but he soon answered with aplomb. Rather than defining or clarifying the term itself, he gave examples of past and current projects and how they have and could improve the local economy. The gentleman nodded in acknowledgement of the answer and no further questions were raised.

These anecdotes show instances where the bureaucratic sphere, with its dominant discourse and practices, intersects with everyday life. Officials' interactions with residents, such as Shōhei or the elderly man, illustrate how an ideal concept or value underlying regional revitalisation policies loses its efficacy outside the bureaucratic sphere. For those who are not invited to institutional rituals such as the CCNJ or the local Assembly meetings, the elements that legitimise the concept of *sōzō nōson*, such as expert insight or bureaucratic formalities, are absent. Without the right environment to foster collective agreements, ambiguity seemed to prevail.

Anthropologists have recently sought to gain a better understanding of how bureaucracy operates in the real world by exploring the social lives of bureaucrats, describing the everyday workings of bureaucracies in a way that truly captures their "banality" (Mathur 2017; see also Bernstein and Mertz 2011). In this context, ambiguity has been discussed as an integral element in understanding the institutional workings under neoliberal systems of governance, exploring the loopholes of organisational practices (Hull 2012; De Genova 2002; Tuckett 2015) and elucidating the diverse ways in which individuals cope with bureaucratic challenges (Abma 2000; Best 2012a, 2012b, Nielsen 2011; Pinker 2015). By using ambiguity as a conceptual lens to examine the everyday practices of individual officials and their subjective perceptions of policy ideas, we can shed light on the complexities and nuances of bureaucratic processes that might otherwise be overlooked.

The implication of ambiguity has been particularly relevant in public policies invested in the idea of creativity (Cunningham 2011; Garnham 2005). It has been suggested that the "very lack of certainty" (Cunningham 2011: 48) is the essence of the creative industries, where the question of "what the creative industries are, why they are important and thus merit supporting policy initiatives" has been "[taken] for granted" (Garnham 2005: 16). The broad definition of creativity-related policy allows for diverse regional initiatives that are not bound by the specific guidelines set by the central government. The popularity of the creativity discourse lies in its "specific rhetorical purpose within policy discourse" (2005: 16), serving as a shorthand for a range of theoretical and political positions.

In Chapter 2, I argued that the *sōzō nōson* initiatives place more emphasis on changing the image of a rural region, as a strategic slogan to transform the regional atmosphere from one of decline to one of cultural prosperity and creativity. However, the opening anecdotes in this chapter illustrate how the campaigns to create a new rural image can be as confusing as they are hopeful for the region. Based on an understanding of ambiguity as a "social concept that comes into play when people try to make sense of the world around them and act on those interpretations" (Best 2012a: 89), I explore the practical dimension of Tamba Sasayama's implementation of the *sōzō nōson* campaigns with a sense of ambiguity as "a place to begin" (Niezen and Sapignoli 2017: 2).

In the early stages of my fieldwork, I tried to understand the local perceptions of public policy by asking a wide range of people, from civil servants to a retired high school teacher, if they were familiar with local projects such as UCCN or Japan Heritage. Many had heard of these projects but could not clearly explain what they were about. Some pointed out about the unclear linguistic connotation of the term *sōzō*. For example, an official at City Hall once asked me to explain the English translation of *sōzō* and how it was generally understood by English-speaking audiences. I frankly told him that I had no clear idea. Perhaps as a result of my unexpected openness about my lack of knowledge, he shared that he also did not fully grasp its meaning, despite having overseen the relevant projects. It was revealing to know that we were both struggling to grasp a concept we took seriously. He pointed out that the translation of "creative" into "*sōzō*" was misleading. First, "*sōzō*" can be understood as both "imagination (*sōzō* 想像)" and "creativity (*sōzō* 創造)", but, it was only the latter has been agreed as the official meaning. Secondly, he thought that "creative" was better translated into Japanese as "*sōsaku* (創作)" than "*sōzō*", which means creativity but with an emphasis on the making (*saku*, 作). Furthermore, grammatically, "*sōzō*" should be "*sōzō-teki*" to become an adjective meaning "creat-ive". The concept, translated directly from the theoretical debates of the Euro-American context seemed to require a lengthy explanation to be comprehensible in Japanese. However, the linguistic clarity seemed to be a minor matter in practice. For instance, the officials often used the terms *sōzō toshi* and *sōzō nōson* interchangeably, even though the latter was the correct term for the projects they were dealing with.

Instead, what seemed to create confusion around the concept of *sōzō* was the inconsistency of multiple regional revitalisation projects that were linked together despite having little in common in terms of their content or theme. For example, the UNESCO Creative City mark appeared on almost all public posters, banners, websites, and other media promoting local cultural events, exemplifying what Garnham calls the rhetorical power of creativity that "serves as a slogan" for a wide range of public initiatives (2005: 16). These elusive boundaries of creativity as a concept seemed to lead to the question of what *sōzō* exactly means.

In this chapter, I neither focus on the conceptual clarity of *sōzō nōson*, nor attempt to evaluate its validity as a guiding concept of Tamba Sasayama's regional revitalisation policy. Instead, I explore how it is implemented despite the lack of a comprehensive understanding of its conceptual meaning, from the perspective of those directly involved in its formulation and promotion. Based on my interactions with several local government officials, I show that the prevailing self-help ethos, indirectly encouraged by the central government's regional policy, sets the stage. As inter-regional competition has become the basic logic of national policies dealing with regional revitalisation, such as the Abe administration's *Chihō sōsei* policy, local governments feel pressured to make short-term plans for public subsidies, concerned of being left behind. I argue that Tamba Sasayama's attainment of the UNESCO Creative City title is part of their strategies to gain a competitive edge in the race for public subsidies.

The *keshō* of creativity

The Abe administration had pinned much of its hopes on the impact of regional revitalisation on the national economy, and encouraged local governments to participate in the Local Abenomics. The *Chihō sōsei* policy provided highly competitive public subsidies. One of the three main monetary provision schemes was the Allocation Grant for Promoting Regional Revitalisation (*Chihō sōsei suishin kōfukin*, hereby Allocation Grant), which distributed a total of 10,000,000 yen to local governments each year between 2016 and 2020 To receive the Allocation Grant, a local government had to submit a five-year plan called the Local Edition of the Revitalisation Strategy (*Chihō ban sōgō senryaku*), which was evaluated based on seven criteria, including financial independence, public-private partnerships, cooperation between different regions, and relevance to the overall theme of the Regional Revitalisation policy. The plan was evaluated and announced by the committee members of the Prime Minister along with the Council for Overcoming Population Decline and Revitalising Local Economies in Japan (*Machi hito shigoto sōsei honbu*).

However, getting accepted for the grant was only the beginning. In return for the grant, the local government had to spend an equivalent amount from the municipal budget, which was a considerable burden for financially unstable regions. Additionally, the local government had to carry out the projects as originally proposed, hence the grant could not be spent on extra equipment or overtime work. As a result, any additional labour hours or materials required to implement the projects had to be covered by the local government budget, resulting in unpaid work for a small number of local government employees. In fact, it was reported that local governments struggling to plan and manage the five-year Regional Revitalisation schemes outsourced some of the workload to external consulting firms. In 2017, 70 per cent of 1,317 local governments had subcontracted with external consulting firms, most of which were private organisations based in Tokyo, Osaka, and Nagoya, contradicting the main purpose of the Regional Revitalisation policy, which is to reduce the economic gap between metropolitan centres and the rest.[1] The current tendency for local governments to indulge in securing public grants has exposed local government officials to the systematic burdens of multiple roles and long working hours. As Love argues, the central government's policy of decentralisation has only increased the "responsibility of rural collectivities to 'rediscover' the seeds of future vitality in their surroundings" (2013: 117). Tamba Sasayama was no exception.

The Creative City Section (*Sōzō toshi ka*) manages regional revitalisation projects in Tamba Sasayama, such as organising events to promote rural creativity and managing of the UCCN and CCNJ initiatives. It was established in 2012, shortly after the local government shifted the direction of regional policy from development to revitalisation. Behind the creation of this division and the rise of the creativity discourse was Nomura, a former local government employee. From the early stages of my fieldwork, I had heard stories and rumours about him, which seemed to indicate his widespread reputation and influence in the region. He seemed to be the kind of person who has the charisma of what Hansen and Verkaaic call "fantasmic surplus – rumours and circulating stories of certain deeds of these individuals, their past life and career and so on" (Hansen and Verkaaik 2009: 16).

When I finally met him in a café near Sasayama Castle, Nomura introduced himself as the head of a local organisation that provides advise on rural revitalisation policies and business start-ups. He had retired from the City Hall years ago, but still vividly remembered his days as a civil servant. He first came to the region as an agent from the Hyogo prefectural government to help with Tamba Sasayama's debt crisis. With the tip of his hand tracing a downward line, he demonstrated the sudden deterioration of the regional economy around the time of his arrival. The local government was worried about facing bankruptcy, as had happened a few years earlier in Yubari, Hokkaido. With financial constraints and a lack of locally sustainable industries, he had to find a way to reduce public spending while improving the quality of public services. Before reaching the table, he raised his hand slightly upwards and said that it was then that he began to think about the idea of *sōzō nōson*.

It all started in 2011 when he attended the CCNJ conference for the first time. He took part in one of the seminars where the municipal representatives took turns to talk about regional issues and revitalisation strategies. Nomura gave a presentation on the concept of *sōzō nōson*, a term he invented by rewording *sōzō toshi*, and proposed it as a new vision to make rural regions a creative and inspiring space. It should be noted, however, that there were differing opinions as to who first came up with the concept. Later, during the reception, other public officials gathered to discuss the potential of developing Nomura's new concept as a pair of *sōzō toshi*. Confident from his discussions with like-minded people, he took the idea to Tamba Sasayama to form a new conceptual basis for regional revitalisation strategies.

What appealed to Nomura about the concept, however, was not its economic prospects or his understanding of academic debates around the creative industries, but its practicality in reframing Tamba Sasayama's image. According to him, Tamba Sasayama was a different case from Kanazawa, which also promoted traditional craft for regional creativity, as it had a larger budget to build a solid foundation for relevant policies. For the financially struggling region, the rationale behind the idea to promote creativity was simple: to create an innovative image that would increase the chances of obtaining public subsidies. He believed that a fresh vision was crucial to prevent the local government from worsening its future financial situation.

Nomura used the term *keshō*, meaning "to make-up" or "to paint", to describe his intentions in using the concept of creativity. His aim was to use the positive connotation of *sōzō* to make Tamba Sasayama more attractive to potential investors and migrants, and in the applications for public subsidies. However, the projects initiated under the slogan of *sōzō nōson* were not particularly innovative or creative in themselves. For instance, the first project under Nomura's new vision, the 400th anniversary, was not much different from the usual cultural festivals that Tamba Sasayama had held. What was different was that there was conscious effort to be *seen* as creative. Having *sōzō* in the title of the regional revitalisation policy was enough to signal the positive changes and originality of Tamba Sasayama. Resonating with Woods' argument about the diversifying representations of rural space, the campaign for *sōzō nōson* was a promising act for a financially struggling region for "the power and popularity of … ideas" (Woods 2011: 9).

Sennett argues that strong leadership has always been the driving force behind public projects of city planning. He cites the example of a civil engineer who oversaw the construction of London's sewers in the mid-19th century. This engineer made decisions based on his gut feeling and vision rather than scientific calculation: "[o]ne of the truly admirable aspects of Bazalgette's character is that he exuded Victorian confidence without claiming that he knew exactly what he was doing, believing only that he would get it right in the end" (Sennett 2018: 25). Similarly, Nomura's decision to transform the municipality's revitalisation policy was bold and visionary. When he introduced the idea of *sōzō nōson* in 2011, the general mood at City Hall was despondent due to large-scale restructuring. His idea met with mixed opinions from his colleagues, but he convinced them of the potential value of this new concept and preached about the new opportunities it could bring. In the end, his vision was taken on board, and regional revitalisation strategies were refocused on promoting this rather unconventional notion of rurality.

However, Nomura admitted that there had not been enough discussion among the officials about his ideas because of the immediate financial problems Tamba Sasayama was facing. With the debt clock ticking and an immediate solution needed, the concept was adopted without a thorough examination of its specific implications for the region. And soon after the local government had embraced his vision, he had to retire from City Hall for personal reasons. Nevertheless, the projects that Nomura had started continued and produced satisfactory results. Tamba Sasayama chaired the Sasayama Creative Cities Network Promotion Committee and the UCCN network of Japan in 2012 and 2013, and was later successfully nominated for UCCN membership and Japan Heritage. The *Chihō sōsei* policy initiated by the central government in 2015 also motivated officials to further develop the idea of *sōzō nōson* to apply for its five-year subsidies.

Despite the success of the projects implemented under the concept, there was lingering confusion among the post-Nomura generations of local government officials. When he left, leaving behind the ongoing initiatives, it became clear just how significant his influence had been. Echoing what Weber argued about charisma, that there are "territorial or functional limits to charismatic powers" (1978: 243), his absence had left a sense of ambiguity and disorientation behind. Miu's difficulties with the booklet project are an example of the challenges of implementing projects without a solid grasp of the general policy direction. Furthermore, within the existing structure of City Hall, it is difficult for individuals to develop a comprehensive understanding of all the projects they are responsible for. For example, staff rotate between different divisions every three years, so that they are trained to be multitaskers who can deal with the different tasks of the local government. This is more the case in Tamba Sasayama, where a major structural reform of the local government after the merger in 1999 consolidated the local administrative offices into a single office, resulting in fewer employees covering a wider expertise. Miu's lack of understanding of the UCCN project reflects the absence of a guiding figure and the chronic problem in the structure of the local government. Shōhei seemed to be well aware of her difficulties, as the potters were equally frustrated by having to reintroduce themselves each time a new official took over a project in development.

Dealing with ambiguities

Despite the pervasive sense of ambiguity that prevailed among public officials, there were individual strategies for coping with this uncertainty. Yuya, who was in his 40s, had joined the Creative City Section when it had just been formed. His outgoing personality and a good sense of humour set him apart from his colleagues. As one of the most experienced members of the Section, he was responsible for several projects. As the spokesperson for various projects relating to the campaigns to change the public image of Tamba Sasayama, he was the one who communicated most frequently with the locals. Best argues that it is the role of "key actors" to manage "the task of reining in the scope of the policy and ensuring greater clarity in its definition" (2012a: 95). Yuya was the "direct link" (2012a: 94) that connected the concept of creativity to the various projects being implemented under the umbrella concept of *sōzō nōson*. In a way, he had inherited Nomura's role in maintaining the *keshō* of creativity. I was not surprised when he told me of his close relationship with Nomura, often meeting up for a light meal or coffee. Although Nomura was a retired employee, Yuya seemed to continue to seek his advice.

As a native resident of the area, unlike many other City Hall officials who commuted from Sanda or other suburban areas on the outskirts of Osaka, he had a strong sense of pride of his hometown and went the extra mile in the tasks assigned to him. However, explaining Tamba Sasayama's regional revitalisation policy to the public was always a challenge for him. One of them was effectively communicating the abstract conceptual ideas behind the various projects.

To compensate the limit of verbally explaining the concept, he had developed his own visual tools that allowed him to explain in a more accessible and appealing way. One of his favourite methods was to use presentation slides in public lectures or seminars, which were planned in detail to capture the audience's attention and keep them engaged.

One of the usual versions goes like this. At the beginning of the presentation, Yuya introduces himself as an enthusiastic photographer and shows the beautiful pictures of local landscapes and Tamba pottery that he had taken. He then shows a cropped image of an elderly man holding a Tamba pottery and explains the history and tradition of Tamba pottery. Here, he intentionally misleads the audience to assume that the figure is a professional Tamba potter. However, in the following slide, when the image is revealed in its entirety, it shows Yuya standing next to the potter with a young girl who looks just like him. In fact, the potter is his father, who takes Tamba pottery classes as a hobby. This idea was to convey a sense of rural creativity, the value of living in the countryside with its wealth of cultural activities. This part of the presentation always drew laughter from the audience, turning a serious subject into something one can relate to.

However, such an effective communication strategy did not work for everyone. I learned this from talking to Shunsuke, an elderly Tamba potter who lives in Tachikui, when he mentioned about the visit of two foreign guests that Yuya had brought to his workshop. After talking about how international Yuya's working environment was, he asked me if I had heard about Yuya's business trip abroad for the upcoming conference abroad, to which I confirmed that I was already aware of. When I added that I had also attended the UCCN conference earlier that year and witnessed a presentation by a team led by Yuya that explained about regional revitalisation policy and Tamba pottery, he wondered why he had not heard such stories. He then said that Yuya seemed to spend most of his time with Toshiaki, an active member of the *kumiai*. This was partly true, as it was also Toshiaki whom Yuya first introduced to me as a point of contact in Tachikui. He was by far Yuya's closest collaborator, being one of the first potters to take part in the discussions about the campaigns for *sōzō nōson*. Without a sense of connection with the public officials, Shunsuke seemed to find it difficult to grasp the development of the projects he was involved in.

Yuya acknowledged the difficulties of maintaining close relations with the potters in Tachikui, mainly because he was the only staff responsible for maintaining contact with them. Although there were other officials involved, they were mostly dealing with bureaucratic tasks in the office or working on a short-term basis, like Miu. Since it was not possible for him to visit Tachikui frequently, he had to prioritise one or two potters as his main points of contact. He enjoyed the work, getting along with the potters and developing new projects using local traditions. As the plans to promote Tamba Sasayama as the destination of rural creativity seemed to work out successfully, with the recent designation of UCCN and Japan Heritage, he seemed confident in his contributions. At the same time, he was also keenly aware of the limits to his ability, the lack of energy and time to manage multiple projects simultaneously. He was a dedicated City Hall official and a native resident with deep emotional ties attached to the region. However, his passion alone seemed insufficient to sustain the motivation to revitalise his hometown.

Conclusion

Recent works in the anthropology of bureaucracy has discussed ambiguity for its positive aspects, emphasising individual agency and the possibilities offered by the open-ended nature of gaps and loopholes in bureaucratic systems. Bortolotto et al. argues that "bureaucratic creativity is…made possible through the flexibility provided by the absence of clear official definitions" (2020: 76). Contrary to the dominant perception of bureaucratic institutions as rule-bound and rational (Weber 1978), the cracks in the highly ordered bureaucratic world allow creativity to emerge (Abma 2000; Best 2012a,

2012b; Bortolotto et al. 2020; Nielsen 2011; Pinker 2015). Much of their focus has been on the creativity that emerges within the confines of a tightly controlled environment. In this context, a sense of ambiguity is like an oasis in a desert. It tells us not only about the shortcomings of organisational structures, but also about the "strategic advantage" (Best 2012a: 100), "principled improvisation" (Cowan 2020: 28), "spontaneous knowledge" (Billaud 2020: 117), and "the interpretational space" (Nielsen 2011: 278) that allows room for individual agency. As Bortolotto et al. argue, the way individual agents deal with organisational constraints is a "dialectical process between disenchantment and aspiration" in which "the limitations of bureaucratic measures, expressed in sentiments of disappointment and frustration with policy results, trigger creative efforts to meet the utopian principle" (2020: 78; see also Nielsen 2011).

While these works expand our understanding of bureaucratic practices, how can we apply their insights to Yuya's case? While the discussion resonates with how he created strategic devices, such as the presentation slides to explain the confusing concept of sōzō nōson to the public, he also faced difficulties in maintaining close relationships with the potters. Perhaps what we need to consider when examining an ambiguous aspect of a bureaucratic world is not only the efficacy of creative strategies, but also the physical limits, distinguishing between the possible conditions for individual agents to be creative and their willingness to develop creative strategies of any kind.

The ambiguity surrounding Tamba Sasayama's *sōzō nōson* campaign resonates with Peck's analysis of the creativity boom in public policy: "[t]he hard news for civic leaders is that while they can, and must, do whatever is in their power to cultivate creativity, there is no way of knowing where the creative sparks will ignite" (2005: 762). The rapid development of the "creative turn" in the region, driven by Nomura's charismatic leadership and the *sōzō* title that secured public grants, resulted in a shallow logical foundation and deep doubts about the meaning of rural creativity. In a way, Yuya's efforts were an attempt to inherit Nomura's charismatic role, justifying and explaining the effectiveness of the policy to the public with engaging presentation slides. However, his creativity could not alone cope with the heavy workload assigned to him, which proved beyond his creative capabilities.

Note

1 "Seventy percent of local development plans of municipalities in Japan are outsourced and 2.1 billion yen of grant money is returned to Tokyo" (*zenkoku no shichōson no chihō sōsei keikaku no 7 wari ga gaichū kōfukin 21 oku en ga Tōkyō ni kanryū*) (Chunichi Shinbun, 13 Jan 2019, no longer available).

4 Enacting Creativity

Abstract

This chapter documents my involvement in the collaborative project between local actors. Based on Yukari's business plan for a guided tour programme in Tamba Sasayama, I show how her efforts to cooperate with other so-called creative agents of Tamba Sasayama's *sōzō nōson* campaign were met with unexpected challenges such as the rumours and stories about other towns and villages that created emotional barriers in interacting with them. In facilitating a dialogue between Yukari and the Tamba potters, I learned that the cooperation between the local actors required careful plannings based on a discrete understanding of the intra-regional stereotypes. This readily revealed a direct contrast with the presumption of creativity in Tamba Sasayama's UNESCO Creative City report that implied the region as an organic community of creatives that are open to each other and communicate without constraints. As I show, the success of Yukari's long-esteemed project with the Tamba potters was not the result of an unprompted encounter but a deliberate arrangement of their interactions.

Creating social ties in a web of regional stereotypes

A recent study of Tamba Sasayama's entrepreneurial activities shows a clear trend of "*tanbo kaiki*" (return to the paddy field), with a growing number of migrants starting new businesses in the region (Tanikawa and Nakatsuka 2020: 127). A noticeable group of newcomers are the old retirees who settle in through private consultancy services. Compared to young migrants, they are financially well-off and less inclined to seek economic activity to make a living. In an attempt to achieve the lifestyle they have long desired, they indulge in activities related to their hobbies or interests. Nobuo, who recently settled in Tamba Sasayama, had previously worked for thirty years in a furniture store in a city full of trendy fashion brands in Tokyo. He had always dreamed of spending his later years in the peaceful countryside, and Tamba Sasayama was the perfect place. Its geographical location was particularly appealing; a few hours by train takes one to Osaka, Kobe, Kyoto, and other coastal areas in the

DOI: 10.4324/9781003326540-6

north. He runs a café in a renovated *kominka*, an old house to which he has developed a strong attachment. His love for the place is evident in the small vases of flowers carefully placed in the corners, the tastefully decorated tea-room, and the well-kept inner garden. Initially discovered with the help of a local consulting group, the building was in poor condition, with a tilted structure, a leaky roof, and even a small pond inside, the result of years of neglect since the closure of a previous restaurant. Despite the unexpected cost of a year-long renovation, which involved repairing everything from the bottom part of the wooden pillars to the roof above, Nobuo was confident that he had made the right decision. He discovered the unique quality of *kominka*, which is its ability to adapt to the local climate. During the humid summers, for example, the wooden pillars absorb moisture from the air and maintain ideal humidity levels. At the same time, in winter they expand and release water, filling the building with a pleasant woody scent. He truly believed that the building was alive (*ikite iru*) and said that everyone should experience the nostalgia (*natsukashisa*) of living in a *kominka* (Figure 4.1).

While there are people like Nobuo who have settled down in the countryside with an untroubled mind, migrants of a younger age want to venture into a new chapter of their lives. The Sasayama Innovators School, a joint project organised by the local government of Tamba Sasayama and Kobe University, offers 11 months of courses and lectures on social trends and practical skills useful for settling down in the area. The seminar participants come from a variety of regions, from nearby towns in Hyogo Prefecture to the wider Kansai area. The seminar room, known as the Rural Innovation Lab, is conveniently

創造農村

丹波篠山市　地域おこし協力隊

2020/12/20　丹波篠山市企画総務部創造都市課

Figure 4.1 The front page of a report for the Community Cooperative Support programme of Tamba Sasayama.

Source: Tamba Sasayama City Hall (Creative City Section of the Municipal Planning and General Affairs Department).

located at Sasayamaguchi station to accommodate participants who commute from afar. By 2017, over 70 per cent of the course attendees had already implemented or were preparing new businesses in the region (Schrade 2019).

The Community Cooperative Support (*Chiiki okoshi kyōryokutai*) programme has been one of the most effective public initiatives behind the pan-regional mobility of young urban dwellers to rural areas in recent years. Launched by the Japanese Ministry of Internal Affairs and Communications in 2009, it supports young people to move to provincial areas under one to three-year contracts with attractive financial and administrative support from central and local governments (see Reiher 2020). Participants in the programme are sent to depopulated regions across Japan, where they are employed in a diverse range of industries, including agriculture and services, and some even start their own businesses. The aim of the programme is in line with Tamba Sasayama's regional revitalisation policy to attract young and enthusiastic people to the region to rejuvenate local communities. In collaboration with Kobe University, the Community Cooperative Support programme in Tamba Sasayama started with just three participants in 2014, increasing to 21 by 2021. The programme is open for applications from August to September each year, with preference given to candidates who have completed the Sasayama Innovators School relocation programme. Participants can choose from two activities: conducting research on local issues as a university affiliate or working as an apprentice or part-time worker for a local organisation. During my fieldwork, six members lived in the area and were involved in various private and public sectors, such as a guesthouse, bakery, agricultural school, and wild meat processing shop. What they have in common is that they use local resources, such as Tamba black bean or game meat from wild boar hunting, in ways that support local industries. Programmes such as art residencies have also attracted artists to the region.

Alongside the small, but notable, influx of retirees and newcomers, locals are also starting new businesses. For instance, a group of young university graduates opened a co-working space in 2018. Founded by two young U-turn returnees (urban dwellers returning to their hometowns in rural areas), the space provides a platform for business networking in the region, IT services such as web design, and community events such as public lectures and barbeques.

Yukari is a young female migrant who recently moved to Tamba Sasayama from Tokyo, where she had worked for several years. I first met her at a seminar on the Community Cooperative Support programme. She was the only woman on the panel, and her presentation summarised her journeys in Tamba Sasayama over the past three years. She had worked with a group of farmers to promote local agricultural products and had recently attended a food fair in Tokyo to promote Tamba black bean. As her three-year contract with the programme was coming to an end, she wanted to develop her own project based on her years of experience working with the local people. She hoped to create an English tour guide programme for foreign visitors, which seemed to fit with the local government's interest in making the region more international. Yukari wished to create a private and customised tour programme, and one of its central themes was the Tamba pottery culture of Tachikui. After the seminar, she came up to me and asked if I was the foreign researcher who had appeared in the newspaper last year. I said yes, and she that we exchange contacts.

A few days later, we met again in a local café. Knowing the place well, Yukari recommended which drinks and cakes to take, and we sat in the corner. As much as I was curious to know more about Yukari and why she had chosen to settle in Tamba Sasayama, she was equally intrigued by my presence in the quiet countryside and the subject of my research. I came to realise that I was more unusual than she was: I was a Korean working in a German research institute who had decided to do research on Tamba Sasayama during a year's stay there.

Yukari was confident in her decision to settle in Tamba Sasayama. Originally from a small town near Osaka, she moved to Tokyo in her early 20s to study at an elite university. After graduating, she stayed in Tokyo and worked at a branch office of a foreign company. She later moved to part-time work, which continued for several years. She spoke positively about the transition from a regular job in a large company to smaller part-time jobs, explaining that the latter were more enjoyable. Working in a local shop was one of the best times of her life as she met people from different backgrounds. However, as she entered her thirties, she felt insecure about living on short-term contracts. It was then that one of the regular customers introduced her to the Community Cooperative Support programme. Without hesitation, she applied for the opportunity that would change the course of her life. Among many rural destinations, she chose to move to Tamba Sasayama because it was one of the closest to her hometown. Having spent her 20s in one of Japan's most densely populated areas, the prospect of living in a completely different environment seemed refreshing.

During the three years she lived in Tamba Sasayama, Yukari had become firmly established in the local social networks. In fact, she had made several public appearances in local media and whenever I mentioned someone I knew in town, she already knew that person. She had also worked closely with many local farmers and shopkeepers. Through her experiences of communicating with local businesspeople, she had gained knowledge of the area's history, people, and market. Based on these social networks and the information she had gathered, she began to develop a new business idea.

However, the network of locals that she had built up did not extend to the wider Tamba Sasayama area, and in particular to a group of people she had long wanted to connect with: the Tamba potters in Tachikui. She had met them several times at local festivals but not long enough to build a lasting relationship. She had put off responding to a request from one of her first clients to organise a one-day Tamba pottery course because of her lack of connections with the potters. There were official channels through which young business entrepreneurs could meet up with the potters, such as public projects organised by the local government. However, it was difficult for an entrepreneur like her to get support since such initiatives favoured start-up

NGOs made of several members or individuals with years of business experience already. I could agree with this from my experience of attending a meeting between the potters and young migrants in the area, organised by a local government official a few months ago. They were all established entrepreneurs who had been running their businesses for a number of years.

I initially thought that the male-dominated culture and atmosphere of the Tamba pottery community might have made her reluctant to approach them, as observed in cases where female migrants struggle after moving to rural communities with rigid gender roles (Klien 2020: 25–46; Traphagan 2017). However, the potters have made efforts to open up their community to outsiders and have recently recruited more women than men, either as apprentices in their workshops or as staff for the pottery classes. Her reluctance rather seemed to stem from the prevailing regional stereotypes about the potters and the people of Konda town.

Having lived in Tamba Sasayama for several years, she had acquired local knowledge not only related to her business interests, but also about the rumours and gossip circulating among her friends and colleagues. As her social network was mostly confined to the central area of Sasayama town near the Sasayama Castle and the eastern part of the municipality, she seemed to have become accustomed to hearing that side of the local stories. Although she did not describe them specifically, knowing that such ideas might be biased, I knew what kind of regional stereotypes one could have heard, being one of the few newcomers to the region. For example, there were sayings about certain attitudes of the people in Konda town, especially those in Tachikui; that they have a "different way of thinking" (*kangaekata ga chigau*) from those living in central Sasayama town and how "strong-minded" (*ki ga tsuyoi*) they are.

The potters were aware of such stereotypes, and some agreed with it. However, they have been taking steps to become more open and welcoming, such as accepting apprentices from outside the village, regardless of gender. They have recently been discussing about expanding the geographical boundaries of membership of the *kumiai* to include people living outside of Tachikui. One candidate interviewed for membership during my fieldwork was a young female potter who lived in the central area of the Sasayama town, near City Hall.

When I heard Yukari's unfulfilled wish to meet the potters, I told her how I had built up close relationships with some of the potters in Tachikui. I mentioned that I was free to visit their workshops and had even been invited to their homes for meals. She seemed impressed, considering that I had only lived in Tamba Sasayama for half a year. After our conversation, she asked if I could help her meet the potters in person.

A few days later, when I was at Shōhei's workshop preparing his orders, I told him about Yukari's request. When I suggested that she speak to the *kumiai* staff about her interest in working with the potters, he warned me that being too formal could complicate matters. Instead, he suggested that she approach through personal connections. He identified himself as the gatekeeper to the potters' community and suggested that I bring Yukari to his workshop. Then I asked him if he knew her by any chance. Since both Yukari and Shōhei were close to Yuya, who manages public projects in the Creative City Section, I wondered if Yuya had ever mentioned her or the Community Cooperative Support programme. He had no idea about other regional revitalisation initiatives other than the ones that he was directly involved in.

The day had finally arrived for my arranged meeting for Yukari and Shōhei. I picked Yukari up from the old building where we first met and drove to Shōhei's workshop in Tachikui. He greeted us with a big smile as soon as we entered, and we sat around the dusty table behind the electric wheels. I did not have to lead the conversation, as Shōhei and Yukari were excellent speakers. Yukari introduced herself and the project that she wanted to work on. She brought a small brochure of a private guided tour programme written in Japanese and English, one of which was a walk around Tachikui. After Yukari finished presenting her business plan, Shōhei expressed his concern and suggested that she try something different from the usual strategies used in projects organised by the local government. He mentioned a recent group tour organised by the Tourism Division at City Hall, which brought buses of tourists to Tachikui. While the initiative was successful in attracting visitors to this village in the deep mountains, the programme did not take into account the benefits to the potters. The tight schedule of the one-day tour package made it difficult for the tourists to look around the village and visit the potters' shops and showrooms. It was a half-baked project for the potters, who wanted to use the opportunity to show their work to outsiders. They wanted a tour programme that covered the whole village, including their private shops, not just the public facilities such as museums.

A few weeks later, while attending a morning pottery class at Shōhei's workshop, I heard that Yukari had successfully organised a guided tour programme. She had brought a group of visitors from abroad to Tachikui. I was surprised that her plan had developed so quickly after our meeting with Shōhei. When I asked what had happened, Shōhei said that her business plan sounded convincing and well prepared, so he promoted it at a *kumiai* general assembly (*sōkai*), one of the largest gatherings of the Tamba potters. Her business ideas were generally well received by the members. Since then, the director of the *kumiai* office and Yukari have communicated directly by email, leading to the first English-guided tour in Tachikui. Discussions about another future project were also underway. Shōhei shared an email that Yukari had sent to all *kumiai* members regarding the new project, asking for permission to visit their workshops. Her plans seemed more structured than my impromptu fieldwork.

I was impressed by the rapid progress of Yukari's long-awaited plan, but it was also revealing to know the extent to which the key local actors in Tamba Sasayama's revitalisation policy were socially disconnected. Although festivals such as Dekansho or the Historic Street ART Festival brought together artists and local entrepreneurs from across the municipality, their daily lives were generally unrelated and physically distant.[1] The potters of Tachikui were particularly isolated from the recent economic boom in the central Sasayama area. For example, the headquarters of a renowned company that renovates *akiya* (unoccupied houses) and runs *akiya*-turned-hotels was located near the castle town. The company was widely known for transforming old buildings into sophisticated shops and accommodation, expanding to other regions in Japan. However, most of the renovation projects, including the hotels they managed, were concentrated around Sasayama Castle town. Other local businesses recently set up by young entrepreneurs, such as a local beer brewery, an organic restaurant, and a coworking space, were also located in the same area. This was presumably due to the relatively convenient public transport system and the attractive townscape of old houses, which seemed to inspire new business ideas.

Not only was there a physical distance between the entrepreneurs and the potters, but other factors also limited their interactions. Once, I was invited to visit the showroom of one of the renowned artist potters in Tachikui. The sophisticated interior design, with its wooden furniture and concrete walls, was reminiscent one of Andō Tadao's architecture. He told me a story about how the room was renovated. Initially, a well-known local renovation company approached him and suggested that his buildings renovated as part of the regional revitalisation project. Having heard about successful *akiya* projects in the news and from his acquaintances, he thought they might be able to give him some helpful advice. However, the project did not go as the company had hoped, as he refused to take part because of what appeared to be his personal views against the people of central Sasayama town. He said that the staff changed the plans too often, leading him to withdraw from the project. He then attributed the staff's misbehaviour to the general nature of the people of central Sasayama. Whether or not he was exaggerating his impressions or not, the fact that he addressed what sounds like a regional stereotype seemed to resonate with the initial hurdles that hindered Yukari's business plan. A similar attitude was evident in Shōhei's initial reaction when I first told him about Yukari's project. The first thing he asked was where she lived. When I told him that she lived in a village on the eastern edge of the municipality, he immediately categorised her as a member of the Sasayama Castle townspeople tribe, as if this had any significant relevance to her personality.

I wondered if the strong sense of distance between Konda town and the rest had anything to do with the recent municipal merger. According to Cohen, "[a]s government becomes bigger and more remote from the constituent elements of society; as its economics appears to become increasingly centralized and institutionalized, so it loses credibility and relevance as a referent of people's identity" (2000: 106). He suggests that one of the failings of the current government is its size, which leads to a feeling of "under-represented and inadequately understood" (2000: 106). As I discussed in Chapter 1, the 1999 municipal amalgamation sparked disputes between residents of different towns, particularly those of Tachikui and Konda town who saw no incentive to merge with their neighbouring districts. However, the issue of municipal identity or the lingering tensions between the towns were sidelined in favour of regional revitalisation, as mismanagement of the post-merger development left the local government with heavy financial debts. The villagers of Tachikui often implied that they were different from the people of Sasayama, who were either city bureaucrats or saw themselves as decedents of old aristocrats. They sometimes referred to places outside Konda town as "over there" (*mukō*), as if the only distinction in the region was between "us" and "them". The stories of Yukari and the potters illustrate how mutual stereotypes exist among the residents of Tamba Sasayama, depending on their respective town and village affiliations.

However, the official discourse of *sōzō nōson*, which emphasises a harmonious community of creative individuals, undermines the complex and challenging dynamics of local social fabric. The *Tamba Sasayama: The City of Crafts and Folk Arts Monitoring Report* shows the ideal narratives and images of local creative projects that contradict the experiences of the local people.

Re-presenting the local social context

As Tamba Sasayama entered its fourth year as a UNESCO Creative City, the local government was required to submit a Membership Monitoring Report to the UNESCO Creative City Network headquarters.[2] The report is important in many ways. First, it is a requirement for renewal of UCCN membership. Second, the meetings held to prepare the report – Japan Heritage Creative City Promotion Assembly from 2018 to 2019 – provided an opportunity for local government officials and various local stakeholders to exchange ideas about regional revitalisation on a regular basis. Towards the end of my fieldwork in 2019, the officials were in the process of finalising the report that would highlight how regional initiatives had contributed to the development of Tamba Sasayama into a creative place (Figure 4.2).

As Tamba Sasayama is a Creative City of Crafts and Folk Arts, the report focused on the projects related to Tamba pottery, such as the "International Biennale of Gastronomy and Pottery", the "Tamba Ware New Products Development Project: The Tamba Style", the "32nd Incheon Ceramic Festival", Tōki Matsuri and Haru Monogatari. It showed the centrality of Tamba pottery in Tamba Sasayama's regional revitalisation policy, and described Tamba Sasayama as a prime example of rural creativity. It addressed the Tamba Sasayama Model (Figure 4.3) and the basic agenda behind the regional revitalisation policy: "Tamba Sasayama continues to actively disseminate information as a pathfinder of the sustainable rural model while preserving and passing down its indigenous culture and traditions along with fostering successors and welcoming creative synergies" (Sasayama City Hall 2019b).

However, the self-proclaimed title of the Tamba Sasayama Model lacked any clear explanation of its philosophy or economic rationale. Instead, it was accompanied by bullet points of key words, images, and catchy slogans. In

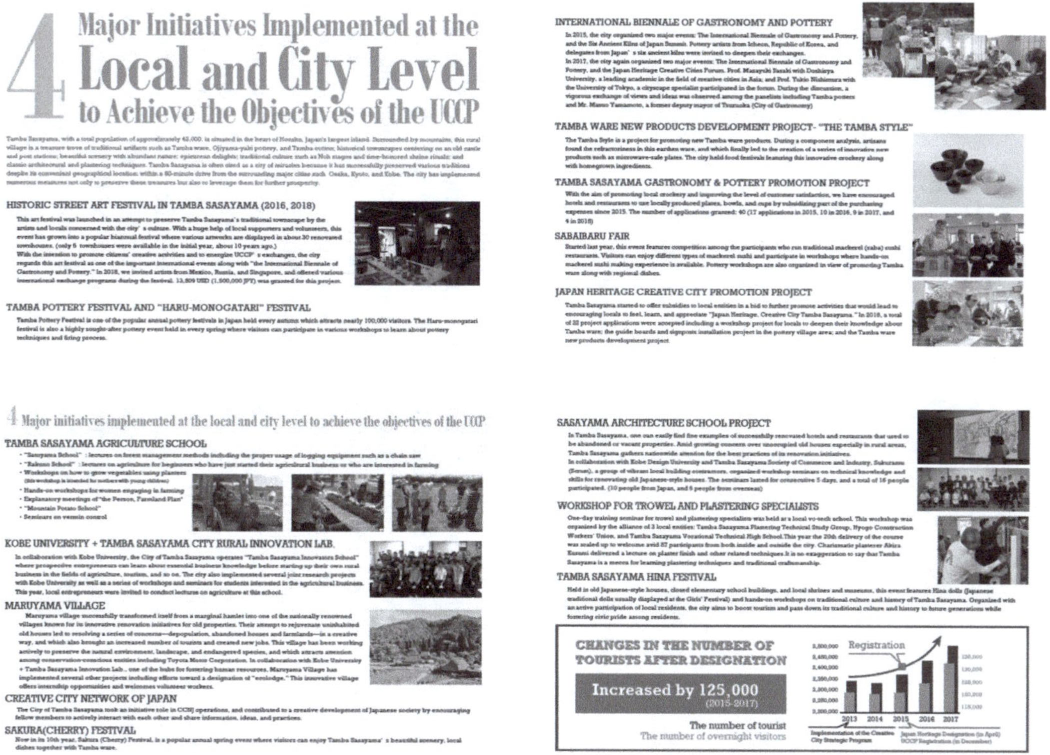

Figure 4.2 Major Initiatives Implemented at the Local and City Level to Achieve the Objectives of the UCCP (UNESCO Creative City Program).

Source: UNESCO Creative City Network.

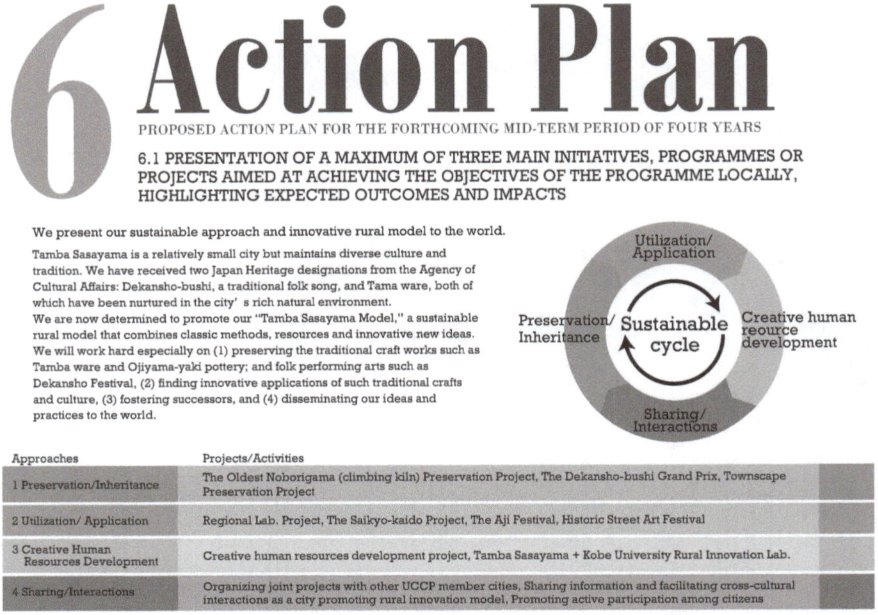

6 Action Plan

PROPOSED ACTION PLAN FOR THE FORTHCOMING MID-TERM PERIOD OF FOUR YEARS

6.1 PRESENTATION OF A MAXIMUM OF THREE MAIN INITIATIVES, PROGRAMMES OR PROJECTS AIMED AT ACHIEVING THE OBJECTIVES OF THE PROGRAMME LOCALLY, HIGHLIGHTING EXPECTED OUTCOMES AND IMPACTS

We present our sustainable approach and innovative rural model to the world.

Tamba Sasayama is a relatively small city but maintains diverse culture and tradition. We have received two Japan Heritage designations from the Agency of Cultural Affairs: Dekansho-bushi, a traditional folk song, and Tama ware, both of which have been nurtured in the city' s rich natural environment.
We are now determined to promote our "Tamba Sasayama Model," a sustainable rural model that combines classic methods, resources and innovative new ideas. We will work hard especially on (1) preserving the traditional craft works such as Tamba ware and Ojiyama-yaki pottery; and folk performing arts such as Dekansho Festival, (2) finding innovative applications of such traditional crafts and culture, (3) fostering successors, and (4) disseminating our ideas and practices to the world.

Approaches	Projects/Activities
1 Preservation/Inheritance	The Oldest Noborigama (climbing kiln) Preservation Project, The Dekansho-bushi Grand Prix, Townscape Preservation Project
2 Utilization/ Application	Regional Lab. Project, The Saikyo-kaido Project, The Aji Festival, Historic Street Art Festival
3 Creative Human Resources Development	Creative human resources development project, Tamba Sasayama + Kobe University Rural Innovation Lab.
4 Sharing/Interactions	Organizing joint projects with other UCCP member cities, Sharing information and facilitating cross-cultural interactions as a city promoting rural innovation model, Promoting active participation among citizens

Figure 4.3 The Action Plan of the Tamba Sasayama Model.

Source: UNESCO Creative City Network.

addition to initiatives related to Tamba pottery, several other projects were also listed as key achievements, such as "Tamba Sasayama Agriculture School", "Kobe University + Tamba Sasayama City" and "Rural Innovation Lab". Although the ongoing projects were mostly unrelated to each other, the concept of *sōzō nōson* was described as a unifying concept that presents a clearly defined goal. In the Action Plan, the various projects were grouped into four clusters – "Preservation/Inheritance", "Utilization/Application", "Creative Human Resources Development", and "Sharing/Interactions" – where activities related to Tamba pottery were cast under "Preservation/Inheritance" (Figure 4.3). The clusters were then structured within the Sustainable Cycle, with visual diagrams showing their relatedness. As if to reflect the underlying premise of creativity in the *sōzō nōson* discourse, the Action Plan also emphasised both the innate ability of individuals and the synergy of their social cooperation. For instance, while it stressed the need to enhance individual talents – "Pursuing the betterment of people's life by fostering and welcoming creative talents" – it also highlighted the importance of their interconnections – "Pursuing new possibilities through active information dissemination and cross-cultural collaboration and enhancing a sense of civic pride among citizens" (Sasayama City Hall 2019b). The projects of different themes were then complemented by a demographic chart showing collective achievements with two key moments: the introduction of the Creative City Strategic Program in

2013 and the designation of Japan Heritage and UCCN in 2015. These milestones were the turning points for a surge in tourists and overnight visitors to Tamba Sasayama (Figure 4.2). The quantitative data seemed to confirm the effectiveness of the Tamba Sasayama Model.

After pages of descriptions, statistics, and images showcasing the positive effects of public projects in regional revitalisation, an illustration of Tamba Sasayama City appeared on the last page (Figure 4.4). Key local cultural products were portrayed in silhouettes: Dekansho dancers; Ōjiyama ceramics; Tamba pottery; and Tamba black bean. The colourful letters and the cartoon-like images of traditional artefacts conveyed a youthful atmosphere, and the combination of vivid colours seemed to suggest their vitality, as if the various local products were contributing to the common vision of rural creativity.

The various projects, with different themes and objectives, were presented as components of a cohesive framework of the "innovative rural model" (Sasayama City Hall 2019b). However, the assumed organic and harmonious coexistence of the local creatives gives us little clue of the complex process of the bonding that Yukari and Shōhei, the two key agents behind the revitalisation policy, had to go through. Yukari's bumpy path to becoming a local entrepreneur was only possible through her confrontation with the local constraints emblematic of rural areas where communities are bound by rumours and stereotypes.

Wilf provides a similar account in the business world. He describes the case of the company Lego, which recently abandoned fixed office spaces as part of its new strategy to encourage "organically emerging forms of the transaction of ideas and bottom-up contractual relations" (2020: 4). The underlying assumption was that if employees were exposed to people from different departments, they would be more likely to interact with each other, and in doing so, generate new ideas. In practice, however, they found it difficult to adapt to the nomadic working style and were reluctant to interact with strangers. He argues that the company's assumption that creating a flexible working environment will encourage creative ideas essentially ignores "the lived reality of context" (2020: 15). The dominant idea behind the company's

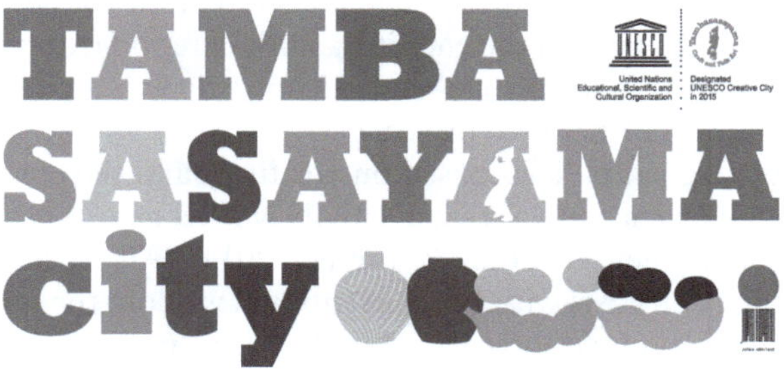

Figure 4.4 A graphic illustration of "Tamba Sasayama".

Source: UNESCO Creative City Network.

initiative reflects the prevalence of neoliberal ideology that expects individuals to be exploratory and entrepreneurial: "if the right communicational context … or the work environment is built, the right economic or organisational activities that lead to economic efficiency or innovation will inevitably and automatically follow" (2020: 13). In this context, individuals are seen less as autonomous agents but more as "quasi-mechanical devices that deterministically and automatically react to specific communicational contexts in the form of specific communicational activities such as the exchange of the right kind of information that can lead to innovative products and ideas" (2020: 13).

This resonates with the way in which the *sōzō nōson* policy regards the presence of multiple actors in the area as a sign of creativity in the region. It is as if they are willing to network and communicate as long as there is mutual recognition, especially if that recognition is through the paternalistic care of the local government policy. Although their names do not appear in the tidy diagrams that interweave the various projects into the abstract designs of the Action Plan and Sustainable Cycle, Yukari and Shōhei are the ones among the many who contribute to Tamba Sasayama's promotion of local vitality and creativity. Rather than proposing a viable plan for the future or addressing the limitations of public events based on "the lived reality of context" (Wilf 2020: 15), the report seemed to be invested in magnifying the results of various initiatives that are broadly lumped together as the Tamba Sasayama Model, disregarding the intra-regional stereotypes that are essential to understanding the very creativity that emerge in rural social settings.

Conclusion

Based on Yukari's efforts to establish a guided tour programme in Tachikui, we gain insight into the complex social fabric and stereotypes that shape and influence the actions of those involved in shaping Tamba Sasayama's new rural representation. Her initial enthusiasm was dampened by persistent rumours and negative perceptions of people from other parts of the municipality, particularly the potters, which led her to doubt the viability of her project. Far from being spontaneous, the dialogues and negotiations between Yukari and Shōhei were characterised by their meticulous attention to the particularities of the local social context. In the end, it was this careful arrangement of their interaction, grounded in locally embedded knowledge, that paved the way for her successful launch of her own project.

As Campbell argues, policies based on creativity and the creative economy rely on a "teleological narrative" that creativity *will* become increasingly important in the emerging new economy (Campbell 2014: 997; see also Kong 2014: 4). This approach contrasts with the conventional wisdom that public policy is based on precise economic forecasts. Tamba Sasayama's efforts to create an image of a creative village assume that local actors will contribute to making Tamba Sasayama a creative place, regardless of the project's goals or their feelings about them. The emphasis is less on the experiences of local actors than on presenting the successful model of Tamba Sasayama as a creative village. Kato argues that regional revitalisation policies in Japan may be nothing more than a "common illusion" (*kyōdō gensō*) of bureaucrats (2015: 3). Without being imagined from within the complex social contexts of the region, rural creativity may remain a mere illusion of a few policymakers.

Notes

1 Dekansho, or *dekansho bushi*, is a local folk song that has been sung by the people of Tamba-Sasayama for over 200 years since the Edo period. It is sung at *bon* in summer, which is an annual Buddhist event comforting the spirits of the dead and commemorating ancestors.

2 https://en.unesco.org/creative-cities/content/reporting-monitoring.

Figure 4.5 The main shopping street near Sasayama Castle.

Figure 4.6 Sasayama Castle area.

Figure 4.7 Streets behind City Hall.

Figure 4.8 Sasayama Castle.

Figure 4.9 On the way to Tachikui from the central Sasayama area.

Figure 4.10 Sue no sato.

Figure 4.11 *Saitō goma* held in front of the oak tree in Kami-Tachikui.

Figure 4.12 Street signs of pottery workshops and the MCART in the background.

Figure 4.13 Houses in Kami-Tachikui.

Figure 4.14 Gas tanks from a workshop in Shimo-Tachikui.

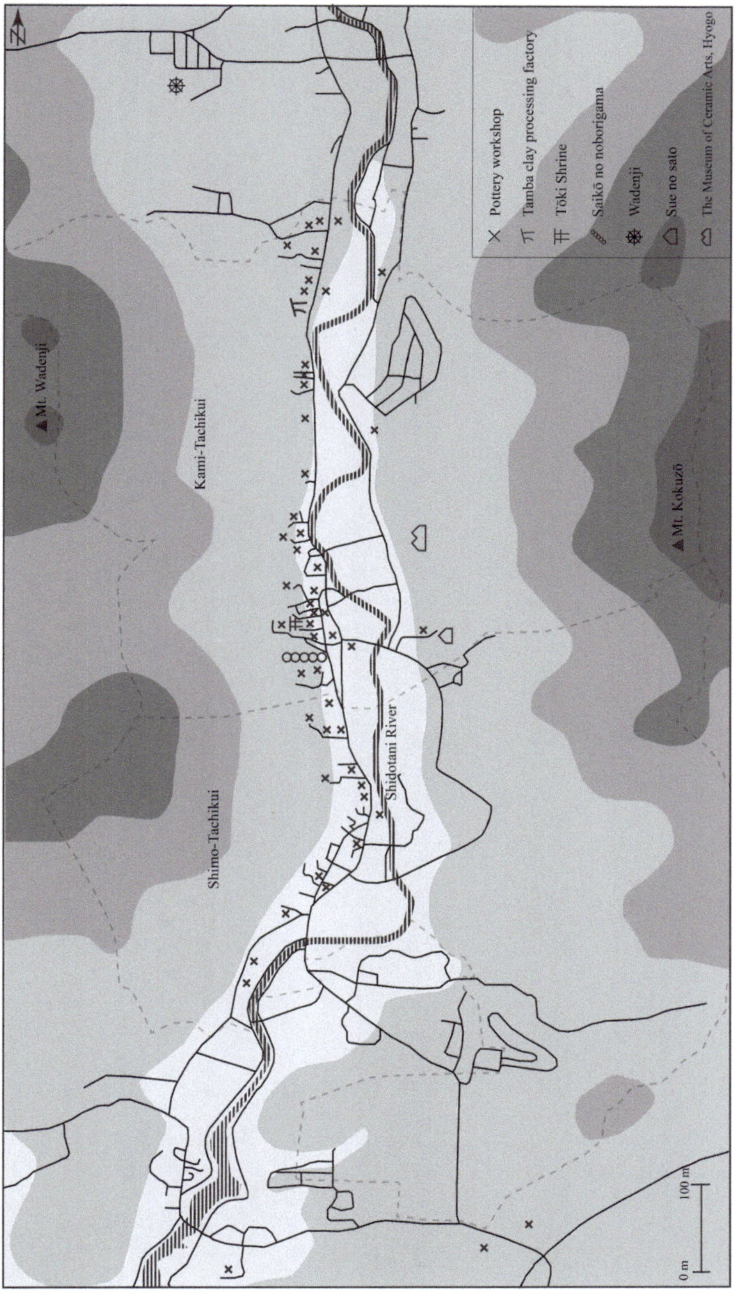

Map 4.1 Tachikui.

Part Two
Tachikui

The previous chapters have outlined the general socio-economic context behind Tamba Sasayama's regional revitalisation policy and its campaign for *sōzō nōson*, focusing on the institutional aspects of local government. The neoliberal turn in various sectors of society, which had been underway since the Nakasone administration in the 1980s, bloomed in the early 2000s during the Koizumi, is exemplified in Tamba Sasayama's case: its birth as the headliner of the Great Heisei Amalgamation policy in 1999, one of the key policies that marked the nationwide trend towards decentralisation, soon turned into a source of debt about a decade later, putting it at the risk of financial collapse. In the process of reorienting Tamba Sasayama's policy direction from development to revitalisation, creativity emerged as the new guiding concept. The rise of the new rurality discourse of *sōzō nōson* reflects the municipal struggles to live through the neoliberal orders of 21st-century Japan.

Having explored the national and municipal contexts of Tamba Sasayama's regional revitalisation strategies, I now zoom in on the more intimate social fabric of the local residents who are involved in the process of promoting Tamba Sasayama's new rurality. Although the ultimate goal is to revitalise the once economically depressed region, not all actors share the same aspirations, nor do they participate with a single, coherent objective in mind. In the interlude, I briefly touch on the history of Tamba pottery production in Tachikui and the lives of the potters. The potters' perspective allows for a renewed understanding of what regional revitalisation means and how it is conceptualised and experienced in the scale of the locals' everyday lives. Having existed in roughly the same location for centuries, with the social and economic life around the Tamba pottery tradition continuing for several generations, village life in Tachikui offers a different angle to understanding the dynamic changes that Tamba Sasayama underwent in the last 20 years. By contextualising the potters' relationship with the local government and their role as creative agents within the broader history of Tachikui, we can better understand how the new discourse of rurality is intertwined with diverse aspects of their lives, from village social relations to collective craft practices.

DOI: 10.4324/9781003326540-7

Interlude

A Brief History of Tamba Pottery Industry

A history of Tamba pottery

Tamba pottery is one of the Six Ancient Kiln sites that represent medieval ceramics in Japan, produced since the late Heian period (794–1185). Their beginnings are known to be linked to the fall of the Heian meritocracy, when Sue potters, who had produced ceremonial and decorative wares under a centralised system, scattered across the island to start making daily wares. Early kiln sites are found on the borders of the ancient provinces of Tamba, Settsu, and Harima, a vast region roughly in the location of the modern Hyogo Prefecture. Some of the known areas are Sanbontage, Tokorari, Genbei, Tasaura, and Inariyama, which are not far from Tachikui (Aoki 1976: 28). At the Tōki Shrine in Kami-Tachikui, a story is passed down of a potter named Furoyabu Sōtaro, who is known to have spread pottery production and kilns in the region in the 9th century (Rhodes 1972: 31). Notable features of Tamba pottery are known to have developed towards the end of the Kamakura period (1185–1333) (Sugimoto 1969: 85, in Kleinberg 1979: 95).

Until the late Muromachi period (1333–1573), the types of Tamba pottery produced were mainly limited to *tsubo* (narrow-necked jar), *kame* (wide-mouthed pot), and *suribachi* grinding bowl with combed inner surface), which were standard designs found in medieval Japanese pottery. The stability of the manor system and the development of agriculture in the 11th century increased agricultural productivity, leading to an increased demand for containers such as jars for seeds and water (Cort 2001: 60). The earliest Tamba pottery from this period is a grain storage jar (Nakanishi 1971), but its use was varied, as evidenced by a jar found in Takarazuka filled with Chinese coins (Aoki 1976: 26). The clay used at this time was of poor quality, dug up from the ground near the kiln site, similar to the clay obtained at Bizen and Shigaraki at this time (Cort 2001: 83). The dominant ceramic technique suitable for the condition of the clay was the coil method. The body of a jar, for example, was made of long threads (*himo*) of clay that were layered on top of each other. No glaze was applied at the time. This rough and unrefined nature of early Tamba pottery, fired in a tunnel kiln (*anagama*), is called Old Tamba (*kōtamba*) and covers the early Kamakura to Momoyama period (1573–1615).[1] Tunnel kilns

DOI: 10.4324/9781003326540-8

were built in tunnels dug into mountain slopes, and they were far from efficient, as water interruptions under the ground made the temperature inside the chamber unstable, prolonging the firing process to more than two weeks. However, it was precisely this prolonged firing process that allowed the wood ash to accumulate on the shoulder of the pottery, creating the natural glaze (*shizen'yu*) of a rusty greenish colour that is appreciated as the charm of Tamba pottery.[2] As Nakanishi remarks, the "accidental" result of the tunnel kiln firing created the "great beauty" of Tamba pottery (Nakanishi 1971).

Later, the introduction of advanced ceramic techniques, such as the construction of climbing kilns (*noborigama*), brought about significant changes in the styles of Tamba pottery.[3] The Momoyama period, which lasted for about four decades in the late 16th and early 17th centuries, was a transitional period that ended the chaotic Sengoku period and saw Japan unified under the leadership of three great *daimyō* (feudal warlord): Oda Nobunaga, Toyotomi Hideyoshi, and Tokugawa Ieyasu. One of the decisive events that gave Tokugawa Ieyasu the authority to establish the Tokugawa shogunate, marking the beginning of the Edo period (1615–1868), was Toyotomi Hideyoshi's two unsuccessful invasions of Korea in 1592 and 1597 and his death in the following year. Soon after his son Toyotomi Hideyori was appointed as the new shogunate by the Council of Five Elders (*go-tairō*), Tokugawa overthrew the reign of the young Toyotomi and gained the ultimate status of shogun.

However, the social and cultural legacy of Toyotomi Hideyoshi outlasted his death and was continued, some of which were definitive in the lives of the Tamba potters in terms of their future economic and social prospects. For instance, the rich tea culture, such as the tea ceremonies so highly regarded by Toyotomi, peaked in the Edo period and became the centre of elite culture. This subsequently led to a growing demand for domestically produced tea utensils. By the 17th century, the fine Chinese porcelains favoured by the aristocracy could no longer keep up with the growing demand, and collectors began to seek alternative products from local manufacturers. Tea masters in Kyoto, for example, began to use various tools produced in Seto, Shigaraki, Bizen, and Tamba kilns (Cort 2001: 165). It is suggested that Matsudaira, the first daimyo of the Sasayama domain (*han*), commissioned potters in Tachikui to produce tea utensils (Kleinberg 1979: 101). The tea ware they produced ranged from tea bowls (*chawan*), water containers (*mizusashi*), to water dispensers (*kensui*). Records show that Kobori Enshū, a famous tea master in the early Edo period, used products from Tachikui (Yanagi 1956: 15–18). Although Tamba pottery in the Edo period was still largely perceived as everyday ware, "[setting] the standard for glazed wares in western Japan" (Cort 2001: 211), the production of costly tea wares shows the diversification of its products from the simple medieval wares.

The mass production of Tamba pottery was only made possible by the introduction of supporting technological developments. In particular, the introduction of climbing kilns at Tachikui triggered mass production for markets in Kyoto and Osaka, marking the realisation of the industrial revolution of Tamba pottery (Aoki 1976: 32).[4] The firing time was reduced to one-third of that of the tunnel kiln, and the long snake-like shape of the kiln allowed for large-scale firing. Also, the improved quality of clay from designated sites allowed for shaping into various forms. Artificial glazes, such as red clay (*akadobe*) and later Tamba black (*tanbakuro*), were also widely used, as were various glazing techniques, including slip trailing (*itchin*) using bamboo tubes. With the ability to build climbing kilns on less steep slopes and closer to the flat lands of hamlets, kilns gradually moved from Kamaya to Shimo-Tachikui (the lower Tachikui) and Kami-Tachikui (the upper Tachikui), marking the beginning of the village kiln (*satogama*) period from the mid-18th century. These changes during the Edo period created a new generation of Tamba pottery and marked the end of the *kōtamba* era (Nakanishi 1971).

Climbing kilns have recently lost much of their technical appeal, with many potters now using gas or electric kilns. However, they continue to have significant symbolic value as a representation of the Tamba pottery culture. For example, the Tamba climbing kiln building skill was designated as a National Intangible Treasure in 1957. This played a major role in Tamba Sasayama's designation as a UNESCO Creative City of Crafts and Folk Arts in 2015 and as a Japan Heritage site in 2017.

A history of Tamba potters

During the Edo period, the reformed domain (*han*) system required residents to be registered in a designated domain. They were subject to strict taxation and tight control over local craft production. When political power shifted to the Tokugawa military regime, the new daimyo Matsudaira Yasushige took over the Sasayama domain, and the Onobara domain was renamed Konda. Unlike the Tamba kilns, which were located in a mountain hamlet far from Sasayama Castle, the Aoyama kiln, which produced expensive porcelain products similar to Kyoto and Sanda wares, was under the direct control of the local government. Although the Tamba kilns had a reputation for making tea caddies (*chaire*), the Aoyama pottery was considered more suitable for the markets of luxurious tea utensils. It is difficult to determine the extent to which officials interfered with the pottery production in Tachikui; however, a domain-controlled guild (*zakata*) in Shimo-Tachikui suggests some political influence. The potters affiliated to the guild system were instructed to produce specific products, such as sake bottles (*tokkuri*) decorated with symbolic animals and plants. Compared to the Aoyama potters, however, they were relatively independent. The profit from guild production was small, and the sale of everyday wares from neighbouring hamlets continued to be the main source of income for the village potters (Kleinberg 1979: 103).

Another important authority in the production of Tamba pottery during the Edo period was the middlemen (*ton'ya*). By the early 17th century, Osaka had become the commercial centre of Japan. The middlemen were the ones to "[bring] rurally produced goods into the urban market" (Cort 2001: 237), trading in the bustling marketplaces with various daily wares produced in Tachikui. By 1850, there were five middlemen in Kami-Tachikui, equivalent to the local brokers (*nakagai*) of Shigaraki pottery (Cort 2001: 237). As Tamba potters began to sell their products to a wider area of Kansai, they were exposed to different styles and techniques from other kiln sites. This exposure led to experimentation with unique designs and skills. Among the first kilns to gain a reputation were Naosaku, Ichifusa, and Kayū (Nakanishi 1971). The Naosaku kiln continues to this day, and visitors can witness its famous Tamba white-glazed sake bottle (*shirotamba tokkuri*) in the display room in Shimo-Tachikui.

The Meiji Restoration in 1868 and the abolition of the *han* domain system in 1871 brought an end to the Tokugawa military regime, which also halted the *zakata* production. Meanwhile, the development of the railroad system increased competition from other regional kilns, such as Seto and Karatsu, which produced cheaper daily wares that were more popular than Tamba (Aoki 1976: 48). The Tamba pottery industry faced many challenges, including economic instability, social upheaval, and, not least, the depletion of high-quality Tamba clay (Nakanishi 1971). Despite these difficulties, the potters were able to survive the turbulent period by producing sake bottles, which were still in demand, and by growing rice and other local crops.

The outbreak of the Russo-Japanese war (1904–1905) and the militarisation of the Japanese empire brought significant changes to the Tamba pottery industry. Although production continued, it was marked by instability. The onset of massive industrialisation led to an increased demand for industrial products, such as jars for sulphuric and nitric acid, which were ordered from chemical factories in the Osaka, Kobe, and the surrounding Kansai area. War-related materials, such as surface materials for land mines, were also in high demand. For a brief period after World War I, unglazed flowerpots became popular among the new middle class in urban areas (Kleinberg 1979: 108). Tamba potters had to adopt new machinery and management techniques for mass production. Despite these efforts, pottery remained a difficult livelihood during the war. Intense economic regulation by the central government and the conscription of young men for war-related services drove many households out of pottery production by the mid-20th century. Many of those who had been engaged in farming and pottery on a part-time basis (*hanno hanto*, 半農半陶) had to become full-time farmers again. Tachikui began to lose its identity as a pottery village, and the tradition of pottery production gradually declined.

With the end of the Asia-Pacific war, the ceramic markets flourished again, reviving pottery production in Tachikui. Due to the shortage of industrial raw materials such as steel and glass, everyday items such as bowls, cups, and jars were supplemented by clay products. However, the post-war special procurement did not last long, as other cheaper industrial materials again replaced them. Then came about the folk craft boom (*mingei būmu*) in Japan, associated with economic growth, domestic tourism, and a growing sentiment for *furusato* (Idegawa 1988: 245–47). It reached Tachikui in the early 1970s, which was later than other *mingei* craft sites that had already joined the tide, and dramatically changed the entire pottery production scene of the village (see also Kleinberg 1979: 117, 138). Yanagi Muneyoshi's philosophy of "ordinary functional art" (Kikuchi 2004: 1), which had already gained popularity in the 1920s, spread through various media and campaigns in the post-war period, leaving a noticeable impact on the craft market. Whether the nationwide consumer boom in folk craft products was "deliberately set out" (Singleton 1989: 15) or was connected to the national ideology of "cultural nationalism directed towards the creation of a Japanese national identity" (Kikuchi 2004: 95), it was clear that Tamba potters were thriving. Sales increased and visitors flocked to Tachikui. What had been one of many regional potteries began to be recognised as *mingei* pottery and received heightened public attention. Ikuta Kazutaka, a famous disciple of one of the key members of the folk craft movement, Kawai Kanjirō, moved to Tachikui from Kyoto during this period. His presence in the village influenced many young villagers to aspire to traditional craftsmanship. The Prefectural Tamba Pottery Production Laboratory (*Kenritsu tamba yōgyō shikenjyō*), established in 1948 with the financial support of the Hyogo prefectural government, carried out various experiments to revive the old techniques of Tamba pottery from the Edo period (e.g., a traditional glazing technique of *akadobe*). The old skills, almost lost in the economic turmoil of the Meiji Restoration and the wartime period, were rediscovered and appreciated.

In his book *Ceramics of Hyōgo* (*Hyōgo no yakimono*), published in 1976, Aoki records the general atmosphere of the Tamba pottery industry at that time. He remarks that "owing to the folkcraft movement, the true aspect of Tamba pottery could be recognised again in the world" (*mingei undō ni yotte kōtamba no kachi ga yatto hiroku yo ni saininshiki sareru youni natta*) (Aoki 1976: 49). The increasing number of connoisseurs of Tamba pottery and the nationwide "boom of yakimono" (*yakimono no bumu*) was "unprecedented" (*mizoū*) (1976: 49). By the late 1970s, most of the workshops in Tachikui were equipped with electric wheels and gas kilns. Potters were also confident in identifying themselves as full-time potters (Kleinberg 1979: 296). The various names that had been given to the pottery produced in Tachikui, such as Tachikui pottery (*Tachikuiyaki*) or Tamba Tachikui pottery (*Tanbatachikuiyaki*), were also unified as Tamba pottery (*Tanbayaki*) during this period.

Along with the growing demand for Tamba pottery, Tachikui received increased attention as one of the pilgrimage sites of Japanese traditional crafts. In the post-war period, domestic tourism flourished with Japan's remarkable economic growth and the expansion of the middle-class lifestyles (see Creighton 1995). In response, tourist facilities were built in Tachikui from the early 1970s. In a local newspaper circulated in Konda town, *Kōbō Konda*, published in 1968, an article discussed the Konda Town New Scheme (*Konda-chō shinkō keikaku*). This scheme aimed to build the Tamba Pottery Hall (*Tanbayaki tōgei kaikan*) through cooperation between the Hyogo prefectural government, Tamba Tachikui Pottery Cooperative, and the Konda town office.

However, the end of Japan's economic growth since the burst of real estate market in the late 1980s brought the craft boom to an end. The middle-class lifestyle that had supported the ceramic market was no longer sustainable in the shift from the general middle-class society (*sochūryū-shakai*) to the gap society (*kakusa shakai*) (see Chiavacci 2008). Profits from the sale of products were no longer sufficient to sustain the many household businesses. Potters had to supplement their income by offering pottery classes to tourists and even opening tea rooms.

It was not until Tachikui became part of the new municipal district of Sasayama in 1999 that the local government made significant investments in the Tamba pottery industry. The construction of the Museum of Ceramic Art, Hyogo (MCART), and the establishment of Sue no sato, a cultural complex for Tamba pottery, were just the beginning. The central role of Tamba pottery in the designation of the UNESCO Creative City of Crafts and Folk Arts and Japan Heritage made Tachikui the symbol of Tamba Sasayama's local culture. Placards and signs bearing the UNESCO and Japan Heritage marks were placed throughout the village. Tamba potters became the key collaborators with the local government, playing a central role in promoting the Tamba Sasayama culture in return for the growing currency of their cultural value and financial support.

Despite the effective cooperation between the potters and the local government, their relationship also masked underlying tensions rooted in both recent and distant memories of local history. As noted in Chapter 1, the process of municipal merger was uneasy. The residents of Konda town, particularly those from Tachikui, rejected the proposal of the amalgamation committee (led by the representatives from Sasayama town) to join the plan. The economic complacency of Konda town was the reason for their objection, but the people that I spoke to also referred to the deep-rooted tensions with the people of the central Sasayama area, which seemed to stem from generations of memories of serving the feudal lords of the Sasayama domain in the Edo period.

In 1869, the villagers of Tachikui, burdened by rising taxes and a severe famine, wrote letters to higher officials asking for tax relief. However, their living conditions were hardly improving. Frustrated by the ignorance they encountered, they rebelled against the ruling class, along with other villagers in the Konda area. Of the 52 rebels who were arrested, 23 were from Tachikui (Yabūchi 1955: 165–8). A story about one of these uprisings became legendary in Tachikui. Once an administrator visited the village to conduct a survey. By this time, the villagers were full of rage against the merciless bureaucrats and were seeking to express their anger. They greeted him by offering him a bowl of hot udon. The poor man did not know that they were waiting for him to disarm himself. As he began to slurp the noodles, a villager hit him on the back with a stick. The udon noodles burst out of his mouth, creating a scene. The aftermath of the attack is unknown, but it seemed to convey the prevailing antagonism towards the ruling authorities in the central Sasayama area.

Despite a troubled past, the common concerns about a declining and ageing population forged a new companionship between the potters and the local government. The potters needed the public support to sustain the Tamba pottery industry, and the local government sought the potters' involvement as cultural representatives in regional revitalisation projects. Underlying the interdependence, however, were lingering memories of the past, creating a fuzzy relationship that could be described as neither antagonistic nor intimate. An elderly potter who had once been in the front row of the crowds protesting against the amalgamation policy was now one of the core members of the *kumiai* discussing public projects with the local government officials. The potters' participation in regional revitalisation policies is therefore underpinned by a complex structure of feeling specific to the history of the village. How this plays out in the wider socio-cultural context of Tamba Sasayama requires a closer look at their everyday lives and craft practices.

The second part of the book explores the potters' complex and sometimes conflicting roles as creative agents of the region, organising cultural events and festivals to showcase the rural creativity of Tamba Sasayama. The chapters analyse their diverse strategies for managing their evolving relationship with the local government. By examining the various forms of cooperation, I show how the municipal campaign for rural creativity is translated into their everyday lives, from their village social relations to the collective activities of the pottery cooperative. On the one hand, they try to take advantage of opportunities to promote Tamba pottery, stimulate sales, and attract visitors to Tachikui. On the other hand, they struggle to balance the traditional and modern paths of the Tamba pottery industry, which in turn becomes an act of strengthening their knowledge of Tamba pottery and their identity as Tamba potters.

Notes

1 This period is also known as the *Anagama* period because of the widespread use of *anagama* at the time. Others refer to it as the Inariyama period, named after Inariyama, which was the largest kiln site in the Tamba area at the time (Nakanishi 1971).

2 For technical explanations of how the natural glaze is formed during the kiln firing, see Rhodes 1972.

3 Strictly speaking, the kilns found in Tachikui today are *waridake-gama* (split-bamboo kilns), which are lower and smaller than the typical *noborigama* found in other areas of Japan or Korea. Due to their length, these kilns are also called *hebi-gama* (snake kilns). However, as Kleinberg observed in the 1970s (1979: 98), and as I saw during my fieldwork, the potters and the villagers generally refer to the traditional climbing kilns in Tachikui as *noborigama*.

4 However, it is uncertain how the skills of building climbing kilns and firing techniques were transferred from Kyūshū, where Korean potters had been relocated after Toyotomi's invasion of Korea, to western Japan and the Tamba kiln sites. The use of the spinning wheel (*rokuro*) in a clockwise direction, as opposed to other kiln sites that spin counterclockwise, is similar to that of the Korean potters, which the Tamba potters claim as indirect evidence of the presence of Korean potters in Tachikui in the past.

5 The Taskscape of Tachikui

Abstract

In Japan, train stations often provide an entrée gate to local cultures. Just by wandering around corridors or rest areas, one can get a glimpse of the region's main tourist spots. The cultural artefacts and images that decorate the space inform us the cultural highlights of the area. The first thing one notices when arriving at the Sasayamaguchi train station is the municipal theme song Dekansho. Past a ticket gate is a corridor spread sideways with local products displayed in various themes. Right in front of the wall facing a Family Mart is a huge municipal map showing the wider area of Tamba Sasayama. Several places are pinpointed with star marks, such as the Sasayama Castle town in the central Sasayama area and the Tamba pottery village of Tachikui. Next to the map is a giant poster of an older man firing a climbing kiln, which stood out for the lively image: an intense fire bursting out of a traditional kiln and a potter taming it with a wry face. Without any spoken words attached, the image conveyed a folksy atmosphere of the traditional craftspeople. Over the next months of my fieldwork, this image of an experienced potter reappeared in different medium, on the UCCN webpage of Tamba Sasayama, in an introductory booklet of *sōzō nōson* and other promotional materials, representing Tamba Sasayama's core regional value of rural creativity.

In the present and following chapters, I examine the representation of Tamba pottery in Tamba Sasayama's *sōzō nōson* campaign from the Tamba potters' perspectives. The social contours of their lives in Tachikui are as complex and dynamic as they can be, contradicting the routine image used in the promotional materials for the municipal revitalisation initiatives. Rather than directly resisting the invented images circulating in public, the potters facilitate their social relations rooted in the village to cope with the tension between the external and internal aspirations envisioned in the Tamba Sasayama's regional revitalisation movement. This chapter illustrates the kin and neighbourly relations of the village that set the backdrop for the potters' involvement in Tamba Sasayama's regional revitalisation projects. As the following chapters will further illuminate, what the potters' social lives and craftsmanship fixed on the village space tell us is not the resilience of traditional modes of living against changes but the flexibility in embracing them.

DOI: 10.4324/9781003326540-9

As I drove my old grey Toyota along the national highway 176 away from the Sasayama Castle area, the picturesque mountains that seemed so far away drew closer. I navigated the winding roads up and down the hills, eventually reaching a place cut off from the central town areas.

The first sight of the village was a scene of a vast rice field between Mt. Kokuzō and Mt. Wadenji. The natural landscape perfectly demonstrated why a pottery village was created in this area. The Shitodani River provided plentiful water for clay production, and Mt. Wadenji had gentle slopes suitable for building a climbing kiln. Piles of wood were stacked every corner of the village, covered by patchy slate roofs to protect them from getting wet. I had heard that visitors could sometimes see black smoke puffing from the chimneys of the kilns, but with the summer days still hot and sizzling, it was unlikely that any firing will take place soon. One striking scene was the constant passing by of small white trucks with yellow number plates. I later found out that they were the potters' main vehicles, carrying loads of clay from the Tamba clay processing factory or making deliveries to shops (Figure 5.1).

Kami-Tachikui and Shimo-Tachikui are densely populated with houses, pottery workshops, and kilns, so close together that it is difficult to tell them apart from the outside.[1] Kami-Tachikui is centred around a giant oak tree that enshrines a fox deity. Every January, a priest from Wadenji, a local temple in Tachikui, performs a religious ritual called *saitō goma*, praying for the well-being and safety of the villagers.[2] Next to the shrine is *Saikō no noborigama* (the oldest climbing kiln), and above it is a community cemetery with the two or three most common surnames in the area, such as Ichino and Shimizu. The streets in front of the oak tree are decorated with Tamba pottery tiles. Wood scraps, gas tanks, and pottery shards are scattered around the houses. Climbing kilns can be found in random sights, next to potters' houses and deeper in the forest. The steep hills and irregular layout of the streets seem to have been created by the development of pottery production. The topography of the village is suitable for building kilns, but not for living, as an elderly resident told me how difficult it is to walk around the hills.

Shimo-Tachikui is located just a few minutes' walk south of Kami-Tachikui. The land is relatively flat and less hilly. The houses and pottery workshops are located close to a well-paved road, but are exposed to the noise of vehicles,

Figure 5.1 The natural landscape of Tachikui.

Figure 5.2 The cultural landscape of Tachikui.

including the large transport trucks that travel along prefectural route 282. Most of the shops are new, including the workshops of the two potters who are newcomers to Tachikui (Figure 5.2).

Symbolic signs seemed to ensure that Tachikui was a pottery village. Placards of UCCN and Japan Heritage are placed at every corner of the village. A huge billboard welcomes visitors with the slogan, "Tamba Sasayama: Japan Heritage, UNESCO Creative City (*Tanba Sasayama: nihon isan yunesuko sōzō toshi*)". Mt. Kokuzō is home to Sue no sato and the Museum of Ceramic Art, Hyogo, built by the prefectural government in 1985 and 2005 respectively. Sue no sato, which literally means the "village of pottery", is a public facility that organises various cultural activities around Tamba pottery and which also houses the office of the Tamba Tachikui Pottery Cooperative (*Tamba tachikui tōjiki kyōdō kumiai*, hereafter *kumiai*). While it has a modest exterior, in the old-fashioned public architecture style of the 1980s, the Museum of Ceramic Art, which exhibits traditional and modern ceramics, boasts a simple and sophisticated exterior.

The landscape of Tachikui has all the ideal elements of a traditional pottery village: the natural environment (clay, river, and mountains) and the cultural symbols (UCCN and Japan Heritage). It is an example of the nostalgic landscape of rural life combined with the vitality of cultural practices and creativity. From this perspective, the poster at the train station, depicting an elderly potter and the fierce fire coming out of the climbing kiln, seemed to have well captured the essence of life in Tachikui.

However, these ideal scenes also obscure the social practices embedded in the landscape. Ingold argued that we need to move beyond the "insistent dualism" (Ingold 1993: 154) between "the naturalistic view of the landscape as a neutral, external backdrop to human activities, and the culturalist view that every landscape is a particular cognitive or symbolic ordering of space" (1993: 152). Neither view can fully address how "through living in it, the landscape becomes a part of us, just as we are a part of it" (1993: 154). Rather than the symbolic contour of a landscape, we should examine "those who spend time there" (1993: 156) and "the kind of activities" they engage in (1993: 156). Only through the social relations woven into the land they inhabit can we see the "more-than-visual dimensions of life" (Stasch 2017: 452). As Stasch argues, "space is not an abstract container in which people secondarily act and think", but it entails and is created by "distinctive forms of activity, thought, feeling and social or political relating" (2017: 443). In this context, Ingold proposes the concept of "taskscape", which emphasises the labour activities in space (1993: 158). Based on the "dwelling perspective", we should examine the accumulated social panorama beneath the surface value of a landscape, tracing "an enduring record of and testimony to the lives and works of past generations who have dwelt within it [the landscape], and in so doing, have left there something of themselves" (1993: 152).

In this chapter, I outline Tachikui's taskscape, focusing on the social lives of the Tamba potters and other villagers and exploring what lies beyond the idealised representations on station posters or in other public spheres. I examine the changing social panorama of the village under the fluctuations of Tamba pottery production from the post-war to the post-bubble period.

Between potting and non-potting households

In *Folk Art Potters of Japan: Beyond an Anthropology of Aesthetics* (1997), Brian Moeran illustrates how economic and technological developments in the pottery production system, such as in the use of traditional pottery tools (e.g., the clay crusher) and techniques (e.g., the way pots are stacked in the kiln), transform the village social structure. Traditionally, the social organisation of Sarayama village in northern Kyūshu has been shaped by the flow of water. Depending on the water pressure, the water-powered clay crushers pound different amounts of clay. This meant that the location of the crusher was crucial to pottery production, and it depended on the social and political status of the potters in the village. However, the mechanisation of pottery production no longer required the use of clay crushers, which affected village politics around water control. Gas and electric kilns allowed potters to work individually, dismantling the collective production system. As the pottery industry grew during the post-war folk craft boom, the economic status of potting and non-potting households expanded, creating tensions between them. The latter were discontented that the "potter's interests were often put forward as 'community' interests" (1997: 162). As the potters were the "tourist attraction" (1997: 162) and the main economic actors in the village, their opinions held more power. As a result, some community matters were decided without hearing the views of the non-potting villagers. The post-war transformation and prosperity of the pottery industry in general had led to a decline in community solidarity.

However, this is not always the case. From what I observed in Tachikui, the potters were flexible in adapting to broader socio-economic changes in ways that did not undermine existing social relations in the village. The relationship between potting and non-potting households has certainly changed with the economic and technological development of the Tamba pottery industry, but the non-potting households continued to participate in the pottery-related activities. The interests of the non-potting households were accommodated within the changing Tamba pottery industry, with pottery-related events creating new platforms for community activities in the place of the rapid disintegration of traditional village corporations.

Written records indicate that until the 1950s, over 50 per cent of the households in Kami-Tachikui worked for pottery enterprises in the village, either as full-time or part-time workers (Kleinberg 1979: 218–241). In the early 1970s, when demand for folk craft products was high, majority of the households in Tachikui took up the pottery business, and mass produced Tamba pottery. Compared to the production of acid jars and planters, which were less complicated to make, folk craft products required more workers to operate various machines and tools, such as extra electric wheels and spray guns for glazes. The labour pool of family members was insufficient to meet the market demand, and many workshops hired their neighbours. Those employed on full-time contracts were mainly recruited from neighbouring families with close kinship to the workshop owner, often younger brothers, to throw the wheel, fire the climbing kiln or sometimes run the workshop. They supported the pottery business of their father or elder brother, who are the head of the main household (*honke*), in return for the latter's financial assistance in establishing their independent branch households (*bunke*). While the head of the branch household was rewarded with a monthly wage, the work of his wives was often taken for granted. The *ie* ideology was a strong backbone of many pottery enterprises until the early 1970s (see Kleinberg 1979) Without the flexible and relatively cheap labour of close relatives, the potters could not have saved enough margins to continue the pottery business. Part-time jobs available for the non-potting households were mostly minor tasks, such as glazing, kiln loading and unloading, and packing.

As the folk craft boom waned after its peak in the 1970s, large orders were gradually replaced by smaller orders from shops and restaurants. Extra-household labour was no longer needed, except during the firing of a climbing kiln, when the potter would reach out to relatives or friends in the village. Various subsidiary occupations, such as professional kiln builders, traders, and wood experts, became obsolete. Kiln builders were key figures in the Tamba pottery industry, until at least the 1980s, when several potters used climbing kilns. One of the potters who still fires extensively in his climbing kiln said that a kiln builder had in-depth knowledge of kiln construction methods and could give advice on repairing old ones. However, such an expertise was no longer needed as many started using gas or electric kilns. Since the passing of the last kiln builder, there has been no expert in the village. As for the traders, the Great Hanshin Earthquake, which hit the trading networks in Kobe, seriously affected their businesses, causing many to close down completely. There were two shops in Tachikui during my fieldwork, but neither was operating. On the other hand, a wood expert, who prepares firewood for the firing session in climbing kilns, is still in business. His expertise lies in drying the firewood so that it burns with the right consistency and cutting it to the right size to fit into the stokehole. The elderly man was quick to answer any questions about firewood. He mentioned that pine trees used to be the most popular species, as it produced the greenish ash glaze, but due to the recent increase in price, hinoki is now replacing it. As the only wood expert left in the village, he doubted that anyone else would want to follow in his footstep.

Compared to the peak of folk craft production in the late 1960s and 1970s, the economic cooperation between the potting and non-potting households in Tachikui has declined significantly. However, this does not necessarily mean that the economic links between them have been completely severed. The dominant occupational group in the village is still the Tamba potters, and the number do not appear to have changed significantly in the 2000s where the majority of the residents in Kami-Tachikui (over 60 per cent) and a slightly smaller but noticeable number in Shimo-Tachkui (around a quarter) were still directly involved in the pottery production (Takeyasu 2007: 58) (Figure 5.3).

Instead of the burgeoning sales that forced the workshops to seek additional labour from the villagers, the potters' recent efforts to attract more tourists to Tachikui seemed to stimulate new economic cooperation in the village. One obvious change in the local business scene in Tachikui is the opening of finely

Figure 5.3 Construction of a new café in Kami-Tachikui.

decorated restaurants and cafes (Figures 5.4 and 5.5). This change was partly triggered by the release of the village's private lands, which until recently was almost impossible to obtain without a personal connection to the locals. The tight land ownership of village households seemed to have eased as they had seen the growing number of tourists coming to Tachikui. In the case of a Spanish restaurant that opened next to the Shidotani River, the young and prominent chef had moved her prestigious restaurant to Tachikui for her fondness for a potter's work. Her cuisines are inspired by Tamba plates and utensils. Other recent openings – a *kake tamago gohan* (egg on rice) and a kaiseki restaurant, a café, and a judo studio – have also added to the diversity to the village's

Figure 5.4 Tōki Matsuri.

economic life. One might expect some tension between these newcomers and the existing residents, given the closed nature of the village's social network. However, the villagers I spoke to were delighted to have youthful energy in Tachikui, even if they thought the prices in the new shops were too high.

The potters' commitment to boost tourism in the village also led to new forms of social activity among the villagers. According to Nakane, "in any village in Japan there have always been local corporate groups" (1967: 133). Although her observation is based on the generalised account of village societies, it nevertheless provides an index for tracking the transition of village-wide interaction between households. In Tachikui, there are Old Folk's Association (*rojinkai*), Women's Association (*fujinkai*), and Children's Association (*kodomokai*) that are formed based on residents' age and gender. However, they take up much less of the villagers' social activities than in the past. The Old Folk's Association, comprised of older male residents, could be seen regularly on Tuesdays at a playground near the Shidotani River, where they played gate ball, a typical sports activity in many elderly associations (Kalab 1992; Traphagan 1998). When I spoke to one of the members, he expressed concern that it would be difficult to continue the activity as the members were getting older and weaker. However, he noted that it is not always a matter of age that inevitably dismembers the group. It is the lack of group spirit that makes people less interested in community sports nowadays. The Young Men's Association (*seinenkai*), formed by younger male residents, seemed to have similar problems, where social activities seemed scarce, apart from the communal duty of managing the fire safety facilities. The Women's Association was no exception, representing the entire female population from the 20s to 70s. Yōko, who runs a small grocery shop in Kami-Tachikui, was the group leader when she was in her 40s. At that time, the members often spent time together, going on short trips or getting together for tea. They also had a social ritual of lending each other their *tomesode*, a ceremonial kimono for a married woman. She noted, however, that young wives no longer organise social events among themselves, preferring to be alone. The women's ocarina club had no one below the age of 60s. The Children's Association was almost non-existent, as there were few children resided in the village. However, this led to some positive changes in the local festivals, such as the *sumō matsuri*. What used to be a boys-only event is now open to girls.

Instead of tethering to the weakening age associations, the villagers reunited around the Tamba pottery festivals. Two of the largest ones held in Tachikui are the Tōki Matsuri in autumn (late October) and the Haru Monogatari in spring (early May). Haru Monogatari is known for the firing of the oldest climbing kiln and opening days of the potters' workshops. Tōki Matsuri is similar but attracts more visitors as autumn is the peak tourist season, with mountains tinged in red and orange. During these two festivals, non-potting households also participate in the festivals in their own way, selling street food, small handcrafted goods, or home-grown vegetables at street vendors and in their garages. Yōko was selling *oden* in front of her house, and one of the young members of the Woman's Association, who seemed half-hearted to the group, was also standing in the parking lot of her house selling local tea leaves, chatting pleasantly with customers. It was hard to see how the villagers could benefit from running temporary parlours, but, as one old resident remarked, it was entertaining to do something together with the neighbours. The Tamba pottery festivals had become one of the most important events, inviting all villagers to come together, regardless of age or gender. The potters actively sought their participation in the festivals, emphasising that the invigoration of the Tamba pottery industry was dependent on the revitalisation of the village (Table 5.1).

In addition to restoring social gatherings between the potting and non-potting households, the potters were among the most dedicated members of the *rinpō*, a neighbourhood organisation of the village. The traditional activities of the *rinpō* used to be the preparation of funerals and weddings, the organisation of festivals, and the renovation of communal facilities. Due to the declining and ageing population, arranging weddings ceremonies has become a rare activity, while attending funerals has become the most common excuse for gathering. Other communal duties still practised were grass mowing (*kusakari*) and festival organising. To some extent, it is natural that the potting households are the dominant members of *rinpō*, as they *are* the most common occupational group in the neighbourhood (Table 5.1). For instance, when I asked Yōko about the schedule of *sumō matsuri*, the main organiser she named was a young potter who was the leader of one of the subgroups of *rinpō*. She noted that his father was also a leader, who took care of communal matters. The potters took the collective duty of the village seriously and sometimes excused themselves from *kumiai* meetings. For example, an interview with one potter had to be cancelled as another potter had asked him if they could swap shifts for mowing. At a time when the general participation rate is low due to the declining and ageing population of the villagers, the dominant role of the potters in village affairs was appreciated, far from the Onta potters that were seen as "big headed" (Moeran 1997: 162).

Table 5.1 The *rinpō* organisation in Kami-Tachikui

Rinpō		*Total number of members*	*Number of potters*	*Percentage of the potters*
Group 1	*Rinpō* 1	11	8	72%
	Rinpō 2	10	2	20%
Group 2	*Rinpō* 3	10	4	40%
	Rinpō 4	10	3	30%
Group 3	*Rinpō* 5	10	6	60%
	Rinpō 6	9	4	44%
Group 4	*Rinpō* 7	8	4	50%
	Rinpō 8	9	4	44%
Total		77	35	45%

Note: The data are based on the *rinpō* organisation of Kami-Tachikui in 2019.

Some potters felt a strong sense of responsibility to rejuvenate the village economy. During an official meeting between members of the *kumiai* and young entrepreneurs from Kobe, organised as part of the UCCN projects, one potter spoke about his visions for the Tamba pottery industry. He said that *monozukuri* (making things) would not suffice to sustain the pottery industry without *machizukuri* (community building). He emphasised that potters should simultaneously seek ways to improve their work and village life. A similar point was made by another potter who held a leading position in an assembly of commercial activities in Konda town. He argued that for the Tamba pottery industry to thrive in the long-term, the wealth must be shared with the entire town community. He suggested that a closer business ties be established between the Tamba pottery industry and other businesses in Konda town, such as an *onsen* complex, restaurants, and shipping companies. By the end of my fieldwork, some of his ideas had been implemented in the form of a discount voucher that could be used in all the shops and restaurants in Konda town.

Looking at the participation of non-potting villagers in the various economic and social activities of the Tamba pottery industry, and the role and involvement of the potters in the social affairs of the village, we can see that the development of the local pottery industry can accompany the consolidation of the village community.

If the Tamba pottery industry, and the role of the potters in general, is so important in sustaining the social and economic activities of the village, the internal relationships of the potters are equally significant. How do they keep the group spirit alive amidst the growing individualisation of the Tamba pottery industry?

Between potting households

In Moeran's observation of the Onta potters (1997), the transition from a collective to an individualised system of pottery production deteriorated their group solidarity. A sense of egalitarianism had disappeared as collaborative pottery making, such as cooperative firing, was abandoned in favour of new individualised techniques.

On the other hand, the Tamba potters have been able to manage and control the changing economic and social panorama of their community by reorienting and reinterpreting the traditional social relations. The modernisation of the production system in Tachikui – the mechanisation of clay production, the introduction of gas and oil kilns, and the diversification of marketing channels – has not weakened their social ties. Although these changes have created tensions among the potters, as the social orders around gerontocracy have weakened and incomes have diversified according to individual reputation, they have not eradicated their existing social relations. Rather, the shifting gender dynamics and the traditional kin ties demonstrate the vitality and flexibility of the Tamba pottery community that constantly adapts existing norms and relationships to changing social conditions.

Changing gender dynamics

According to Kleinberg, between the 1950s and 1970s, the number of male workers from non-potting households receiving wages from pottery production in Kami-Tachikui declined due to out-migration. However, the number of female workers from non-potting households, both from within and outside the village, had increased (Kleinberg 1979: 183, 199). Similar to Guth's argument that the "unknown craftsmen" we typically assume to be men are often women who are "active participants in many crafts" (Guth 2021: 12), female workers in Tachikui played a significant role in the development of the Tamba pottery industry in the post-war period. In the absence of male wage labourers in the village that commuted to the cities, they supported the growing demand for folk craft products. In other words, they were the ones who played a crucial role in transforming the public image of Tamba pottery into a *mingei* craft.

One aspect that appears to have changed significantly from the employment is the nature of the tasks performed by women in the Tamba pottery production. By the 1970s, female workers, including wage labourers from non-potting households or within kiln owners' households, performed tasks that did not require special skills, such as clay pugging, glazing, packing, loading and unloading kilns, and shop keeping. Although they were also given the task of throwing on a jigger wheel, they were very few. Even during my fieldwork in 2018–2019, female workers were mainly seen at shop counters or during kiln unloading or packaging. At Sue no sato, female part-time workers were mostly employed at ticket counters, pottery classes, shops, and restaurants. In the office of *kumiai*, two women were employed for administrative job.

While these occupations seem to imply that women continue to be employed on the fringes of the Tamba pottery industry, there is an increasing number of professional female potters and apprentices in Tachikui. In one workshop, where many aspired to become apprentices to the master potter who was known for his unique techniques and record of winning prestigious awards, more than half of the apprentices were women. The potter noted that young men today are no longer interested in potting and tend to look for more stable jobs, as potters' incomes have become so unstable in recent decades. However, an increasing number of female students were willing to continue in the profession after graduating from art schools. This growing pool of female apprentices seemed to be creating a different gender dynamic for the future of the Tamba pottery industry. In *kumiai*, where not a single female potter is registered as a member, there was an ongoing discussion about accepting an application from a young female potter from a neighbouring town. The general ageing of the membership seemed to be forcing potters to rethink traditional gender roles.

Looking at the work of the existing female potters in the village, whom all are daughters of established potters, there is a strong individuality that distinguishes their work from that of the fathers. They exceled in terms of the modern ceramic techniques and had exhibitions in prestigious galleries that their fathers had not experienced. The number of female potters is still far below the number of male potters, but the small yet growing number signifies a change in the gender perception of the Tamba pottery industry. Women are no longer seen as back-ups for the main jobs preserved for male potters, but as potential leaders to run their independent kilns and possibly the *kumiai*.

Continuing kin ties

Kin-based cooperative activities are crucial to understanding the potter's everyday lives. *Ie*, a corporate residential group, is a crucial element in the organisation of pottery workshops based on a household-based production system. While conventional discourse argues that there has been a shift from the "household-to-household networks based on the *ie* and *dozoku* systems" to "person-to-person networks" (Otani 1998: 279), I argue that the former is still relevant when it comes to labour relations in Tamba pottery production. When Kleinberg (1979) conducted her fieldwork in Tachikui in the 1970s to study the kinship and the economic systems of Tamba pottery production, she observed two dominant types of kinship relationships: *shinrui* and *dōzoku*. In her analysis, they played an essential role in facilitating the village's limited labour pool. While her emphasis on the importance of ideology and family structures in the analysis of a village society is in line with the prevailing academic paradigm of structural functionalism at the time (Ryang 2004: 101–166), it is worth exploring their continuing relevance in contemporary village life.

In my interviews with the villagers, including potters and non-potters, they readily acknowledged the *shinrui* and *dōzoku*, but implied that they were no longer relevant in their everyday lives. Their lukewarm responses seemed to invalidate their practicality as kinship terms. However, they did not become obsolete or completely disappear from their daily contexts; they were simply practised in different forms than in the past. Their prevalence in everyday activities was evident when they were examined "in light of their current structure and adaptation to complex and rapidly changing situations" (Nakano and Brown 1970: 200). In my observations, *shinrui* and *dōzoku* were crucial elements, or at least, guiding ideas that shed light on how the Tamba pottery production system manages to sustain itself amidst the prevailing demographic challenges in the village.

Shinrui, also known as *shinzoku* or *shinseki*, is a category of a specific set of households. The ego's blood or marriage ties determine the bilateral kinship, usually extending to first cousins, both cognate and affine relations. It is a practical rather than an ideological entity, being sustained by "moral rights and obligations of the members to each other" (Nakane 1967: 32). In Kleinberg's observation of Tachikui in the 1970s, the *shinrui* relations were manifested in "weddings, births, funerals, sick-calls, hōji [maintenance] and house building or house-razing" (1979: 64). Although most of these activities are no longer customary, which is also related to the declining role of *rinpō*, there are still communal tasks that require *shinrui* relationships. Befu argues that there are three significant activities surrounding the *shinrui* relations – "economic assistance, participation in life crisis ceremonies, and visiting on special occasions" (Befu 1963: 1332). I focus on the economic assistance to show how the *shinrui* relations are still a partial but essential part of the Tamba pottery production.

In a climbing kiln firing, the first thing to be done is to heat *kamaguchi* (literally the "mouth of the kiln", referring to the first chamber). When the temperature reaches around 1300 degrees, the potters work in pairs to pull the fire into the final chamber. To create a natural glaze on the surface of the pottery, the potter must control the movement of the fire so that it moves to the next chamber at a steady pace and temperature, which requires at least two people to throw firewood into stokeholes on parallel sides of the kiln. Each throw must be carefully calculated based on the colours and movements of the fire. In the past, when climbing kilns were fired collectively by a group of potters, it was easy to find partners. However, as more potters use individual gas kilns, fewer are accustomed to using traditional climbing kilns, making it harder to find assistants with the necessary skills. Even if a person has sufficient knowledge of the climbing kiln firing, an ideal candidate needs to be close enough to spend days and nights together during the firing process. In my experience of attending three firings and two pre-firing preparations, the assistants were either family members or close relatives: In two cases, they were household members, and in the other three cases, they were relatives.[3] In the latter case, one of the assistants was a former potter who now lived outside of Tachikui. Although there were other potters nearby who knew how to use the climbing kiln, the older potter invited him since they were comfortable being around each other. In the other two cases where relatives acted as assistants, the younger was the nephew, and the older was his uncle. When the younger potter had a firing session with two of his contracted staff who were university graduates, his uncle had come over to help. For the nephew, his uncle was a reliable expert in climbing kilns and someone he could casually ask for demanding tasks such as training staff. The nephew returned the favour by helping his uncle with the subsequent firing.

The number of cases I have presented here may not be sufficient to make a solid argument. However, they do show how important *shinrui* relationships still are to those that continue to fire in climbing kilns. Given the symbolic value of the climbing kiln in representing the historical value of Tamba pottery, particularly in the designations of the UNESCO Creative City of Crafts and Folk Art and Japan Heritage, *shinrui* relationships do play a role in keeping this vital tradition alive.

Dōzoku is another form of kinship based on a hierarchical relationship between the potters of the main and branch households. Traditionally, the eldest son, or sometimes the eldest daughter, continues the main household and receives most of the inheritance. The younger ones establish branch households with economic support from the main household. The branch household may form a new main household, thus creating a new genealogical line. The reciprocal ties based on *dōzoku* were effective when rice farming was the main livelihood of the village. It lost its importance with the diversification of

Table 5.2 *Honke* and *bunke* relations of pottery workshops in Tachikui

	Surname group	Honke *(main household)*	Bunke *(branch household)*	*Relations between* honke *and* bunke
1	Ichino	Workshop 9	Workshop 10	Brother
2		Workshop 11	Workshop 20	Brother
3		Workshop 14	Workshop 1	Brother
4		Workshop 10	Workshop 21	Father-son
5		Workshop 12	Workshop 15	Brother
6	Shimizu	Workshop 23	Workshop 25	Brother
7	Ōgami	Workshop 38	Workshop 36	Brother
8	Others	Workshop 46	Workshop 45	Father-son
9		Workshop 57	Workshop 58	Father-son

Source: The information is based on interviews, surveys, and the information on the official webpage of *Tamba tachikui tōjiki kyōdo kumiai.*

economic activities and the decline of family farms. However, it is still relevant in the socio-economic relations of the potters.

Potters used the terms *honke* (main household) and *bunke* (branch household) to describe the structural relationships between workshops. Based on the archival sources provided by the *kumiai* and interviews with the potters, I identified 17 workshops linked in *dōzoku* relationships (Table 5.2), with one workshop overlapping with both brother and father-son ties at the same time (workshop 10). Of the nine pairs, six were in the brotherhood, where the eldest son of the family took over the workshop of the main household and the younger son established an independent branch. The common aspect that I found was that most of the *bunke* workshops produced a distinct style of work to that of the *honke* workshops. Take the case of workshop 45. The potter was trained at an art school and the shop looked like a modern gallery. On the other hand, his father's workshop (46) produced daily ceramics such as large bowls and thick cups in a simple *mingei* style. Instead of inheriting the prestige of the father's tea wares, the son had forged his own path as an artist potter.

Although most *bunke* workshops had their own concepts and designs, they were not completely independent regarding the knowledge and economic support they received from *honke* workshops. For instance, if a *honke* was a member of the *kumiai*, the *bunke* workshop had the privilege of joining the group at a reduced membership fee. Access to existing sales channels was also a considerable advantage for a newly established pottery business. For practical purposes, many young potters still relied on the *dōzoku* relationship.

Another kinship tie, although which tend to create tension among the potters, was *ittō*, which is a "[g]roup comprising houses that, in general, all bear the same surname" (Kleinberg 1979: 61). In Tachikui, the surname Ichino accounts for half of the members of the *kumiai* (Table 5.3). One of the first pieces of local knowledge I acquired was not to refer to villagers by their surname, as they could be confused. According to a study of the social structures of Tachikui conducted by Kyoto University in the 1950s, the high intermarriage rate in

Kami-Tachikui was the reason for the expansion of the Ichino group (Yabūchi 1955: 165–202). When I asked the potters for their thoughts on the dominance of a few surname groups, they were reluctant to discuss it as it was deemed a sensitive issue of the internal village politics. According to Kleinberg's observation in the 1970s, the *ittō* relations are manifest as a "bounded pressure group" when political rivalries are contested (Kleinberg 1979: 64). During my fieldwork, a project group for a new brand of Tamba pottery was formed by the potters with the same surname. The identity of an *ittō* group seemed to serve as a basis for developing a business cooperation at the expense of excluding others.

For some potters, the continuing relationships with *shinrui*, *dōzoku* and *ittō* were burdensome, and they cut themselves off from these kin ties altogether, for instance by resigning from *kumiai* membership. However, such cases were very few and far between, as it gave exclusive access to the Tamba clay produced on the *kumiai* budget. The potters seldom used the terms *shinrui, dōzoku*, or *ittō* in their daily conversations, nor did they seem to consciously appropriate their economic values. Nevertheless, the cooperative activities facilitated by these embedded relationships were fundamental to the survival of individual kilns. In other words, it was based on the deep sense of connectedness through these kin ties that sustained the contemporary taskscape of the Tamba pottery industry.

Between individuality and community solidarity

However, the potters' social relations are characterised not only by cooperation but also by competition. As much as the products they make resemble each other's for the identity of Tamba pottery requires a certain standardised designs and colours, there is always a tension between the potters alternating between cooperative and competitive modes. In practice, this is experienced as a balancing act between the conformity to group solidarity and the freedom to express one's individuality. The potters alleviated this tension, at least in part, by creating a symbolic boundary that separated each workshop from the others, despite the predominant collectivism. By using *yagō* (house name) as a "nickname" (Yamamoto 1992: 85) of the household-based workshops, potters kept their distance from others while maintaining a strong sense of community solidarity.

The origin of *yagō* is thought to date back to the Muromachi period, long before the establishment of the *ie* system (Kuwayama 2001; Ochiai 2000). Prior to the Meiji Restoration in 1868, only those of the samurai class and above were granted a surname (*myōji*). The surname represented the family's generational history and marked one's elite status. Wealthy merchants could negotiate a family name with a failed samurai. However, commoners who could not obtain one instead used *yagō*. It had no official record and was recognised only by a small group of close acquaintances in a closed village context (Partner 2009: 23). It provided a wide range of information about an individual and their household, "such as family history, occupation, reputation, and community ties" (Thompson 2004: 63). In addition, *yagō* was often used as a second

Table 5.3 The generations and references of *yagō*

Workshops	*Surname groups*	*The generations of* yagō	*The references of* yagō
1	Ichino	1	geographical location
2		1	
3		1	first name
4		1	first name
5		1	first name
6		1	
7		2	first name
8		2	
9		2	Specialty
10		2	first name
11		2	first name
12		2	first name
13		2	first name
14		2	first name
15		2	first name
16		3	first name
17		3	first name
19			Specialty
20			reference to Tamba pottery
21			reference to Tamba pottery
22			reference to Tamba pottery
23	Shimizu	2	first name
24		2	reference to Tamba pottery
25		2	first name
26		2	
27		2	reference to Tamba pottery
28		2	
29		3	
30			
31			
32	Ōgami	1	
33		2	
34		2	first name
35		3	first name
36			
37			reference to Tamba pottery
38			geographical location
39	Ōnishi	2	first name, reference to Tamba pottery
40		2	first name, reference to Tamba pottery
41		2	
42		3	first name, reference to Tamba pottery
43		2	first name

(*Continued*)

Table 5.3 (Continued)

Workshops	*Surname groups*	*The generations of* yagō	*The references of* yagō
44	Others	2	first name, reference to Tamba pottery
45			reference to Tamba pottery
46		1	geographical location
47			reference to Tamba pottery
48		1	
49		2	first name
50		1	first name
51		2	first name
52		2	first name
53		2	geographical location
54			first name
55		2	reference to Tamba pottery
56		1	
57		1	first name
58		1	first name
59		3	first name
60		1	

Source: Information based on interviews, surveys, and the information on the official website of *Tamba tachikui tōjiki kyōdo kumiai.*

Note: The workshops are all located in Tachikui, but they also include those that are not members of *Tamba tachikui tōjiki kyōdo kumiai.*

name to distinguish between the overlapping surnames that were common in a small and isolated community (Thompson 2004: 66; Yamamoto 1992: 85; Chang 2007: 392). However, it lost its importance when the state passed a law under the Meiji Restoration in 1875 requiring to obtain family names, which was a prelude to the introduction of *koseki*, the family register system. Nevertheless, *yagō* did not disappear and continued to be used in private contexts (Chang 2007).

In Tachikui, the use of *yagō* expanded rapidly following the expansion of ceramic markets and the individualisation of pottery production systems in the post-war period (Kleinberg 1979; Moeran 1997). As shown by the generations of *yagō*, most of them range from one to three generations (Table 5.3). With the development of the Tamba pottery industry in the early 1970s, there was a demand for brand names from collectors who wanted to use them to confirm the market value of the potters' work.

Yagō imbues the household enterprise with historicity, giving it a sense of "continuing, transgenerational nature" (Kleinberg 1979: 305). It is a common practice to refer to a potter by the *yagō* with whom he is associated. For example, when a son took over his retired father's kiln, old customers referred to him by the *yagō* of his workshop rather than by his name. When I asked if it was confusing to be called by *yagō*, he said it was a way of inheriting his father's

Figure 5.5 An outdoor bazaar during Tōki Matsuri.

reputation. *Yagō* helped to perpetuate household histories and the social value associated with it.

At the level of the pottery community, however, it reflected the tension between the growing desire for individuality and the collective identity as Tamba potters. The use of *yagō* was in part a strategic act of balancing between the collective identity as a Tamba potter and the individual maker (Table 5.3). The composition of the Chinese characters reveals different references to *yagō*, giving clues to the identity of the potters and which element they used to display their individuality or sense of belonging to the Tamba pottery tradition. Of the 44 workshops that responded to the multiple-choice survey, the majority named their *yagō* after the name of a potter (29 cases), followed by references to Tamba pottery (13 cases), the geographical traits of the workshop location (4 cases), and the specialty of the workshop (2 cases). About 30 per cent of the *yagō* deliberately made reference to Tamba pottery by using *tan* (丹) from *Tanba* (丹波). Some imply both the group identity as a Tamba potter and their individuality as in the case of "Tansui", who use *tan* from Tamba and *sui* from the potter's surname.

The practical value of *yagō* as a buffer between the individual and group identity was manifest during collective events. Every year during the Tōki Matsuri, an outdoor bazaar is set up at the playground of a middle school in Tachikui. Apart from the same white canopies installed in two rows, the interiors of the stalls varied with hand-made decorations from each workshop. The potters put considerable efforts in making their stalls distinctive. They set their tables in different structures, and some even brought their display shelves and small embellishments, such as table clothes and lighting, to add a touch of uniqueness. Despite the attempts at differentiation, no single shop stood out significantly. The extra features seemed to attract just enough attention to draw the line from one shop to another. As the aim of the event was not only to make a profit but also to promote Tamba pottery, extravagant spectacles that might disrupt the harmonious atmosphere of a traditional pottery community was avoided. Participating in the outdoor sales was an arduous task of competing with others while submitting to the group solidarity. Under these restraining conditions, the *yagō* sign functioned as the most obvious way of expressing one's fame and social prestige, albeit in an understated manner. It allowed the potters to symbolically demonstrate their individuality without externally flaunting it. Each *yagō* was written and displayed in a uniform format: black letters on a white wooden board hung at the edge of the canopy. It was the most obvious way of distinguishing the identity of the workshop from that of others. Whether by coincidence or not, the shops of renowned potters had minimalist displays. *Yagō* seemed to serve as a marker of market value and as a buffer, allowing the potter to keep their individuality alive without disrupting the collective identity as a Tamba potter.

The layers of social relations embedded in Tachikui, although laid out in a relatively static manner, reveal how contextually dense the cultural representation of Tamba pottery is. While the image of an older potter in the poster seem to embody the vitality of the Tamba pottery industry, his identity as a Tamba potter only persists based on the ongoing social life in Tachikui. In this context, the continuity of the community is as important as mastering pottery skills or preserving the local tradition, and is inextricably linked to the continuation of their craft. It is only by mapping out the complex "taskscape" (Ingold 1993) of Tachikui that we can better understand the potters' experiences of Tamba Sasayama's regional revitalisation policy.

Conclusion

Ingold notes that "[t]he temporality of the taskscape is social…not because society provides an external frame against which particular tasks find the independent measure, but because people, in the performance of their tasks, *also attend to one another*" (Ingold 1993: 159–160). Beneath the simplistic image of Tachikui are complex social relationships that keep the village community alive. The village consists of multiple relationships and components that are "perpetually under construction" (1993: 163), such as the potters' use of *yagō*, the persisting traditional kin-relations, and the changing gender roles. Despite the changing conditions of the pottery industry, the cooperative relationships between the potters and villagers continued to sustain the social and economic activities of the village. As Rosaldo and Narayan note, "mundane everyday activities become as much the locus of cultural creativity as the arduous ruminations of the lone artist or scientist" (1993: 5). It is through the potters' complex social relations intertwined in Tachikui and their multiple roles within the village community that we can better understand how they build cooperative, albeit conflicted, relationships with the local government in their involvement in reshaping Tamba Sasayama's public image.

Notes

1 Although some people include Kamaya, a neighbouring village on the border of Sanda municipality, as part of Tachikui, in this chapter, I focus on Kami-Tachikui and Shimo-Tachikui. The only two Tamba pottery workshops operating in Kamaya have their main household (*honke*), and the second workshop in Shimo-Tachikui.

2 *Saitō goma* is a ceremony unique to Shugendo, in which wood and straw are piled up outside and Buddhas and Bodhisattvas are invited to burn them and ward off evil. Through the ritual, the villagers pray for various wishes, from national peace to safety at home. It is said that the ritual began in Kami-Tachikui during the Taishō period, when an infectious disease took away many young children in the village.

3 It is usually male members of the household who take on the role of assistants in firing the kiln, although there are exceptional cases where the potter's wife or mother takes on this role. To this day, however, the work is still widely perceived as a male domain.

6 The Secular Side of Craftsmanship

Abstract

This chapter elucidates how the municipal campaign for new rurality manifests in the daily lives of locals, based on the potters' involvement in municipal promotional activities. Given the declining membership and ageing population of the Tamba Tachikui Pottery Cooperative (*Tamba tachikui tōjiki kyōdo kumiai*), which have been threatening the sustenance of the Tamba pottery industry, they had little option but to form a closer tie with the local government. In return for financial and administrative support for the Tamba pottery industry, they began participating in public events that required their demonstration and performance of traditional crafts, introducing them to a range of unfamiliar and tedious tasks such as attending meetings and completing paperwork. Previously, as members of the *kumiai*, their collective practices revolved around the production and distribution of Tamba pottery and Tamba clay. Now, their focus has shifted to promotional activities, in which they have limited experience or knowledge.

In the earlier stages of my fieldwork, I was plunged into places such as workshops and kilns, as potters were generous enough to open up their private space and share their thoughts about pottery making. At the time, many of our conversations revolved around ideas about craftsmanship, tradition, and the history of Tamba pottery, which was, in fact, information that I could easily find in books and museum catalogues.

It was not until I had spent months visiting and mingling with the potters, especially with Shōhei, that I began to see unexpected sides of the potter's social life. While the extended history of Tamba pottery in Tachikui instilled a symbolic sense of unity among the potters, membership of the *kumiai* seemed to foster a sense of unity based on shared concerns about the future of the Tamba pottery industry. Many seemed more preoccupied with the collective duties of the *kumiai* than with their individual schedules in their workshops such as the administration of the organisation, the maintenance of the clay processing factory, and the cooperative projects with the local government. Sitting in a grey office room with bundles of documents filled with bullet

DOI: 10.4324/9781003326540-10

points, the everyday life of the potters could not have been more distant from what I had imagined a few months earlier.

Once I realised their dedication to collective tasks, which seemed far removed from the conventional images of traditional craftspeople, I began to perceive the underlying tension between the potters and the local government regarding municipal revitalisation projects. On the surface, their relationship appeared to be a simple matter of give and take, with the local government attracting the potters to regional promotional activities for their cultural aura, and the potters participating for the financial support and increased social prestige they gain by attending local ceremonial events. However, it was also forged on the basis of the local government officials' limited understanding of the potters' notion of craftsmanship. While they expected the potters to have a natural talent for traditional craftsmanship, they seemed to dismiss the fact that this involved tedious tasks of office meetings and bureaucratic work that the potters were unfamiliar with. There was little understanding of the potters' social life, which revolved around the *kumiai* activities and trivial tasks that sustained the Tamba pottery industry. Despite the generous support of the local government, the potters sometimes felt that the officials took their contributions for granted. They could cope with the increased duties and longer working hours of promoting Tamba pottery, but not the feeling of being disrespected for their sincere efforts.

This chapter explores the potters' dilemma of projecting an idealised image of traditional craftspeople while simultaneously coping with an increasing burden of administrative responsibilities. These responsibilities, which mainly revolve around the organisation of events, force them to shift their daily routines towards less creative tasks such as attending meetings and dealing with paperwork. This aspect expands the conventional realms in which the practices and notions of craftsmanship have been centred on. Discussions have often revolved around the moral and political implications of craft against the dominant ideologies of modernisation (Adamson 2010; Kikuchi 2004). Also seen as indicative of the national identity and traditional forms of social structure in Japan (Herzfeld 2004), various studies have traced the transformation of craft practices under the development of modern technologies in the post-war period. Some of the key aspects that scholars have examined are the centrality of kinship relations in the craft economy (Kleinberg 1979; Moeran 1997), the regional symbolisation of craft (Han 1995), the artification of craft (Moeran 1990, 1997), the apprenticeship system (Singleton 1989), and the modernisation of the production and distribution system (Daniels 2001; Moeran 1997; Moon 2011; Paredes 2017). However, we cannot fully capture the expanding scope of craft practices in contemporary social contexts if we limit our notion of craft to its traditional domain. The prominence of craft industries in the recent rise of the rural creative class discourse (Luckman 2015) calls for a renewed dialogue on the idealisation of craftsmanship in place-making strategies. In Japan, where the local traditional crafts are increasingly envisioned as *the* cultural capital to revitalise the rural economies in the face of ageing and declining population (Matanle 2007; Hong 2009), we need to see how the idealisation of craft industry in the context of regional revitalisation initiatives affects the everyday craft practices.

I examine the changing socio-economic conditions – the ageing and declining population and the growing interest in local crafts as critical elements of regional revitalisation – as they are internalised into the existing social relations of the local craftspeople and their changing perceptions of traditional crafts in this process. Based on an analysis of the social organisation of the *kumiai*, I examine the potters' strategies for sustaining their pottery businesses (see also Kawamoto 2020; Tachibana 2022). Based on the transition of its organisational identity from a collective producer of Tamba clay to a promotional agency of Tamba pottery and Tamba Sasayama's cultural persona, I demonstrate how the potters incorporate promotional activities as a new genre of craft practice.

Craftspeople: The new creative class?

One of the grand narratives during the rapid industrialisation of the 19th century was that machines threatened manual skills. As Banks notes, "[t]he effect of industrial capitalism was to usurp the craft model", in which "the meaningful and concrete character of pre-industrial craft labour" was undermined by "the purely abstract labour of the emerging industrial system" (2010: 307; see also Adamson 2010; Sennett 2008). Against this backdrop, the life of craftspeople and their traditional social milieu in village societies, workshops and guilds were reinterpreted as emblems of untainted humanity, most prominently in the Arts and Crafts movements of the late 19th and 20th centuries (Adamson 2010; Kikuchi 2004). More recently, under the conditions of the capitalist system, the spirit of craftsmanship has been revived as a potential remedy for the demoralised work ethics of contemporary societies (Ingold 2000; Sennett 2008; McRobbie 2012).

However, craftsmanship is not always inherently opposed to or counteracting dominant political and economic dynamics. Its social implication is multifaceted and can vary across context. With the recent popularity of the creativity discourse in public policy, the idea that craftspeople can be the key actors in revitalising local social and economic life is gaining attention. This is, in part, due to the rise of the creative class theory, popularised by Richard Florida, which sees the creativity of human agents as the driving force behind regional economic growth (Florida 2003). For creative capital to emerge, the role of a specific group of people is essential, as they provide local communities with inspiration and ideas. It could be argued that creativity is a universal human quality, not a tradable capital. However, the very prevalence of creative class theory is evidence of the general agreement that creativity *is* an asset to be managed. In this context, it is the contribution of creative individuals that matters in regional revitalisation policies, not just local products or cultural elements. Local creatives are the "magnet" (Pratt 2008: 114) that attracts tourists and investors.

More recently, discussions of the creative class have extended from the urban-centred notions of creativity to rural social contexts. The protagonists have tended to be artists living in "'buzzy' or 'edgy' urban neighbourhoods" (Bell and Jayne 2010: 209), such as those working in the fashion, music, or the new media industries. However, in the "post-productivist era" of the countryside (Wilson 2001), where there has been an economic transition "from agricultural production, to become a site of consumption, tourism and recreation" (Bell and Jayne 2010: 210; see also, Woods 2007), the notion of the creative class is being adapted to individuals involved in the rural economy (Luckman 2012). In particular, as Bell and Jayne argue, craftspeople have been identified as a new category of the rural creative class with their "unique selling points" (2010: 212): "traditional arts and crafts and music tend to be explicitly represented in terms of aesthetic content and networks" as they contain "a particular sense of rural identity" (2010: 212; see also Troy Chen 2018).

The rise of the creative class in rural contexts seem evident in the case of Tamba Sasayama. Although the label of being "creative" has only appeared recently with Tamba Sasayama's successful designation as a UNESCO Creative City of Crafts Folk Arts, they have always played an active part in the regional economy since the Edo period. Under the patronage of the Sasayama domain, the Tamba potters produced special types of pottery with distinctive paintings that showed regional identity, enabling the region to catch up with the growing ceramic markets in Japan. Later, when the post-war *mingei* boom revived the Tamba pottery industry, it was once again promoted by the Konda town and Hyogo Prefecture, and Tamba pottery was promoted as a key cultural capital for local tourism.

The potters' rise as the rural creative class of Tamba Sasayama, however, is contradictory, looking at the figure that illustrates the decline of crafts in Japan. Since the enactment of the Act on the Promotion of Traditional Craft Industries in 1974, the craft industry has been supported by the central government, and there are now more than 200 officially recognised traditional craft industries. Recently, however, the market has been shrinking rapidly. According to Kakiuchi and Takeuchi (2014), the approximately 205,000 employees listed in the Japanese government's official records in 1990 had fallen to just 73,000 by 2010. While many other sectors within the creative industries are in decline, with the exception of "software and computer services", the craft industry has experienced one of the most pronounced shrinkage. Against this gloomy outlook, one of the authors offers a contrasting view in another paper published in a few years later. Kakiuchi (2016) proposes a hopeful outlook for the traditional craft industry in Kanazawa, a city known for its established history of Japanese craft culture and the model case for Tamba Sasayama's regional revitalisation policy. Citing statistics that show a recent increase in the number of tourists to the region, she highlights the contributions of local craftspeople. The traditional crafts have been the "basis of the city's brand image of cultural creativity, a valuable asset for tourism and a potential foundation for innovation" (2016: 106).

The optimistic outlook on crafts in Japan, despite the statistics showing its decline, can be attributed to the prevailing perception of traditional crafts in the cultural context of Japan. Craftspeople are often seen as the living embodiment of Japan's unique national culture, such as in the expressions of *shokunin kishitsu* (the spirit of craftspeople) or *shokunin bunka* (the culture of craftspeople). In his acclaimed book *The Craftsman*, Richard Sennett articulates how the craftspeople's ethos of "doing good for its own sake" (2008: 37) provides moral exemplar against the insensate work ethics of capitalist societies. He deliberately avoids using the term "creativity" since "the word carries too much Romantic baggage – the mystery of inspiration, the claims of genius" (2008: 290); however, his caution seems less attentive in the cultural context of Japan, where he reflects on an idea of romantic and spiritual values enshrined in some kind of national spirit. Japan is "a nation of craftsmen" (2008: 30), where the practice of craftsmanship is an innate quality and an example of the "cultural imperative to work well for the common good" (2008: 30). Compared to the disheartened Soviet construction workers of the 1970s and 1980s, Japanese economy flourished during the same period since company employees were motivated to work with a "sense of mutual and self-respect" (2008: 30). Popular media and the corporate sphere project similarly romanticised understandings of craftsmanship. The NHK documentary programme, Project-X, presented the mythical concept of *monozukuri* – "the obsessive devotion to technical perfection" (Shimoda 2013: 254) – as one of the key elements that enabled Japan's miraculous post-war economic growth. In the business sector, Japanese service professionals abroad, such as sushi chefs, "utilise traditional Japanese work ethics in marketing their services" (Aoyama 2015: 275).

Moeran argues that traditional craftspeople in Japan are easily fetishised due to their "detached manner" (1990: 223; cf. Mead 1960: 15).[1] In his essay on the discourse of tradition in Japan, he expresses concern that traditional potters are idealised with a naïve understanding of their everyday lives:

> … people have an image of traditional craftsmen working alone in undisturbed peace, at one with their natural surroundings. As a result, they are unaware of the fact that to the rural craftsmen, nature is not something to be contemplated aesthetically in a detached manner. Rather, it is the environment in which he has to survive, it provides the materials with which he works; it is the source of his success and of his fears. Clearly, people idealize nature only when they are not directly involved with it in a struggle for survival.
>
> (Moeran 1990: 223)

The natural surroundings of their workplace, seen from afar, give the impression of a peaceful and harmonious life; however, from the potters' point of view, craftsmanship is part of their everyday struggle to make a living.[2]

The rise of the potters as the new rural creatives in Tamba Sasayama's regional revitalisation initiatives is promoted against the backdrop of the widespread discourses and media representation that emphasise the internal cultural values of traditional craftsmanship. Just as Tamba pottery was upheld as the regional cultural emblem of *sōzō nōson* for the pervasive discourse of the innate moral value of rural crafts, the potters are believed to possess an innate skill or manner that makes them the rural creatives.

In this context, the tension in the potters' participation in Tamba Sasayama's regional revitalisation policy stems from the disparity between the reality of making a living as a potter and the idealised views of traditional craftsmanship. For instance, the potters considered the planning and implementation of promotional activities as a collaborative effort *with* the local government, however, the officials' involvement in the actual preparation was limited. Once the subsidy had been allocated, they seemed to pay little attention to how a project was planned and carried out. When the potters organised a local pottery course for participants from the Kansai area, together with the Tourism Division at City Hall, some of the potters openly expressed their frustration at the absence of officials. They had expected them to come and see how the courses were being run, but the officials seemed to assume that everything would be fine.

However, as mentioned in Chapter 3, it is almost impossible for local government officials, who are chronically understaffed and overloaded with multiple tasks, to visit every event venue. At another off-site event held at a well-known tourist site in Kobe, a local government official in charge of the project had actually turned up on the second day, but only for a few hours. Knowing how long it took to travel all the way from Tamba Sasayama to the venue, I could see how committed he was to the collaborative projects with the potters. However, his short stay could not have allowed him to grasp the overall issues on the ground. In this context, the way in which the potters' behind-the-scene efforts were overlooked in promotional activities stems from a combination of factors such as the lingering effects of neoliberal reforms, which have left City Hall officials overworked and understaffed, and the enduring influence of the national cultural representation of traditional craftsmanship, which portrays it as an inherent cultural trait of the potters. Ironically, the more the potters' lives became intertwined with promotional activities that portrayed their culture as creative, the more they were exposed to bureaucratic tasks.

I shed light on how this contradiction is experienced in the potters' everyday lives by analysing the evolving organisational structure and activities of the *kumiai*. I explore the complexities of the organisational restructuring that lie beneath the polished surface of their idealised representations.

Tamba tachikui tōjiki kyōdo kumiai

Before the current form of the *kumiai* was established in 1950, there were a number of attempts to unite the individual pottery workshops in Tachikui into a collective entity. Before the Meiji Restoration, the potters, who were part-time farmers, were grouped under the production system of the Sasayama *han* patronage. However, with the political revolution that established a new system of government in Japan, they were disintegrated into separate household-based production units. Barely surviving the economic turmoil of the war years, many had abandoned pottery production by the late 1920s.

Table 6.1 The post-war development of *Tamba tachikui tōjiki kyōdo kumiai*

	1937	*1948*	*1950*	*1954*	*1956*	*1957*	*1963*	*1968*	*1973*	*1978*	*1979*
A	Establishment of Tamba Pottery Industrial Cooperative		Establishment of Tamba Pottery Industrial Cooperative (42 members)				Establishment of a modernised clay factory, start a group purchasing of basic clay ingredients		Purchasing a land to dig Tamba clay in Sanda	Initiation of Tōki Matsuri	
B		Establishment of Prefectural Pottery Production Laboratory in Kami-Tachikui (prefectural)		Restructured as Hyogo Tamba Pottery Production Laboratory (prefectural)	Restructured as Hyogo Tamba Pottery Instruction Center (prefectural)			Closure ofthe Center (prefectural)			
C						The Tamba climbing kiln building skills designated as the National Intangible Treasure					Acknowledgement of Tamba Tachikui Pottery Traditional Craftsmanship by the Minister of Economy, Trade and Industry

1985	*1988*	*1990*	*2005*	*2006*	*2007*	*2015*	*2017*	*2018*
Renamed into Tamba Tachikui Pottery Cooperative					Initiation of *haru monogatari*			Tamba pottery registered for the regionally based collective trademark
Establishment of Sue no sato (municipal)	Establishment of a tourism center within Sue no sato (municipal)	The building and firing of the Heisei kiln in Sue no Sato (municipal)	Renovation of tourism center into Yokochō, a themed sales booth (municipal)	Management of Sue no sato based on Designated Manager System (municipal)		The symbolic firing of *Saikō no noborigama* to celebrate Japan Heritage designation		
						Tamba Sasayama designated as UNESCO Creative City of Craft and Folk Arts with Tamba pottery	Tamba pottery designated as Japan Heritage (*nihon isan*) as one of six ancient kilns in Japan	

Source: The webpage of the *Tamba tachikui tōjiki kyōdo kumiai*, The 50 years history of Industrial Testing Laboratory (*Hyōgo ken kōgyō shōrei kan* 1968: 174).

Note: A refers to developments of *Tamba tachikui tōjiki kyōdo kumiai*, B, collaborations with external entities, and C, official recognitions of Tamba pottery tradition.

In 1937, the Hyogo prefectural government ordered to "'rationalize' the local ceramic industry" (Kleinberg 1979: 112). As a result of this initiative, a number of potting households in Tachikui joined together to form an organised group of cooperatives, which later became the Hyogo Prefectural Ceramic Association in 1942. During this time, land mines were produced in the village, whether willingly or not. After Japan's defeat in the Asia-Pacific war, the cooperative broke away from the prefectural government to form an independent organisation. However, as Kleinberg notes, the long-term influence of external authorities – the Sasayama *han* patronage and the national and prefectural governments – on the production and distribution systems of the Tamba pottery industry had deprived the potters of any professional management skills for running a cooperative. In January 1950, the cooperative went bankrupt and the organisation split into two independent entities. However, with the repayment of debts by the former managerial officials and the prefectural policy of revitalising the prefectural industry, the potters were able to reunite into a single cooperative eight months later.

The current organisational structure was established under the Small and Medium-Sized Enterprise Cooperatives Act (*Chūshō kigyō tō kyōdō kumiai hō*) in 1950 with a total of 42 members. As of 2018, the number has increased to 51. The basic requirement for membership is to have a workshop set up in Tachikui and, in some cases, in Kamaya village, and, although implicit, a newcomer should be someone from within the social and kinship network of Tachikui. However, an apprenticeship or internship with an active member grants an informal qualification for application, and further efforts have recently been made to loosen the ties to the village networks.

Regarding the role distribution, there is the *san'yaku* (three roles), as the potters call them, which consist of a president (*rijichō*), a vice president (*fukurijichō*), and a financial accountant (*kaikei buchō*) (Figure 6.1). They share responsibility for the organisation's overall management together with the director of the *kumiai* office (*jimukyokuchō*). They hold separate meetings to discuss sensitive issues such as financial affairs or the administration of bureaucratic businesses with the local government. The president represents the group at external events, while the vice president manages practical administrative matters. The financial accountant oversees the budget plans for various businesses, such as municipal and community-wide public projects, the renovation of public facilities, and the management of clay processing factories. Gerontocracy is not so evident in the directorship, as experience in *kumiai* activities or social standing among the potters is what counts most. Two of the *san'yaku* were relatively young, in their mid-50s, and well acquainted with various issues in and outside Tachikui. As the leadership positions in the *kumiai* became increasingly involved in promotional activities, which required an ability to follow the latest consumer trends, younger potters were seen as better suited to the job.

Below the *san'yaku* are the nine project committees (*jikōinkai*), each consisting of a chair (*iinchō*), director in charge (*tanto riji*), and members (*iin*), except for the clay factory management section, which *san'yaku* directly oversees.

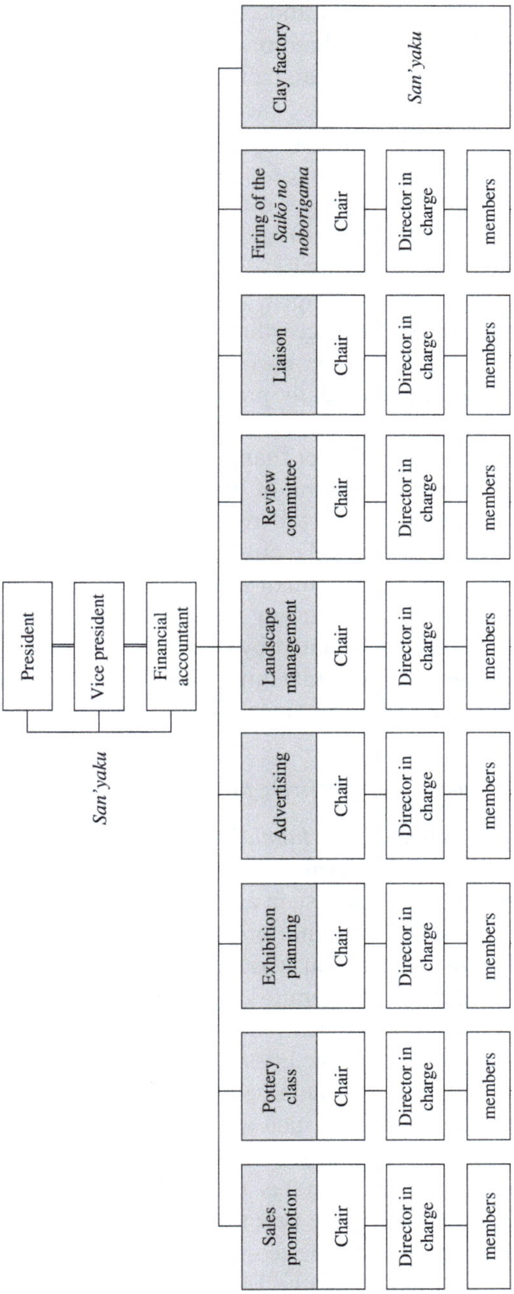

Figure 6.1 The organisational structure of the *kumiai*.

Source: Tamba tachikui tōjiki kyōdo kumiai.

Each committee fulfils distinct roles. For instance, when there was a meeting with the local government about an abandoned tennis court near Sue no sato, the *san'yaku* and a member of the Landscape Management Committee were present in the room. The board of directors (*rijikai*), consisted of the *san'yaku* and the chairs of the eight committees, facilitates meetings to discuss the progress of various projects managed by each committee. The *kumiai* office is comprised of the office director and staff that manage various administrative tasks such as writing reports, checking the budget balance of the *kumiai* and sometimes, assisting the organisation of external events.

The three positions of the *san'yaku* and the eight chairs from the project committees are democratically elected every two years. In practice, only the position of financial accountant is open, and the eligible candidates are the chairs of project committees. The succeeding posts – vice president and president – are based on a system of promotion, with the financial accountant becoming vice president and eventually president. There is a tacit agreement about the term of office of president: unless there is a significant failure in his duties, the same person can stay longer than the two-year period. Suppose that the president remains in office after end of his term. In this case, the vice president and the financial accountant will remain in position unless someone objects and decides to resign. From the outset, the flexible incumbency system seems vulnerable to the monopolisation of directory positions. However, as the majority avoid having a title for the heavy responsibilities that follow, serving for a longer period is rather appreciated by others (cf. Moeran 1997: 82–83).[3] As if reflecting the burden of the leadership, there has not been a delay in the promotion track in the last five terms since 2009.

Production: Keeping the Tamba clay processing factory running

When the potters first established the *kumiai*, the goal was to catch up with the changing market trends and modernise the production system of the Tamba pottery industry. Although products such as planters, wide-mouthed pots, and grinding bowls were in modest demand, profits were low. Under Japan's rapid economic changes during the post-war period, there was a growing demand for industrial ceramic products from chemical factories located in the Osaka and Kyoto areas. Although there have been requests for industrial containers since the 1930s, few workshops had the facilities to handle the large orders. By the 1950s, the *kumiai* had attempted to increase the productivity of each workshop by introducing advanced machinery such as electric wheels, gas and oil kilns, and motor-powered jigger wheels, based on loans provided by the prefectural government. However, as Kleinberg notes, the prefectural government did virtually nothing to help potters acquire new tools as its organisational structure was still immature. It was not until the economic revival of the Tamba pottery industry during the folk craft boom in Tachikui in the early 1970s that the *kumiai* could introduce the various private and public funding programmes to the potters to improve their workshop facilities (Figure 6.2).

Figure 6.2 The remaining building of the Tamba Pottery Industry Experimentation Centre.

From early on, the practical aim of the *kumiai* was to ensure stable production and distribution of Tamba clay. In 1963, the potters established a clay processing factory in Kami-Tachikui. Traditionally, the preparation of fine clay in the pottery production process took significant time. It took up to 40 days to produce popular daily utensils such as grinding bowls or large jars, which included stages of washing and pounding the clay before the shaping and firing processes (Kleinberg 1979: 180–90). The Tamba Pottery Industry Experimentation Centre (*Tamba yogō shikenjō*), established in 1948, contributed significantly to the development of new pottery techniques and the establishment of the Tamba clay processing factory in 1963. The factory was an important lever in the time management of the production process. The potters were able to concentrate on the shaping and glazing processes, as all they had to do was to purchase lumps of clay from the factory at a reasonable price, and to process them through a pug mill machine that was equipped for each workshop.

The potters emphasise that one of the main factors contributing to the competitive advantage of Tamba pottery in the ceramics market is the availability of affordable and high-quality clay. Members can purchase the clay at a relatively lower price than in other pottery villages that rely on the supplies from private clay shops (*tsuchiya*). In Bizen, for example, demand for local clay comes from all over Japan, and the price of the clay fluctuates regardless of the

Figure 6.3 Stacks of processed clay at the Tamba clay processing factory.

situation of the local potters in the area. In contrast, the *kumiai*'s strict control over access to and price of the Tamba clay keeps its price stable, allowing its members to sell their products at a more reasonable price than other traditional pottery brands. At Yokochō, an official sales platform within Sue no sato, one of the most common reactions from the customers was that the products were affordable for their decent quality. Therefore, it would not be an exaggeration to say that the most important role of the *kumiai* is the management and operation of the Tamba clay processing factory. In contrast to the prevailing discourse that suggests mechanisation in traditional craft sectors undermines the communal spirit of craftspeople, the modernisation of clay processing in Tachikui brought the potters together to seek "inter-workshop cooperation", at least in "financial" terms (Kleinberg 1979: 189). The potters had to work together to maintain the stable management of the Tamba clay processing factory.

There are two main sources of income that sustain the *kumiai* and the factory, which can be divided into a fixed income and an additional income. The fixed income consists of a membership fee that potters pay to the *kumiai* when they first join and a monthly fee that they pay regularly until they retire. The initial membership fee can be burdensome for some potters in the early stages of their careers. However, the reclaiming of the initial membership fee in their retirement and an additional retreat bonus provides a financial safety net for the self-employed potters. Additionally, the membership system is of a significant advantage to an inheritor of a member's workshop, who receives a discount on the membership fee. This explains the common practice of membership inheritance within households.[4]

The fixed income, consisting of the joint financial assets, based on the membership fees and monthly fees, is used in maintaining the clay processing factory, the *kumiai* office and Sue no sato. For instance, the salaries of nine full-time office staff and around 20 part-time workers hired to run Sue no sato – at the ticket booth, pottery classes and Yokochō – are paid by the fixed income. While some of the operational cost of Sue no sato, being municipal property, are partly subsidised by the local government, the management of the factory is the sole responsibility of the *kumiai*. The costs of running it include the salary of a technical manager, the occasional refurbishment of machinery, utility bills, and the cost of procuring the essential ingredients of Tamba clay. As important as the smooth operation of the factory is, its annual budget is kept separate from the general budget. One of the most controversial issues during my stay was the considerable cost of repairing the old machinery. The debate was about whether to replace the old ones or to continue using them after some repairs. Some opposed the latter option, as the cost of making partial improvements would eventually add to the cost of revamping the entire facility. Others refuted the former, arguing that the cost to obtain new machines would be too much to spend when there were multiple other issues to deal with. Although I was left out of the conversation, unable to figure out how the discussion had developed, it seemed clear that the problems concerning the clay processing factory were of great concern to the potters.

However, the ageing and retiring members of the *kumiai* have raised concerns about the management of the clay processing factory. According to a survey conducted by the local government in 2016, the number of potters in the *kumiai* will decrease dramatically in 30 years (Table 6.2). Many of the potters I spoke to seemed to agree with the findings of the survey. The problem of depopulation was directly related to the sustainability of the *kumiai* itself. Fewer members meant less financial capacity to run the organisation. Since its

Table 6.2 The estimated number of *Tamba tachikui tōjiki kyōdo kumiai* members in 30 years

Age group	*Present*	*In 10 years*	*In 20 years*	*In 30 years*
60s	25	15	14	12
50s	15	14	12	5
40s	14	12	5	?
30s	12	5	?	?
20s	5	?	?	?
Total	69	46+?	31+?	17+?

Source: Tamba Sasayama's report for the *Zenkoku chiiki rīdāyōsei juku 28 kisei* published in 2016.

financial stability depended on the collective wealth of its members, a high number of imminent retirees meant a significant loss of membership fees. The number of members also determined the amount of the monthly fee, as it was shared between them. If the number of members fell dramatically, as the survey predicted, the remaining members would have to pay a higher monthly fee, which could affect their interest in the membership. As one senior potter anticipated, if the potters do not find the high fees of the *kumiai* worthwhile to contribute, they will leave, putting the organisation in financial turmoil.

In sum, the potential lack of financial contributions to maintain the clay processing factory in the near future posed several challenges. Firstly, the factory has been instrumental in saving potters considerable time and energy, allowing them to focus on other aspects of their craft, such as developing skills or promoting their work. However, any intervention in the stable supply of clay could disrupt the established work patterns and cause delays in the production process, thereby affecting individual businesses. Secondly, the Tamba clay produced in this particular factory over the last few decades has been a crucial element in determining the authenticity of Tamba pottery. The skills of the potters have been trained on the unique properties of the clay, such as its viscosity, and any changes to the current state of the Tamba clay could affect their craft techniques. This, in turn, could have a ripple effect on the quality of Tamba pottery as a whole, affecting its market competitiveness.

Promotion: Keeping promotional activities going

In this context, the additional income was at stake in place of the membership fee and the monthly fee, which might decrease in 30 years' time due to the retirement of senior potters. Commissions from the sales revenues in Yokochō and the pottery classes in *Sue no sato* were two of the most important sources of additional income. However, as a survey of the Tamba pottery in 2003–2004 showed, one of the biggest declines since the 1990s was in sales from Yokochō, which had accounted for almost 20 per cent of the total sales, followed by that from shops attached to individual workshops (Takeyasu 2007: 58–59). The potters saw the need to increase the number of tourists visiting the village, as both of these major sales routes were based on direct sales to visitors. As Takeyasu points out, "it was important that Tachikui as a region becomes an attractive area that attracts people, in addition to the charm of Tamba pottery" (2007: 58). One of the potters who have been central contributors to the promotion of Tamba pottery emphasised that appealing to young people is essential as they will substitute the existing customers who have become economically less active. If they became regular customers of Yokochō and the pottery classes, there was a glimpse of light that the *kumiai* would find a new source of financial stability.

The increase in promotional activities is evident in recent years. Of the 202 activities in 2018–2019, 67 were tasks related to the advertisement and promotion of Tamba pottery, such as festivals, press exposures, and other public events (Table 6.3). *Kumiai* office staff managed the administrative work associated with

Table 6.3 The promotion-related activities of *Tamba tachikui tōjiki kyōdo kumiai* in 2018–2019

Year	*Month*	*The number of collective activities (the number of promotion-related activities)*	*Promotion-related works*
2017	April	12 (6)	External events, festivals etc.
			Press conference of the Haru Monogatari
			Sakura matsuri
			Refurbishing the *Saikō no noborigama*
			Visiting Kobe area for the preparation for the Haru Monogatari
			Visiting the Tamba area for the preparation for the Haru Monogatari
	May	12 (3)	The 11th the Haru Monogatari
			Meeting for reviewing the Haru Monogatari
			Article coverage of Tamba Sasayama monthly magazine
	June	19 (4)	Meeting on Tamba Sasayama's *hina matsuri*
			Meeting of advertising group
			Meeting on Tamba Sasayama's *hina matsuri*
			Meeting on the establishment of *Rokkoyō* of Japan Heritage
	July	28 (5)	Meeting on Tamba Sasayama's *hina matsuri*
			Meeting with Tamba Sasayama Commercial and Tourism Department
			Meeting with Sun Television Broadcasting Station
			NHKBS interview and film shooting
			Visit of the director of the Japan Heritage
	August	16 (3)	NHK Broadcasting Station shooting
			Festival of *monozukuri*
			Presentation of the Japan Heritage subsidy
	September	14 (4)	Meeting with Sun Television Broadcasting Station
			Meeting on Tamba Sasayama's *hina matsuri*
			Location hunting for Sun Television film shooting
			Location hunting for TV Osaka
	October	14 (4)	Magazine coverage of Tamba pottery workshops
			Meeting with Sun Television Broadcasting Station
			Film shooting of Sun Television Broadcasting Station
			Meeting on Tamba Sasayama's *hina matsuri*
	November	14 (6)	Exhibition of Tamba pottery at the Japan Heritage Forum
			Japan Heritage Forum
			Exhibition of Tamba pottery at Exhibition of Tamba Sasayama
			Tourism seminar
			Tamba Sasayama Mackerel Festival
			Tamba pottery class at a local elementary school
	December	20 (9)	*Rokkoyō* Summit
			Japan Heritage seminar at a local elementary school
			Hyogo Cultural Exchange
			The 1st Haru Monogatari meeting
			Refurbishing street signs in Tachikui
			Tachikui street tour program
			Seminar of Tachikui street tour program
			Meeting with Tamba Sasayama Commercial and Tourism Department
			Meeting on Tamba Sasayama's *hina matsuri*

(*Continued*)

Table 6.3 (Continued)

Year	*Month*	*The number of collective activities (the number of promotion-related activities)*	*Promotion-related works*
2018	January	18 (11)	*Huku bukuro* sales festival Meeting of Haru Monogatari event group Tamba pottery class at a local elementary school Meeting of Haru Monogatari *tari* advertising group Interview from *Hyogo Gokoku* The 2nd Haru Monogatari meeting Tamba pottery class at a local elementary school Meeting of Japan Heritage promotion committee Tamba pottery class at local elementary school Meeting of Sakura matsuri Meeting of Japan Culture and Culinary Tourism Promotion Committee
	February	15 (6)	Tamba pottery class at a local elementary school Tamba pottery class at a local elementary school Meeting on Tamba Sasayama's *hina matsuri* Tamba pottery class at a local elementary school Parent-child pottery making class Meeting with Hankyu Magazine
	March	20 (6)	Meeting of Haru Monogatari advertising group Special exhibition at MCART Location hunting for Sun Television film shooting The 3rd tourism seminar Hankyu pottery class Meeting of Haru Monogatari
	Total	202 (67)	

Source: Tamba tachikui tōjiki kyōdo kumiai.

these activities. The potters focused on public events, but they also engaged in bureaucratic tasks. Festivals, press interviews, and pottery classes usually only took a few hours or days. What occupied most of their time and energy is the administrative work involved in these activities. In the case of the three-day Haru Monogatari in May, there were at least seven meetings before and after the event, not to mention the many informal meetings that took place off the record. As shown in Table 6.4, there were 153 sessions related to event preparations in 2017–2018.

As the *kumiai* received public support from the local government, the potters were responsible for the planning and organising of events, not to mention the bureaucratic procedures. Budget management was particularly demanding, as detailed plans had to be submitted to the local government. In contrast to the flexible modus operandi of the initiatives managed solely by the *kumiai* budget, public funding required definite plans and results. The *kumiai*

Table 6.4 Meetings of *Tamba tachikui tōjiki kyōdo kumiai* in 2017–2018

Year	*Month*	*San'yaku meeting*	*Project committee meeting*	*Other meetings*
2017	April	2	3	3
	May	2	2	4
	June	1	7	10
	July	1	8	9
	August	1	10	3
	September	1	13	9
	October	1	5	12
	November	1	6	-
	December	1	6	2
2018	January	1	12	3
	February	1	4	2
	March	1	4	2
Total		14	80	59

Source: Tamba tachikui tōjiki kyōdo kumiai.

office held regular meetings and discussions to ensure that the plan met the bureaucratic norms. In this process of meeting deadline or double-checking the budget plan, the number of meetings increased, sometimes to the extent that the potters complained about the lack of time spent in their workshops.

The administrative burden was likely to intensify as the promotional activities of the *kumiai* have increasingly relied on the financial support from external authorities. In 2017–2018, they received eight public subsidies from various entities, such as the local government, the prefectural government, and the Ministry of Economy, Trade and Industry to fund public events such as pottery classes, markets, and exhibitions. It is true that the potters deliberately sought external subsidies to substantiate their promotional activities. However, the local government also encouraged them to become more involved in public affairs, such as holding events as part of the regional revitalisation policy. Since the designation of the UNESCO project and Japan Heritage, the *kumiai* has received far more information about public grants from the local government.

Another substantial financial aid the potters received from the local government was the Designated Manager System (*Shitei kanrisha seido*), which the *kumiai* took over in 2006.[5] As generous as the budget for running and managing Sue no sato was, the audit system was equally rigorous. Each year, the *kumiai* submits a monitoring report to the local government's Department of Financial Affairs (*zaimu ka*) on the management of Sue no sato, including an assessment of how the current performance could be improved. Based on the annual performance, a decision was made on the upcoming renewal of the contract. The main criteria for the audit are the number of visitors to Sue no sato and the number of participants in the pottery classes. The figures are then evaluated in the context of an annual increase in tourists to Tamba Sasayama. In the example of the 2012–2013 report, feedback from the local government showed concern about the declining number of general visitors to Sue no sato and the pottery class attendants. In response, the *kumiai* demonstrated in the report its plans to increase the advertising budget. They spent more than twice as much on advertisement as the previous year.

When Kleinberg conducted fieldwork in Tachikui in the 1970s, it was the time when the Tamba pottery industry was flourishing with the booming *mingei* market. The potters were so overwhelmed by demand that even during New Year and O-bon, they spent most of their time at work (1979: 80). Back then, successful sales alone could finance the stable management of the Tamba clay factory. The lengthy process of discussing, planning, and reporting on local government subsidies was not part of their duties, nor did they feel the need to do so. However, potters nowadays no longer live the simple lives of traditional craftspeople. The popular image of the traditional craftspeople, alone in their workshop surrounded by nature, is virtually impossible. Whether or not they enjoy the collective duties, the potters have to keep trying different ways to promote Tamba pottery and look for new business opportunities. They have to play the role of administrators, PR managers, and event organisers to adapt to the changing market and prepare for the downsizing of the *kumiai*. Their everyday space extends from a dusty workshop to an unsoiled meeting room.

Conclusion

This chapter demonstrated the complexity of the everyday craft practices of Tamba potters against the prevailing views that romanticise traditional craftsmanship. Underlying the grant-mediated ties of cooperation between the potters and the local government was the shared fate of depopulation: the municipal depopulation and the shrinkage of the *kumiai* members. From the perspective of the social organisation and the collective value of the *kumiai*, the grant-mediated relationship with the local government and the general discourse of rural creativity seems to have been helpful in sustaining the Tamba pottery industry. Although the potters sometimes complained about the burdensome and unfamiliar duties, they knew that their community and the *kumiai* were at risk of downscaling in the near future. They had to prepare for future risks that might affect the stable supply of Tamba clay and were convinced to embrace the new tasks of promotional activities as one of the foremost priorities of their collective activities. The many meetings, paperwork, and organising events were demanding, but in doing so, they hoped to secure their livelihoods and shape the future of Tamba pottery for younger generations.

Notes

1 Margaret Mead argues that distance plays an important role in arousing a sense of newness and creativity:

> Here the sense of freshness of the masterpiece is maintained by the difference between those who live near it and those who have seen it only once at some great ceremony or when they journeyed from a great distance on a pilgrimage, for a coronation, or to see a capital city, or attend the university of a son. For most people, such a painting or statue will be seen only once or twice in a lifetime; those who live close to it…live and feed on the freshness which is contributed by the new visitors.
>
> (1960: 18)

2 For further works on the difficulty of continuing traditional craftsmanship in Japan, see Hwang 2015 and Moon 2011.

3 Moeran observes a similar attitude from the members of the Onta Pottery Cooperative in Sarayama, where potters do not wish to take the leading positions. He describes that "it is an unrewarding task which they [members] do not see as at all prestigious… Increasing contact with the media, local government officials, and various *mingei* organisations has made the job of cooperative leader rather more time-consuming than it used to be, and outside bodies tend to look upon the position as one of importance" (1997: 83).

4 Retirement from the *kumiai* is usually considered equivalent to retirement from the head of the household. However, even after the son/daughter has inherited a pottery business, the retired potter often remains involved in the production process.

5 The Designated Manager System was created by the partial amendments to the Local Government Act (*Chihō jichihō*) in 2003. As a result, the party that holds managerial authority under the System is granted greater autonomy than under the previous Management Commission System (*Kanri itaku seido*). For instance, the *kumiai* has the right to grant permission to another party to use the public facilities of Sue no sato and can set the entrance fee.

7 Whose Tamba Pottery?

Abstract

In previous chapters, I explored the potters' social lives in Tachikui and their collective activities as members of the *kumiai*. I demonstrated how they experience and are influenced by Tamba Sasayama's regional revitalisation policy in their day-to-day lives, particularly in the way they readjust their individual craft practices and the collective activities of the *kumiai*. This chapter shifts the focus to their more critical views on the influence of Tamba Sasayama's regional revitalisation policy on their craftsmanship. I examine the potters' struggle to negotiate their own interests and those of the wider region. I discuss the contradiction in the representation of Tamba pottery in the regional revitalisation projects, in which the more Tamba pottery is promoted as the emblem of rural creativity, the more its style becomes monotonous in the public eye. The proliferating images of Tamba pottery in the public sphere undermined their efforts to innovate the Tamba pottery industry and overshadowed their evolving aesthetic visions. While they could cope with the unfamiliar administrative tasks, they were rather cautious about the way in which Tamba pottery was projected in promotional events and distributive materials as a *mingei* craft. Except some potters who deliberately branded themselves as the successors of *mingei* philosophy, most sought to find a balance with contemporary styles so that they can appeal to both elder customers who prefer *mingei* products and younger ones who seek unique designs. In their pursuit to take control over the public representation of Tamba pottery, they re-examined the essence that makes it Tamba pottery in the first place, namely the *tsuchi* (soil) and *tochi* (land). In contrast to the fleeting ideas about Tamba pottery, circulating through the *sōzō nōson* campaign, the reference to the materiality of Tachikui created an axis through which they could freely expand their creative ideas about Tamba pottery, uninterrupted by the external gaze.

DOI: 10.4324/9781003326540-11

Winter is the season for firing the climbing kilns in Tachikui. I was invited to Hiro's first firing of the year in his old garage in mid-January. It was a simple building built in patches of woods and slates, conveniently located on a slope by the Shidotani River. The air under the roof was warm and thick with smoke. The kiln to my left from the entrance stretched down to the lower ground, where Hiro was squatting in front of the bright golden flame, doing *han'yake*, the process of drying and warming up the *kamaguchi*. He had just finished using an oil burner to raise the temperature and was now throwing in extra firewood.

Firing a climbing kiln was all about repetition. He did not stop throwing firewood at approximately five minutes intervals, even when I was there chatting with him for hours. He had more than a day's work ahead of him, as it took about two full days for the last chamber to be fully heated. Meals were delivered by his eldest son, and boredom was alleviated by chatters on the radio. Heating the kiln with firewood took time, but it was the only way to raise the temperature at a steady pace. Only then could the surface of the pottery be beautifully tanned with fire marks.

Later in the evening, the temperature of the *kamaguchi* had finally reached around 1250 to 1300 degrees. Thicker smoke was billowing from the chimney outside the garage. Hiro's wife, Yuki, soon arrived to help. Although she had to go to work the next day, she assisted him through the night, throwing firewood. I could see that they had been working together for a long time. Hiro listened quietly to the cracking sound of the firewood and stared into the burning chamber. When he said, "still once more" (*mada mō ikkai*), they threw more firewood in the chamber, and when he said, "good pace" (*ii pēsu*), they moved on to the next chamber.

Figure 7.1 A view inside a firing kiln chamber.

Hiro's manners around the kiln and firing techniques appeared so effortless that the idea of "*tariki*", the state in which the craftsperson allows the order of nature to unfold through his physical actions, seemed to make sense (Yanagi 1956: 7). However, far from being subconsciously immersed, he paid close attention to the signals from the kiln. Each throw of firewood was assessed with meticulous observation. He watched the colours and movements of the fire to determine whether the kiln was being heated properly (Figure 7.1). He then considered whether to build up the flames. He listened to the sound of the fire swooshing and the wood cracking to judge the condition of the wood itself, whether it was sufficiently dry, in order to adjust the intervals between throws.

Hiro says that each climbing kiln has a unique *kuse* (manner). To master it, one must spend days and nights firing and experimenting with different techniques. In addition, the firing conditions vary depending on the various aspects of a kiln, such as its shape, construction materials, location, and environment. They influenced how the fire moved inside the kiln, where natural glazes formed on the surface of a pot, and how long it took to heat an entire kiln. There was no single method or skill that constituted the best practice of firing a climbing kiln. The only way to master the *kuse* of a kiln was through experience. His family kiln was built about 50 years ago, and he had grown up watching his father build and fire it. Since his father had the techniques that tamed the kiln, all he had to do was watch and mimic the father's movements.

Hiro repeatedly emphasised that the kiln, not the potter, does the firing. One must pay attention to the signals from the kiln and act *upon* them. For example, he never knew exactly how much firewood to throw into each chamber. He kept guessing, muttering to himself, "is it not…?" (*n chigai*) or "roughly…" (*kurai*). He claimed that one cannot learn how to fire a kiln by reading a book. They may outline what actions are acceptable and unacceptable, but in reality, there is no simple right or wrong. One could only make impulsive decisions based on the signals from the kiln. For him, such skills required long-term devotion in the making, whether kiln firing or other processes such as clay preparation, wheel throwing and drying, and this bestowed plain regional pottery the identity of *Tamba* pottery.

However, his philosophy as a Tamba potter conflicted with external ideas of Tamba pottery. He pointed out that the dominant portrayal of Tamba pottery at public events, such as those held as part of Tamba Sasayama's regional revitalisation policy, did not necessarily correspond to the way he and other potters perceived the essence of it. The reputation that they gained through the UNESCO Creative City of Crafts and Folk Arts or Japan Heritage initiatives was undoubtedly a significant leverage in sustaining the Tamba pottery industry. However, this also created the dilemma of being and serving as the local traditional craftspeople: to keep up with the symbolic basis of crafts for regional or national discourses, however abstract and detached they are from their everyday lives.

Initially, cooperation with the local government was established under a single purpose (i.e., regional revitalisation) and value (i.e., rural creativity). The subsequent financial and administrative support provided by the local government helped the potters in expanding the market for Tamba pottery, creating a seemingly convenient relationship. However, this alliance was also a complex process that brought about organisational changes in the potters' community, where the collective duty of the *kumiai* was extended to non-conventional activities of event organisation. While the potters were able to manage these changes within their existing social and economic relationships (Chapter 6), adapting to the subtle symbolic changes of Tamba pottery proved challenging.

Tamba pottery has traditionally been appreciated more for its usefulness as a daily ware than for its aesthetic beauty. Even during the Edo period, when it developed a reputation for luxury goods such as tea caddy, tableware remained the most known product. However, by the early 1970s, it began to be recognised with a particular artistic identity of *mingei* craft. The folk craft boom not only helped the potters' business to flourish, but also aroused the interest of ceramic collectors in the aesthetics of Tamba pottery, which met the "criterion of beauty (*bi no hyōjun*)" of *mingei* such as "naturalness (*shizen*)", "simplicity (*tanjun*)", "tradition (*dentō*)", and "selflessness and anonymity (*mushin/mumei*)" to name a few (Kikuchi 2004: 53). Kikuchi argues that the fundamental theoretical ideas underlying *mingei* are the "nexus between morality and art" (2004: 59), a view influenced by the "English Arts and Crafts aesthetic ideas in the earlier stage, and at a later stage after the Second World War, of Buddhist ideas from Zen Buddhism and tea aesthetics" (2004: 54). Central to the moral trope of *mingei* is the denial of a self-conscious mind or an ego, expressed by Yanagi Muneyoshi in a Buddhist philosophical term of *tariki* (other power). In *Tanba no gōto* (Old Ceramics of Tamba), a monograph which he dedicated entirely to the enchantment of Tamba pottery, he described the old Tamba pottery (*kōtamba*) as an exemplary piece that embodied the beauty of *tariki*, along with *wabi* (austere beauty) and *shibusa* (subtle simplicity) (Yanagi 1956: 9–35). He appreciated the muted and monotonous colours that epitomised the material beauty of natural ingredients.

As part of the folk craft boom that revived the regional craft industry in the post-war period, Tamba potters, along with other local craftspeople throughout Japan, quickly adopted Yanagi's ideas and artistic visions in their work. The production lines of many workshops had changed from planters and sake bottles, which dominated Tamba pottery production until the 1960s, to folk craft products by the early 1970s, when the *mingei* aesthetic became a significant factor in the sales of Tamba pottery. Kleinberg noted that half of the potting households in Tachikui had become folk craft specialists, and the rest were also trying to catch up with the trend, leaving a few kilns producing planters (Kleinberg 1979: 143).

This successful coalition between the *mingei* boom and the revival of the Tamba pottery industry left a lasting influence of *mingei* aesthetics on the identity of Tamba pottery, even after its economic value had expired. The decline in consumerism since the late 1980s had brought the heyday of the craft market to an end, and the number of avid collectors of *mingei* products was shrinking as the population aged and declined. As one potter notes, people used to buy huge and expensive umbrella stands that had no aesthetic value or even functionality just because they had enough incentive pay to spend. This was no longer the case. In place of the bygone folk craft boom, in which Tamba pottery industry had fully embraced the rise of it by transforming the business models (i.e., from middlemen to direct sales through workshop-based distribution) and the aesthetic identity (i.e., from daily wares to *mingei* craft), there was the dilemma of dealing with the ambiguous influence of *mingei* on today's Tamba pottery industry.

The younger generation potters, in particular, were reluctant to embrace the philosophy or economic value of the *mingei* aesthetics, and wished to reduce its dominance in public perception by promoting new designs and styles. For instance, Hiro's idea of an aesthetically satisfying Tamba pottery is concerned with the sense of intimacy. He saw elegant fire marks as a sign of good quality, and the whole process of taming a kiln, such as the time he had spent since childhood by the family kiln, was part of an aesthetic mastery of the beauty of Tamba pottery. However, *mingei*, a concept originally developed by a group of Tokyo-based bourgeois literati, was far removed from the kind of knowledge that he saw from his works (Brandt 2007: 39).

In this context, the potters' motivation to participate in Tamba Sasayama's regional revitalisation policy derived partly from their urge to promote the new Tamba pottery and to attract younger and more trend-savvy customers. Ironically, these efforts to expand the market to a wider audience and move beyond the short-lived privilege of the *mingei* boom had instead created a stronger link between their work and the idea of *mingei*. The images of Tamba pottery in the banners, posters, and other public materials of Tamba Sasayama's public events seemed to emphasise the aesthetic elements of *wabi* or *sabi* rather than the dynamic transformations in the young potters' work. In this climate, some potters felt pressured to realign their work with the *mingei* aesthetics in order to justify their identity as a Tamba potter as promoted in the public materials. Others sought ways to express their own aesthetic visions without being constrained by external gaze.

This chapter examines the conflict over the public representation of Tamba pottery in Tamba Sasayama's regional revitalisation policy and how it inspired the potters, individually and as *kumiai* members, to put forward their own definition and aesthetic standards of Tamba pottery. By taking a closer look at the public events of Haru Monogatari, one of the two main Tamba pottery festivals, I will describe the potters' general perception of the idea of *mingei*. I illustrate the everyday context in which the discourse of *mingei* deprives them of a sense of agency over their own work. Despite their scepticism about the commercial value of the *mingei* aesthetics and their frustration with the persistent expectations placed on the *mingei*-ness of their work, they manage its shifting value within the changing Tamba pottery industry. To maintain the grant-mediated relationship with the local government, while expressing their own opinions on the development of the Tamba pottery industry, they strive to embrace both the traditional ideas of *mingei* aesthetics, and the innovative pieces created by young potters as the essence of Tamba pottery.

What if I do not know what Tamba pottery is?

It was a day before the Haru Monogatari. When I arrived at the *Saikō no noborigama*, there was already a silent crowd of potters, some employees from the MCART and the volunteers for the event. The *san'yaku* of the *kumiai* had ignited the *kamaguchi* and were standing in front of it with their hands together. They were praying for the safety of the two days of firing. After the ritual, I approached Inoshita, a prefectural official from the MCART who oversaw the volunteer activities. I checked my attendance and received a yellow vest written *Tanbayaki* (Tamba pottery) on it. As I put it on, I saw a familiar face coming towards me. Shōhei walked by, bursting into laughter, and asked why I was wearing the yellow vest. I did not understand the nuance of his laughter. I assumed I stood out from the other volunteers, who were at least twice my age.

Half of the volunteers were amateur potters from a local non-profit organisation established by the supporters and admirers of Tamba pottery. They were regulars at the festival. When the group leader found out that I was a researcher, he formally introduced himself by exchanging business cards. He

Figure 7.2 The initiation ceremony of *Saikō no noborigama*.

then began explaining the general history of Tamba pottery and the skills of firing a climbing kiln. Flaunting his erudition, he described how the *machimi* (the flow of the fire) creates patterns on the surface of a pot. According to him, the current firing techniques are limited by the rising cost of firewood. He then told me about a bamboo firing experiment his group had been carrying out, claiming that it would be an epochal change to the traditional way of working with climbing kilns. They had even printed a book with scientific evidence of statistics and graphs showing the time and energy efficiency of the bamboo firing.

When I arrived at the same venue the next day, the potters were still firing, sweating from the fire that had grown aggressive. The group of volunteers for the day was small, less than ten, including myself, and we were stationed in a tent near the kiln. The group leader, who knew the most about the festival's itinerary, explained the rules of the event to the newcomers.

Visitors began to pour in ahead of the official schedule. As the fire inside the kiln became more vibrant and visible, they wandered around the *kamaguchi*, eager to see inside the stokehole. As the potters moved busily around the kiln, throwing firewood, they also chatted with the visitors about the kiln's history and the firing techniques. They looked exhausted, having to keep an eye on the kiln and show hospitality to strangers simultaneously. Not too far away, volunteers were also busy guiding the tourists around and sharing their knowledge of Tamba pottery. I, along with other newcomers, remained in the tent and managed simple tasks like handing out flyers or offering visitor stamps.

The hectic morning schedule was over, and it was finally a break time. The potters had gathered around an empty doorway in front of a shop, enjoying instant noodles, and the volunteers were a few steps away from them, joined in the tent. As there was no lunch provided, we took turns to go to a restaurant nearby. I sat quietly on a stool, noticing how peaceful it was compared to the bustle of the crowds half an hour earlier. It was then that I began to sense an awkwardness in the air. Although the potters and the volunteers were in the same space, they hardly spoke to each other, as if an invisible wall stood between them. A few potters came to collect stationary from the tent, but none seemed willing to strike up a conversation, only a slight bow of recognition as a sign of courtesy. The atmosphere in our tent was somehow dispirited. Some of the new volunteers seemed daunted by the joyful chatter and laughter of the potters, which somehow made them feel left out. When Inoshita returned to the tent after lunch, one of the volunteers voiced his dissatisfaction with the potters' behaviour, pointing out that they were smoking and joking around with each other while visitors were still present. He urged Inoshita to go and warn them about it. Inoshita was in no position to scold or intervene with the potters as he was just an official that happened to take the job of communicating with the volunteers. It was not that the potters had bad manners; they were polite and considerate of those around them. Rather, there seemed to be a sense of disappointment on the part of the volunteer who had expected a closer interaction with them.

I had signed up as a volunteer, hoping to work more closely with the potters during one of the region's most important events. However, it turned out to be the worst plan. There was a subtle dynamic of tension at play, with invisible boundaries separating the potters and the volunteers. I could not have felt more estranged, as my months-long effort to be part of the insiders of the potter's community seemed to be shattered.

But it also raised questions that I would not have posed if I had been in my comfort zone with the potters. What was this sense of unease or distance between the potters and the volunteers? Were there previous conflicts between them? I could grasp the underlying views of the potters behind their attitude a few days after the event. In short, the potters had no negative feelings towards the volunteers and were grateful for their help. However, they had a deep-seated concern that somehow influenced their attitude towards outsiders in general.

I was having lunch with a potter at a local Chinese restaurant. He asked me how I felt about volunteering at Haru Monogatari. I said it was a pleasant experience, leaving out my actual reflection of the days. Then he openly asked why I had decided to join the group of volunteers when I already had a good relationship with him and other potters. When I told him about my new experiences, giving examples of my interactions with the veteran volunteers who had been working at the festival for years, his response was somewhat unexpected. He said that they sometimes try to advise him on firing techniques and that it sometimes gets on his nerves. When I mentioned the bamboo experiment, he said in a disgruntled voice that they did not understand Tamba pottery. He agreed that bamboo could be an alternative fuel to firewood, but it was not a practical method when considering the result of the firing. Bamboo-fired pottery had no economic value as it would not appeal to customers that are fond of Tamba pottery in particular for the surface patterns created by the wood ashes. In his view, people like to give opinions because they do not make pottery for a living but as a pastime. Their knowledge is "written in books" (*hon ni kaite iru*) but not the kind of embodied knowledge that potters have acquired over an extended period of time.

His comments seemed to reflect the potters' general complaints about external views being imposed on and explained about Tamba pottery. He described how it is "frightening" (*kowai*) to hear so-called experts extoll the virtues of Tamba pottery when he has no idea what they are talking about. He then suggested a hypothetical scenario: what if Tamba pottery becomes something that he does not understand? The potters welcomed the increased public interest in Tamba pottery, but not all of the public's expectations matched their visions. One of the continuing tensions between the external and internal perceptions of Tamba pottery has been around the different views of the *mingei* aesthetic. Potters have continually debated its influence on their work, and recent involvement in Tamba Sasayama's regional promotional projects seem to have further inflamed the debate. Despite the economic prosperity that the folk craft boom brought to the Tamba pottery industry, they had reservations about representing the essence of Tamba pottery as *mingei*.

In the earlier stages of my fieldwork, unaware of the potters' general perceptions of the *mingei* representation of Tamba pottery, I had several times expressed how *mingei* ideals had sparked my initial interest in Tamba pottery. My innocent opinions were soon met with a look from the potters that seemed to say, "not again". The image of *mingei* pottery has been the dominant representation of Tamba pottery for decades. One potter, for example, recounted his experience at an exhibition in Tokyo of having his work categorised as *mingei*. Another younger potter remarked after a meeting with local government officials that no other potter would have thought so much about *mingei* if Tamba pottery had not been associated with the labels of Japan Heritage and UNESCO Creative City of Crafts and Folk Arts. He said it could be upsetting to present his work as if *mingei* were the essence of his creation. Despite their conflict over the prominent depiction of *mingei*, the potters could not give it up completely because it was what people expected and, consequently, resonated with what the local government wanted to promote as part of regional revitalisation initiatives.

The potters' dilemma can be better understood using Ardener's concept of "remoteness" (Ardener 2012). He proposes that remoteness or distance as a social construction based on particular power relations between different actors. The "perspective of the specifier" (2012: 531) controls the dominant perception of the other, namely, the specified. It creates the "structural mismatch between local self-definitions and the definitional authority of others" (Brachet and Scheele 2019: 157) by defining the "consciousness of the space" (Ardener 2012: 531) and choosing whom to place in a peripheral position. In this context, the external authorities who highlight the *mingei* discourse are the specifiers, and the Tamba potters who compromise with the *mingei* gaze are specified. However, in his account of the structural links between the specifier and the specified, Ardener implies that the specified are also "aware of the defining processes of others that might absorb them" (2012: 532). There is always the "counterspecification of the dominant" (2012: 531), that is, the responses of the specified to the narratives or images imposed on them. He notes that the specified fall into two categories: event-poor and event-rich. The event-poor have fully conformed to the expected gaze of the dominant by establishing themselves as part of the stable system. The event-rich, on the other hand, are those that are conscious of the "continuous threat" of "self-generating set of overriding social definitions" (2012: 531), attempting to fight back for their autonomy over self-representation. Based on the concept of the event-rich, scholars have demonstrated how the specified overcomes the generalising perspectives, as in the cases of the creation of local heritage (Jørgensen 2011), rural aesthetics (Luo et al. 2019; Park 2014), and market needs (Brachet and Scheele 2019). They demonstrate how those constantly seen and defined by others can also reinterpret the gaze in ways that suit their interests. For instance, Brachet and Scheele show how the Tubu of northern Chad support the external perceptions about them as robbers when trucks and traders need to cross their land. They keep their positions as the sole reliable middlemen for international businesspeople by highlighting the distorted perception of their region as lawless and hazardous, which is not necessarily the case in reality.

Ardener refers to the creative process of self-representation as "abortive innovation" (2012: 532). He describes innovation as an act that challenges the externally imposed notions. His claim that remoteness is a social construct initially gives the impression that epistemic knowledge determines the separation between the specifier and the specified. The strategy to subvert the external would be to reshape or reconstruct the current orders (see Brachet and Scheele 2019; Luo et al. 2019), and innovation would be an endless negotiation of "perception" in this sense (Ardener 2012: 531). However, a careful reading of Ardener's text reveals that he also hints at an ontological conception of remoteness when he mentions that "[t]he social space is a material one" (2012: 527):

> Event-richness is like a small-scale, simmering, continuously generated set of singularities, which are not just the artefact of observer bias (as we have seen, observers commonly perceive only a puzzling blankness) – but due to some *materiality*, that I interpret to be related to the enhanced defining power of individuals.
>
> (Ardener 2012: 531, my emphasis)

Event-richness is not only the conscious appropriation of external perceptions – biases, misconceptions, and oversimplifications – but also something that has to do with materiality, which he argues is "related to the enhanced defining power of individuals" (Ardener 2012: 531). Materiality becomes the means by which people try to find their voice and authority. This perspective allows us to examine how the specified can respond creatively to an external gaze, not only through mere statements or disputes over symbolic aspects, but also through the material groundedness of their knowledge and their physical surroundings, to reclaim power in defining who and what they are.

In light of Ardener's concept of remoteness, I will now turn my attention to how *mingei* components have come to dominate the aesthetic and public representation of Tamba pottery in recent years, and how the potters have maintained a strategic distance from it by securing their own knowledge of Tamba pottery.

Mingei and the Tamba pottery industry

Increased demand for Tamba pottery and tourism to Tachikui was directly influenced by the developing domestic economy and the expanding middle class. By the early 1970s, more than 50 per cent of the potters in Tachikui had transformed themselves into folk craft potters, producing not only daily wares such as rice bowls or coffee cups, but also thick and unglazed sake bottles, which were often used as ornaments for *tokoname* (a space in a traditional Japanese tearoom where one displays her artistic taste) (Kleinberg 1979:

135–36). Visitors flocked to Tachikui to purchase a variety of products, from expensive jars resembling the old Tamba pottery to low-cost souvenirs (*omiyage*). During the Tōki Matsuri, collectors rode around Tachikui on bicycles with small trays attached, allowing them to purchase huge and expensive products. For small-scale, household-based workshops, these direct sales to visitors were a crucial source of income. Restaurants and shops were also important for business, as they placed regular orders. Successful business ties were formed based on "how diligently the potter pursues the popularised notion of *mingei* pottery production" (Kleinberg 1979: 158). As the pottery business grew, extra facilities such as storage buildings were built. Neighbours could see that the potters were prospering, with houses being refurbished. According to the owner of a nearby antique shop, Tamba pottery sold out so quickly that buyers had to queue to purchase popular items like vase or jar. The folk craft boom brought unprecedented prosperity to the Tamba pottery industry.

However, not everyone had such a positive memory of the past. Shōhei called the time a "strange period" (*henna jiki*), saying that the magnific stories about the folk craft boom were exaggerated, given the radical changes in the Japanese economy at the time. He began his apprenticeship in the family workshop in Kami-Tachikui at the height of the folk craft boom. His father, Kazuichi, like many other villagers, had become a full-time potter as a result of the thriving ceramic market. As a teenager, Shōhei was a music club member and aspired to become a music teacher. However, his father encouraged him to enter an art university in Kanazawa. The old practice of working as an in-house apprentice were becoming less common by then, as professional institutions were substituting the role of a master potter. Given that it was customary for the eldest sons of potting households to take over the family business, his decision to abruptly follow in his father's footsteps was not unusual. The typical process for inheriting a family business was to first receive formal education at a university or vocational school, return to Tachikui for a brief period to apprentice with an established potter, and then work as a staff in the family workshop until they had mastered the production and management skills.

For him, the golden age of the Tamba pottery industry was a fleeting moment. Since the real estate market's collapse in the early 1990s, Japan's economy has been mired in a prolonged period of deflation, and the folk craft boom also began to wane. The dwindling ceramic market and the growing production of cheaper plastic and glass items made it difficult for the potters to maintain the usual production lines. Then came the Great Hanshin Earthquake in 1995, which cut the workshops off from their main sales channels based in Kobe. Witnessing these moments of economic turmoil and how the Tamba pottery industry collapsed so quickly on the brink of events, he had realised that the popularity that the potters had enjoyed during the bubble period was abnormal, or as he cynically put it, "too good" (*ii sugita*). The reputation of Tamba pottery seemed hollow. He realised that the many so-called connoisseurs were not really in love with Tamba pottery but were more interested in showing off their hefty spending by buying trendy goods.

Shōhei and other professional potters, the second generation in the post-war period, began to develop their careers in the early 1990s after Japan's economic downturn. Their immediate task was to re-evaluate the existing Tamba pottery production and distribution system. The most significant changes were made in sales management, with potters moving away from relying on middlemen and instead developing their own sales routes. The entire process, from production to distribution and marketing of their products, with the exception of collective sales which were still organised by the *kumiai*, was now managed within a single household workshop.

In this climate, the styles of Tamba pottery also began to diversify. The new generation of potters, who had graduated from art schools with the full support of their families, preferred to experiment with new techniques rather than imitate existing designs or follow the traditional methods. They were reluctant to make replicas of *mingei*-style products and were eager to express their creativity. Even the first generation post-war potters, who had learned the traditional techniques of Tamba pottery through the apprenticeship systems, also supported this new trend. For example, during a public lecture at the citizen's centre entitled "The beauty of Tamba pottery in the past and present" (*Tanbayaki no miryoku mukashi to ima*), Iwai, a potter in his seventies, asked the audience what an authentic Tamba pottery is, pointing out at the pictures he had put on a whiteboard. There was a cup with red and white strokes, a bowl with rainbow-like stripes, and other pottery with unconventional combinations of colours and shapes. The answer was all of them. As one of recognised *dentō kōgeishi* (traditional craftspeople) of Tamba pottery, he could have been adamant about maintaining the tradition. Instead, he was openly sympathetic to deviation from the established norm. He said that it was "an era of different tastes" (*suki-zuki no jidai*) where no standard of beauty prevailed. However, he did not argue that the idea of tradition should abandoned altogether. He believed that what seems creative is the new tradition in 30 to 40 years' time. Another potter made a similar comment when interviewed by a journalist from a local newspaper. When he was asked about the traditional aspects of Tamba pottery, he replied that the diversity of Tamba pottery would become part of its tradition in 30 years' time.

However, the gravity of the *mingei* aesthetics, which have been established as a popular image of Tamba pottery during the folk craft boom, required more than internal efforts of transforming production processes or apply new ceramic techniques. Typical styles of Tamba pottery were constantly promoted in the public media, such as the image of a large jar of 30 to 50 centimetres in height with "multiple layers of bright green ash glaze-flows on a russet ground" (MCART 2015: 9), which is the hallmark of the medieval Tamba pottery. Despite the variety of designs within traditional Tamba pottery, including different glazes (i.e., *akadobe* and *shirotanba*) and shapes (i.e., moulds for sweets), these diversities were often overlooked due to the emphasis on the visual aesthetics of *mingei*, which associated Tamba pottery with ideas of natural beauty. Pieces with modern patterns or colours were often simply categorised as something that was *not mingei*. In other words, *mingei* was still the standard aesthetic criteria of Tamba pottery.

Tamba Sasayama's regional revitalisation policy has provided much-needed financial support and platforms for the promotion of Tamba pottery, particularly through the new campaign for rural creativity. However, the potters' efforts to revamp the public image of Tamba pottery were challenged by this very collaboration with the local government. While the potters were in a transitional phase of balancing out the *mingei* and modern styles of Tamba pottery, Tamba Sasayama's promotion of *sōzō nōson* highlighted its alliance with nature and tradition as the essence of rural creativity. Although there were occasions when the local government emphasised the diversity of styles in public representations, these were soon eclipsed by images of traditional pottery at other events. As demonstrated in Chapter 2, the *mingei* aspect of Tamba pottery resonates with the concept of *sōzō nōson*, as Yanagi's moral vision of local crafts coincides with the idea that emphasises the moral values embedded in "rural" creativity as opposed to urban creativity. The potters were often perplexed by how the public perceived their work amidst the plethora of stories and images of Tamba pottery in promotional materials.

Coping with the lingering *mingei* aesthetics

To illustrate the potters' approach to dealing with the proliferating images of Tamba pottery, I elaborate on two distinct tactics that they employ in their everyday contexts. The first involves negotiating between their personal style and the *mingei* aesthetics to satisfy both existing and new customers of Tamba pottery. The second tactic involves a more subtle approach, aimed at redefining Tamba pottery.

Between shokunin, sakka and dentō kōgeshi

To understand how the potters deal with the *mingei* components, it is crucial to recognise the strategic positioning that they undertake in response to the complex representations of their work in the public sphere, and how they skilfully maintain a calculated distance in order to reap the benefits of the exoticised gaze. The three distinct aesthetic modes in the production lines of Tamba pottery demonstrate the continuing influence of *mingei* aesthetics in the present time.

1 Traditional craftspeople (*dentō kōgeshi*), who are often considered as the equivalent of *mingei* potters.
2 Artists (*sakka/geijutsuka*), whose work is not considered *mingei*, and who create objects that are closely related to contemporary craft arts.
3 Craftspeople (*shokunin*) who do not identify with any of the previous categories or labels.

In a survey of member potters of the *kumiai*, I asked, "what is your working style (*aete iu to honnin no sagyō keikō wa doko ni zokusuru to kangaemasu ka*)?" Those who identified themselves as traditional craftspeople (*dentō kōgeshi*) had earned their reputation in various ways, such as achieving the status of *dentō kōgeshi* by successfully passing the official evaluation conducted by the *kumiai*, winning an award at the prestigious Japan Traditional Craft Exhibition (*dentō kōgei ten*), or mastering the techniques of firing in climbing kilns.[1] On the other hand, individuals who identify themselves as artist (*sakka/geijutsuka*) establish their identity based on their individual careers in ceramic competitions or exhibitions held in prestigious art galleries.

Craftspeople (*shokunin*) is the most common identity with which potters identified themselves. Most of the respondents chose it over traditional craftspeople or artists since it does not denote a fixed image or style of a potter. The ambiguous status allowed them to strategically balance traditional and (post) modern styles. The spatial configuration of their showroom is a good example. It is divided into two distinct areas: on the one side, the typical *mingei* pieces with simple brownish colours, and, on the other side, the unique works of the workshop which reveal the identity of the master potter. Even in the workshop of a younger potter, there were a few pieces that could easily be associated with the beauty of *mingei*, such as the simple non-glazed jars. They seemed to show their connection with the traditional aspects of Tamba pottery, a sign of their belonging to the collective identity as Tamba potters. As there was a dwindling, but still significant, number of older clients who sought *mingei* styles, the shop floor was designed deliberately as a "relational space in which certain actions are possible" (Brachet and Scheele 2019: 164).

The strategic deployment of public expectations of Tamba pottery explains the success of Hiro's workshop, which depended on a subtle balancing between the *mingei* and non-*mingei* styles. For him, the *mingei*-ness of his planters was

Table 7.1 A survey on Tamba potter's self-identification

	Self-identification	*Number of potters*
Single choice	Traditional craftspeople (*dentō kōgeshi*)	10
	Artist (*sakka/ geijutsuka*)	4
	craftspeople (*shokunin*)	16
	Others (*sono ta*)	2
Multiple choice	Traditional craftspeople and artist	2
	Traditional craftspeople and craftspeople	1
	Artist and craftspeople	4
	craftspeople and others	1

Note: The word *shokunin* was used by the potters less with the romantic implication of craftspeople. Here it is used more in its plain, literal meaning; a person who makes hand-crafted goods. The survey was conducted by visiting each workshop in Tachikui between 16 and 24 July 2018, and 40 of the 52 member potters of *Tamba tachikui tōjiki kyōdo kumiai* responded. Respondents made either one or two choices.

valuable because they had a particular market value. The traditional style was something that he pursued not in spite of, but with the changing trend in mind. From his father's generation, his workshop retained the basic design of *yakishime* (high-fired unglazed pottery), a rough earthenware planter with a brown non-glazed tan, as a trademark. When a mountain plant research club from the Kantō region visited Tachikui in the 1960s to co-produce a unique planter tailored for wild plants, only Kazuichi responded to their request. After years of correspondence with the club members, experimenting with different combinations of clay and angles for the drainage hole at the bottom of the pot, he had invented a unique planter for wild plants.

Given the popularity of Kazuichi's planters and his long-term customers, most of whom are avid collectors of mountain plants, Hiro had stayed true to the original design with a plain unglazed surface. Most of the sales profits had come from his father's existing customers. A simple phone call was all he needed to get their orders, as he knew their preferences. He hardly expected strangers to enter his shop floor, as I could see from its unwelcoming atmosphere of dusty tables and chairs. He did not even bother to separate the workshop and shop floor. He knew who his customers were and where they are.

The Tokyo *sansō* (wild plant) fair was one of the key venues where he met his old customers in person. Most of them were wholesalers or shopkeepers in Tokyo and were acquaintances of Kazuichi, meaning they were mostly his father's age. Every year, Hiro would drive his small truck full of planters to Tokyo, a journey that took around seven to eight hours. Once he fell asleep on the highway and the truck almost stopped in the middle of the road. Since then, his son has accompanied him to take turns driving. Despite the arduous journey, it was important for him to attend the fair since keeping close relationships with his loyal customers was essential. However, this year, he had sold less than half of what he had brought to the fair. Considering the time it took to prepare – about two weeks from making, firing, and delivering – the sales was disappointing. Many of his regular customers had not turned up, and he suspected that as they got older their health might have prevented them from going to a crowded place. He was seriously considering whether to attend next year. This was just one of the cases where he felt the need to find a new customer base. He was relatively untroubled by the old-fashioned images of Tamba pottery circulated in promotional materials, as his *yakishime* planters fit comfortably into the conventional image of a *mingei* pottery. However, his recent experience of losing regular customers had led him to redirect his interest towards producing planters in more non-*mingei*-like colours and shapes.

He began to make more business trips to other regions to hold outdoor sales. During my fieldwork, he participated in three events initiated by private companies and organisations: an outdoor sale in Kobe, an online sale facilitated by a company in Tokyo, and an exotic plant fair in Osaka. These new sales platforms required some changes in the design of his planters, as the main customers were young consumers who were less likely to be interested in the *mingei* aesthetics or the history of Tamba pottery. Catering to the tastes of this unfamiliar group of customers was a challenge to break the uniformity of the signature design passed down from his father.

The exotic plant fair in Osaka was Hiro's first major success in finding new group of customers. He had many business connections in plants and gardening, but never with foreign species. He had no idea what plants would fill up the vast exhibition space at the multi-complex centre in Osaka or what would be expected of him there, let alone what kind of planters would suit the tastes of the unidentified visitors. Knowing that they would be mostly young urbanites living in Osaka and the nearby Hanshin area, he decided to bring planters of two contrasting designs: the *yakishime* and the glazed.

As I helped him sort out the glazed planters from the dusty boxes stacked up in the corner of the workshop, I realised that he had already tried producing planters of different sizes, with or without foot, and glazes in all sorts of colours, such as light blue, dark purple, and light green. They seemed to have ended up in the garage. I brushed off the dirt, put price tags on and put them in carry boxes. The other boxes were filled with the *yakishime* planters. They were shiny and clean, fresh from the kiln the day before. Hiro wanted to see which one would be more appealing. I could tell he had already ruled out what the youngsters would prefer seeing a few more boxes of the glazed ones.

The fair was held on the top floor of a building next to the Osaka baseball stadium on a sunny weekend. The venue was set up in two long hallways and was filled with all kinds of exotic plants from all over the world, including Madagascar, Indonesia, and Ecuador. Tall tropical plants were scattered in the air, covering the high ceiling. The event started at 10:00 in the morning, and people rushed in to get their hands on the unique species. There were other side events, such as a talk show by a botanist traveller. In the corner were desks full of gardening magazines and a bar selling organic beers and snacks. The whole place had a hip and quirky atmosphere. Hiro's stall was quiet and peaceful in this jungle of funky shaped leaves swaying here and there. It was only when the customers seemed to have finished treasure hunt, holding plastic bags full of greenery, that they showed interest in Hiro's planters. The crowd of young plant enthusiasts, including stylishly dressed couples, university students, and children who came with their parents, checked out the planters with elated faces. In the end, Hiro sold more than half on the first day, which was a great success.

Over the next few days, my conversations with Hiro were occupied with the invigorating insights that he gained from the fair. The young customers, who had no preconceived notions about Tamba pottery or the *mingei* aesthetics, favoured the glazed ones. However, what seemed to have struck him the most was how the *yakishime* planters were appreciated from an unusual perspective. Some young customers had commented that the rough surface and irregular fire mark, the trademark of traditional Tamba pottery, looked stylish.

The experience at the Osaka wild plant fair was a big step forward for Hiro. At first, he seemed to be torn between the glazed and the *yakishime* planters. Instead of choosing one type of pottery over the other, he decided to bring both to see for himself the reactions of young urbanites. He had ventured into a field he knew little about. The gaze of the customers did not presuppose specific ideas or expectations like those of the local government officials, *mingei* enthusiasts or other so-called experts of Tamba pottery but suggested a new perspective and possibility in his works.

Both the strategic arrangement of shops by potters identifying themselves as *shokunin* and Hiro's personal journey of witnessing the different ways in which his *yakishime* planters were appreciated exemplify the epistemological tactic of redefining the symbolic significance of Tamba pottery. It was achieved by carefully accommodating the gaze of outsiders in the aesthetic representations of their works.

However, to effectively challenge the dominant perception of Tamba pottery on a collective level, a different strategy was required. Although the young customers at the exotic plant fair welcomed Hiro's planters glazed in vivid colours, the dominant perception of Tamba pottery was still very much associated with the *mingei* aesthetics. If every potter who makes traditional styles, like Hiro, turned to modern designs, the identity of Tamba pottery was likely to be questioned. Hence, the challenge was to experiment with new styles on an individual level but without undermining the regional brand of Tamba pottery on a collective level.

Tambayaki trademark and the materiality of Tachikui

Recently, the potters have placed a strong emphasis on highlighting the material aspect of Tachikui as a defining characteristic of Tamba pottery. They have developed a strategy to establish the identification of Tamba pottery based on its place of production. The inherent materiality of the local environment serves as a crucial element through which they assert their understanding of authentic Tamba pottery. By upholding knowledge that requires first-hand experience of the place, they seek to establish an equitable position where they can also assert themselves as authoritative sources in the definition of Tamba pottery.

One of the most common ways in which craftspeople assert their rights to a cultural asset is through "enclosure" (Cant 2019: 131): claiming themselves to be the primary holder of the rights to a certain regional product by "limit[ing] production or trade only to recognised 'insiders'" (2019: 131). Recently, *kumiai* took a new initiative to register Tamba pottery as a brand: the registration of a trademark for *Tanbayaki* (Tamba pottery) brand. Since the revision of the Trademark Law in 2006, the number of trademark registrations for local products has increased. According to Rausch, local place-branding through trademark registration has been used "as a means by which rural areas of Japan … identify ways to address increasingly difficult fiscal circumstances" (Rausch 2009: 68–69). He argues that the growing emphasis on branding is partly due to the emerging discourses of provincial regions as "cradles of creativity" (2009: 65). While his observation focuses on how trademark has become popular as part of the regional development strategy, what I observed in the case of the *kumiai* offers a different story. Their decision to register the trademark of Tamba pottery is not only driven by economic prospects (Rausch 2009), but also by political reasons. It is motivated by a desire to define what constitutes authentic Tamba pottery and to develop standards of knowledge based on the customs of those who live and work in the place of production.

The significance of the trademark lies in the very way in which the local knowledge and aesthetic concepts of Tamba pottery is preserved. In the past, they were mainly passed on in an embodied form based on years of experience and imitation of the master's techniques, such as Hiro's firing skills. However, the trademark documents them in written form, contrary to his philosophy of craftsmanship. It demonstrates explicitly the potters' perception and notion of authentic Tamba pottery against the plethora of images circulated in promotional materials. And its significance lies in the subtlety of not having to verbally express the priority of the local knowledge of Tamba pottery. For instance, the attached guideline served as a basis for the potters to establish appropriate standards for authenticating their work, especially when working with external agencies that may have their own perspectives on how Tamba pottery should be represented. It explained the conditions of the trademark and denoted the original purpose of its issuance, which is to prevent the circulation of counterfeits (*nisemono*) that could undermine the authentic (*honmono*) Tamba pottery (cf. Cant 2019: 129–149). It was important in the very process of articulating and verbalising the local aesthetics of Tamba pottery, which have recently been caught in the tension between what the local government promotes – the *mingei*-ness of Tamba pottery – and what the potters themselves wish to popularise – a new tradition of modern designs. The definition of Tamba pottery in the guideline clearly defines what constitutes a *honmono*: "a pottery that uses the clay collected around Konda area of Sasayama as the main ingredient and is produced in Konda and nearby areas" (*Sasayamashi kondachō shūhen no nendo o shuyōna genzairyō to shite sasayamashi kondachō oyobi sono shūhen de seisan sareta tōjiki*). The definition lacks any reference to a specific style or skill to define the identity of authentic Tamba pottery. Instead, it specifies the location of workshops and the use of Tamba clay. By focusing on the geographical provenance of the production site and the use of local ingredients, potters are able to redefine the very criteria and knowledge that constitutes a *honmono*. By reconstituting the entire criteria based on working *in* Tachikui or working *with* the Tamba clay, they have mitigated the epistemological debates about the aesthetics of Tamba pottery to a minor issue. The potters and their works become authentic through their very existence. As long as the potters produce their work in the workshop located in Tachikui using the designated clay, they do not need to wrestle with external views about the aesthetic representation of Tamba pottery.

This reflects the complex situation of the potters' economic, political, and aesthetic practices. Although the influence of *mingei* has been prolonged by the local government's inattentive promotional materials, the potters are far from resisting the intervention, as it is part of the consequences that come with the financial support they receive. What they have done instead is to declare their everyday craft itself as the essence of genuine Tamba pottery. This subtle juggling of power relations over the knowledge and representation of Tamba pottery is where we see the everyday creativity of the potters as they struggle to maintain their livelihoods and way of life intertwined with Tamba pottery.

Conclusion

This chapter explored the potters' dilemma of maintaining a cooperative relationship with the local government and keeping up with their own vision of Tamba pottery. The proliferation of the *mingei* image in the public sphere was undermining the potters' efforts to promote the diversification of Tamba pottery products and attract new customers. The ultimate challenge for the potters was to maintain a subtle distance from the *mingei* representation so as not to risk creating tensions with the supporters of the traditional Tamba pottery – the local government and the older consumers – while continuing to change the dominant perceptions of Tamba pottery.

The way in which the potters continue the tradition of Tamba pottery is different from the way in which the local government attempts to revitalise the region. The main strategy in Tamba Sasayama's revitalisation plan is to follow new trends and reshape the regional image to meet the expectations of outsiders seeking an ideal rural lifestyle. They are highly conscious of external perceptions and prioritise the needs of potential migrants and tourists. On the other hand, the potters are not overly concerned with meeting others' expectations of their lives and work. Instead, they are invested in managing external views so as not to jeopardise their ideas and lives around Tamba pottery. A common thread in their endeavours is the collective nature of their efforts. Navigating the uncertain future trajectory of the Tamba pottery industry has involved a series of attempts to strengthen their collective identity and social bonds within the village. This seemed to prove the kind of creativity that emerged in the process of revitalising the Tamba pottery industry and the village life in Tachikui.

Note

1 *Dentō kōgei ten*, one of the most prestigious competitions for traditional craftspeople in Japan, has long been considered the main foothold to becoming a respected craftsperson. Despite its declining popularity, it is still regarded as the key platform to put one's name on the list of candidates for the Living National Treasures (*Ningen kokuhō*).

Conclusion

The Rurality of Post-Growth Japan

Post-war Japan has been marked by dynamic social changes. Japan's emergence as a global economic model, fuelled by the myth of growth, inspired and intrigued many of its close neighbours and distant allies. Japanese companies prospered in the global capitalist market, exporting innovative products with cutting-edge technologies, and individuals saw themselves rising into a middle class, broadly understood.

However, the pursuit of economic prosperity in the political and economic climate of the time was complex. There was a caveat to the great leaps made during and after the war. The very condition of globalisation lowered the barriers of the nation state and created a contradictory experience of cultural diversification. The desire for economic development and the anxiety of the vanishing traditional values gave rise to a sense of loss. But any sentimental retrospection, or even the fervour of the ideological movements of the time, could only exist as passing moments in the dominant logic of growth. The sentimental void behind rapid social change was overcome, or overlooked, by the simple means of driving the national economy in the order of global capitalism while preserving, at least symbolically, the spirit of the national identity. The flip side of the dynamic energies that achieved economic development was a longing for "time-honored 'tradition'" (Ivy 1995: 70) and "absolute values that [remain] immune" (Harootunian 2000: xxi). Modernists were against modernity, and capitalists were against capitalism (2000: xxi, xxx).

It was in this context that the peripheral regions, away from the main economic zones around Tokyo, Osaka, and other metropolitan centres, which had not been yet taken over by concrete buildings, gained and regained values during Japan's rapid development. Yoshimi points to the rapid suburbanisation of the outskirts of Tokyo and other metropolitan areas as an extension not only of the urban lifestyle but also de-socialisation and de-historicisation of the hometown (Yoshimi 2009). The construction boom of new towns and resorts, emblematic of Japan's bubble period, robbed its residents of a sense of belonging by placing them in places where there was no family history or neighbourhood ties. The central government's post-war land development programmes had left a critical mark on people's sociality. Massive urbanisation and suburbanisation meant a new age of disconnection. Against this massive spatial

DOI: 10.4324/9781003326540-12

reconfiguration, the landscape of remote villages became the symbolic repository of nostalgic memories and pre-modern ways of life, set against the backdrop of a society driven by sweeping forces of growth.

However, the prolonged economic downturn and social insecurities of the post-bubble period created a different kind of public sentiment, leading to a new discourse on the distant peripheries. For the new generations, who had set their life course in the aftermath of exponential growth, the nostalgia for *furusato* or the search for a lost sense of Japaneseness seemed a world away. The niche lifestyle that fuelled post-war development and the social values that forged strong ties to the family ideology were being questioned. In a society mired in precariousness rather than prosperity, where the ideology of self-responsibility pervaded workplaces and homes, *reclaiming* the self was more important than *crafting* oneself to the social norms (cf. Kondo 1990). In this shifting social climate, the public conception of suburban and non-urban areas began to fluctuate. The peripheries, which had long lacked an aura of its own, with its symbolic tropes created by the (urban) outsider's gaze, came into the spotlight again, this time for its representation of the new *desires* of the time. One manifest example is an emerging pattern of mobility that reverses the rural exodus that has been emblematic of Japan's modernisation (Dilley et al. 2022; Fielding and Ishikawa 2021: Klien 2020; Lewerich 2020; Nagatomo 2016; Obikwelu et al. 2017; Reiher 2020; Takahashi et al. 2021; Takeda 2020; Qu and Zollet 2023). As Takeda notes, moving to provincial areas is no longer seen as a privilege of the middle class, the ownership of a second home, or an affluent retirement, but as a choice made by young people to compensate for the dispiriting experiences of living in urban areas with low wages and long working hours (Takeda 2020: 198). Relocating to rural areas is a practical strategy for igniting one's aspirations in the "periphery" (Manzenreiter et al. 2020). The Kishida government's recent efforts to extend digital connectivity to remote areas of Japan hint at a greater propensity for urban-to-rural migration in the future. This movement reflects how people are gradually becoming alienated from the social norms and cultural traditions that have fostered Japan's economic prosperity and are instead seeking a space where they can find "alternative hedonism" (Soper 2020).

Under the changing social zeitgeist, the symbolic landscape of the rural space is being re-examined. It has become a stage rather than a bunker for what used to be modernity's perils. This book examined the emancipation of the countryside from the rural-backward and urban-forward frameworks (see also Klien 2020), which essentialised the rural periphery as a backup reserve for a society overwhelmed by growth and urbanisation: a place that permanently encapsulates what the post-war trajectories left behind. The notion of the rural, or rurality, is no longer tautological to the non-urban. Instead of nostalgic sentiments or traditional values, rurality, as represented in media and public policy discourses, supports the value of globalisation (i.e., the "global countryside" in Manzenreiter et al., 2020) and heterogeneity (see Hansen and

Klien 2022; Klien 2020, 2022; Rosenberger and Sugimoto 2022). Rural social geography is evolving from a closed network of fixed kin relationships to a conglomerate of diverse actors, ideas, and values that are manifested at multiple scales. Rather than a reflexive space embodying the residues of the ideology of growth, rural space is becoming redolent of alternative life trajectories and social discourses in the growing public recognition of no-growth.

In this reinstatement of rurality, the fundamental idea that defined the geographical core-periphery relations of Japan shifts, from "unevenness" to "evenness". For most of the 20th century, the idea of "unevenness" underpinned the discussions of rurality in Japan, such as in the works of folklore scholars (i.e., Yanagita Kunio) and the grassroots movements (i.e., *Rasukinjin Kyō*). The idea of moral geography was dominant in people's conceptions of space. The main concern was the potential pitfalls of relentless urbanisation, and discussions revolved around the resistance to it, with efforts being made to draw the line between the urban and the non-urban. Remote villages, for example, had their dynamic moments of contention and action, which were often too grand a narrative to resonate with the everyday context. The folklore studies, agrarian ideology, and *furusato* discourse that prevailed until the first decades of the post-war period thrived on the idea that certain aspects of the provincial regions remained immune to globalisation and outside influences. In contrast to the urban concrete jungles that were producing new national representations around corporate cultures, the thatched-roofed houses in remote villages represented what remained untainted. They were sacred in the broadest sense. The more Japan prospered economically, the greater the contrast between urban and non-urban areas. It was precisely in the idea of their relative backwardness that the latter gained the status as the symbolic repository of traditional values.

However, the confidence in the idea of growth has begun to crumble since the 1990s with the prolonged economic stagnation. The debate on ageing and declining populations has been the most visible manifestation of public recognition of the limits to growth. As evidenced by the recurrent reference to "2050" (or, as some say, "2060") as the year when Japan's population will fall to a third of its current size, Japan's future is seen predominantly in teleological terms. The ideology of growth is being challenged in the face of this prospect of inevitable shrinkage. Sustainability is becoming the new headline for public policy, and the campaign for population growth is being replaced by the "re-distribution" of population: the new challenge is to mobilise the population of the metropolitan areas and distribute it throughout the archipelago. Although similar attempts were made in the 1970s under the Fukuda government with the relocation of industrial bases and the expansion of the railway system, they were soon reversed by the Nakasone government's embrace of the neoliberal policies in Japan. In any case, the idea of re-distribution at the time was far from the logic of the socialist welfare system; it resonated with the idea of self-help in the sense of re-distributing responsibility for individual well-being (see Yoshimi 2009).

In this context, the logic of "unevenness" that underpinned the post-war conception of Japan's geographical landscape began to change. It was no longer desirable to promote rural space as a repository of "sacred" values, as this idea created a sense of distance from "secular" life in the cities. If population re-distribution is one of the key strategies for dealing with the stagnating economy, the spatial imaginary of Japan had to be reconstructed based on the similarity and interconnectedness of the urban and the non-urban, where the latter could be seen as an alternative space for an equally satisfying life. In this context, the notion of rurality was revived for the new values that replaced, if not filled the void of, the dominant urban lifestyle. In the transition from post-war to post-growth Japan, the urban-rural continuum is becoming the ideal frame of geographical imagination.

Tamba Sasayama's *sōzō nōson* campaign is a clear example of how this new conceptual framework of rurality is encapsulated in regional revitalisation movement. The promotion of rural creativity, an attempt to reshape public perceptions of rural life, illustrates how the regional image is recreated in line with rising expectations of rural space as a new destination for alternative life values and aspirations, with the hope that newcomers will take the leading role in stimulating the local social, cultural, and economic life (see also Lewerich 2020; Love 2007; Obikwelu et al. 2017: 70–71; Hansen and Klien 2022; Reiher 2020: 233; Takeda 2020; Qu and Zollet 2023). In Tamba Sasayama, the recent migration of craftspeople who opened workshops and galleries in the central town areas around Sasayama Castle was heralded in the local newspaper as an event that "sheds lights of creativity (*sōzōsei ni hikari o ateta*)" in the region (Sasayama City Hall 2021: 34–35). With the growing emphasis on the role of external actors in rural sustainability, either as urban-to-rural migrants or as "relationship population" (*kankei jinko*), a new geographical framework of urban-rural continuum seems to have become the new mantra of regional revitalisation policies in the 21st century (cf. Klien 2020:181–83).[1]

However, the ethnographic findings in this book also highlight the complexity of the urban-rural continuum discourse. While Klien's account of the post-growth tendencies in rural Japan focuses on the *mobility* of urban actors, with the idea of rurality as a "means rather than an end in itself" for urbanites who wish to free themselves from strenuous urban lifestyles (2020: 183), I delved into the ways in which the post-growth discourse manifests itself among those who *remain*, namely the native residents. The campaign for *sōzō nōson* reflects a complex process in which the continuum denotes not only the connection between the urban and the rural but also the continuation of urban-rural divide. It denotes that the local conceptualisation of the new rurality is far from a complete departure from the orthodox discourses on rural space, but a mixture of the traditional symbolic reference to its moral superiority and the recent trends in cultural creativity. According to Robertson, "[t]he promotion of native-place making offers the central government an efficacious way of addressing troublesome political, social and environmental issues under a single rubric" (Robertson 1988: 505). The *sōzō nōson* campaign is also open to a similar criticism. The new "rubric" (Robertson 1988: 505) hardly brought the kind of innovation expected from the urban-rural continuum of ideas, activities, and policies, but continued the urban-rural divide, albeit in a new light. The conceptual development of *sōzō nōson* based on *sōzō toshi* (see Chapter 1) and the sense of ambiguity experienced by local government officials (see Chapter 3) exemplified the prevalent idea of "urban-as-teleology" in the local efforts to re-conceptualise rurality (Chio 2017a: 362). The promotion of this confusing notion of *sōzō nōson*, a deliberate attempt to join the recent creativity boom in rural public policy, was a delayed echo of what had already been rampant in urban policy since the late 1990s. What seemed to persist in continuum was the ideology of self-responsibility that Klien also observes in urban-to-rural migrants, who continue to exploit themselves to foster the alternative lifestyles they seek: "even alternative realities seem to reflect pervasive ideologies of mainstream society" (Klien 2020: 178).

In his analysis of the postmodern transition, Harvey argues that within the increasing fragmentation and transience of capitalist society, there is an urge to "find stable mythology expressive of its inherent values and meanings" (Harvey 1990: 217). In this context, "[s]ocial practices may invoke certain myths and push for certain spatial and temporal representations as part and parcel of their drive to implant and reinforces their hold on society" (1990: 217). Under the growing sense of precarity in the post-bubble Japanese society, rural space becomes the repository of a new "stable mythology" (1990: 217). This time, the alternative values look ahead if not back. However, whether the rural ideals are past-oriented (i.e., *furusato*) or progressive (i.e., rural creativity), without supporting stories of the everyday rural life, they seem only to enliven a hypothetical space that exists only as a future anticipation.

Does the book then simply repeat the arguments of previous works that have critically examined the *furusato* discourse – the associated rural idealisation? Is regional disparity inevitable and recurrent throughout history? The book does not provide definitive answers to these questions; however, it does present a different trajectory of these issues by exploring the various levels – municipal, town, and village – at which the everyday lives of locals are woven into the discourse of new rurality, either as a policy initiative or as village-wide collective activities. I examined the ways in which a new rural value, reflecting the national hope invested in regional revitalisation, is developed, diverted, and challenged by local actors preoccupied with their immediate interests.

One of Bestor's key arguments, running through his seminal works on Tokyo neighbourhood (1989) and Tsukiji seafood market (2004) is the importance of "fixity" (Bestor 2004: 18; see also "traditionalism" 1989: 262) in understanding the profound socio-economic changes in Japan in post-war and post-bubble Japan. He points out that "the fixity and authenticity of place as the locus of action and identity" in Tsukiji market is "not evidence of local isolation and insularity" but "the product of and mechanism for articulating larger spheres of social and cultural relationships" (2004: 18).[2] Even in the celebrated notion of "scapes" (Appadurai 1990), which highlights mobility and fluidity, there is a sense of fixity which denote that "the local view – like a landscape – is not necessarily one of motion and process so much as of stability and coherence in a specific setting or perpetual environment" (2004: 18).

I argue that his advocacy of fixity over fluidity in understanding the changes happening within the local communities of Tokyo, Japan's great urban megalopolis, resonates with my suggestion of "focus over locus" in understanding the rural social landscape. If Bestor saw the neighbourhoods and the seafood market as examples of urban mundanity reflecting broader social changes in Japan in its post-war economic rise and post-bubble decline, Tamba Sasayama's regional revitalisation movement demonstrates the rural mundanity reflecting sentimental changes in the prolonged stagnation of the early-21st-century Japan. If the ultimate goal of the *sōzō nōson* campaign, as advocated by the local government, was the influx of newcomers and the free flow of individuals with creative minds into the region, relying on the dominant current of unrestrained relations (i.e., urban-to-rural migration), the potters of Tachikui have shown how their fixed relations (i.e., kinship and neighbourhood ties) embedded in the village was central to their promotion of the rural creativity. The trivial aspects of their everyday lives held the key to facilitating meaningful change: "'something different' does not necessarily arise out of a conscious plan, but more simply out of what people do, feel, sense and come to articulate as they seek meaning in their daily lives" (Harvey 2012: xvii). As shown in Chapter 7, in contrast to the hybrid and heterogeneous ideas about Tamba pottery that travelled through the *sōzō nōson* campaign, the orientation to the materiality of the village, Tachikui, created a firm foundation upon which the potters could freely express their creative ideas about Tamba pottery. As Bestor notes, "place creates the perception of spatial (and social) fixity in the midst of processual fluidity" (Bestor 2004: 18). Tachikui, with the taskcape of different forms of work interwoven through different social relations embedded in the village (see Chapter 5), was the "place" where there was "the product of and mechanism for articulating larger spheres of social and cultural relationships" (2004: 18). It is on the basis of our understanding of the potters' experience of the new rurality, firmly rooted in their physical and social attachment to their community, that we salvage a possibility of hope for the revitalisation of the Tamba pottery industry, Tachikui, and of the wider region.

However, I do not intend to undermine the *sōzō nōson* campaign as an empty echo in the air. Although a concept influenced by an urban-based theory of regional revitalisation, it was a product of the sincere efforts of local government officials, experts, and many others who cared about the region, and it was their bold attempts to reframe the conventional notion of rurality that have led the way to a variety of unexpected outcomes. Graeber argues that people rarely commit to a particular way of life or set of values, as they "simply stroll back and forth between one universe and another without feeling any profound sense of contradiction or even unease" (Graeber 2015: 231). It was the dissimilarity and contradiction between the potters, local government officials, and young migrants, brought together under the municipal-wide goal of promoting rural creativity, that created the diverse and open-ended futures. The complex intermingling of local visions and practices in Tamba Sasayama's regional revitalisation initiatives, that between the creativity discourse of *sōzō nōson* and the creative practices of potters in their daily lives, showed the case.

Initially, the potters had become involved in public projects in the hope of alleviating the fears of their ageing community and the possible collapse of the stable system that supported the Tamba pottery industry. But the more they became involved in making Tamba Sasayama a centre of rural creativity, the more they were burdened with mundane administrative tasks. The more Tamba pottery was marketed as a symbol of rural creativity, the more the public perceived its style as stale. However, the same experience also provided opportunities to reassess their position within the sweeping force of social and economic changes. The process of coping with the demanding role of creative agents revealed the internal strength of their community: the flexibility to pursue collective activities based on embedded social and kinship ties. In other words, as they were exposed to the unfamiliar tasks of public promotion, they became aware of a new aspect of their traditional community. The most notable example of this self-awareness was the renewed understanding of the intimate kinship and social ties, which had previously been seen as fatal to the creativity of the Tamba pottery industry. They were now seen with greater pride, for it was through these established social relationships that the potters were able to manage multiple promotional activities with greater flexibility. The close social and physical distance between them facilitated spontaneous meetings or the exchange of schedules. It could be argued that this is nothing more than peer pressure, an emotional stress of a group consciousness; however, in the current social and demographic conditions of the Tamba pottery industry, they seemed to prefer the burden of social relationship to the lack of it. Although frustrated by certain representations of Tamba pottery in public promotional materials, they sought to strike a balance between the local government's desire for Tamba pottery to be seen as a municipal cultural symbol and their own authority and knowledge of it. It was when the ephemeral nature of etic creativity was imposed on the existing social contours of their community that the creativity to sustain the Tamba pottery industry and the village life emerged.

In this course, the conventional practices we associate with traditional potters such as pounding clay, throwing a wheel or firing a kiln, were no longer the dominant components of their craft. The realm of everyday craft practices was changing in its adaptation to wider social changes. In the process, the potters have come to grips with a new source of inspiration to navigate the uncertain times. Although the symbolic trope of Tamba pottery continues to fluctuate as the idea of rurality changes, it has always been their sense of tactility that has guided them through the economic and demographic crisis. Tamba pottery was not just a cultural product but their livelihood, and Tamba Sasayama was not an abstract space of ephemeral values but a place of residence. Their daily lives were closely intertwined with the historiy of the land where Tamba pottery had been produced for centuries, and they were constantly reminded of the material quality of the space: the *tsuchi* (soil) from which they crafted Tamba pottery and the *tochi* (land) on which they lived. Over time, the efforts to embrace the new rural ideals proposed by the municipal revitalisation campaign gradually transformed the potters' community and led them to creatively shape their own future. The process also reduced their dependence on outside influences, leading them to craft a more self-determined path and foster a new hope for what lay ahead.

Existing ways of life in itself encapsulates the potential to live and think differently. Rather than *discovering* the value of rural things, which underpins the authority of the outsiders' gaze, a more attentive *awareness* of their value in the context of the local everyday lives offers a more plausible scenario for Japan's future. The signs of regional revitalisation can be found in the very fabric of everyday life. It is in our sincere recognition of what is already there that have persisted despite being overshadowed by the grandiose achievements of economic growth that we find clues to navigate the post-growth era.

Notes

1 *Kankei jinko* refers to a group of people who travel or do business in areas remote from their place of residence and create social and economic ties with the locals regularly or irregularly.

2 Bestor's ideas about "fixity" based on his observation in the Tsukiji market resonates with his earlier work on Tokyo's neighbourhood, where he suggests the concept of "traditionalism": "traditionalism – as an active agent creating and recreating images and meanings that attach to the social forms around which people organize their lives – is an index not of isolation from but of integration with the broader society" (1989: 262).

Epilogue

A visit to Tamba Sasayama in four years. The trip lasted four days, and I had made a one-page summary of the book to talk to the main interlocutors from my fieldwork and get their feedback, concerns, or thoughts on the book.

At first glance, not much had changed in the central area of Sasayama Castle. The main streets with shops and restaurants behind the City Hall building were remarkably quiet, as I had somehow expected. But the pandemic had left its mark on the local communities.

According to C-san, an official at City Hall, the area had seen an increase in newcomers in recent years, most of whom are craftspeople. As we got out of the car and walked around the area, I could see new cafes, galleries, and restaurants delicately decorated with an ideal rural atmosphere. For example, a minimalist gallery displayed everyday items such as ropes, vases, chairs, and other vintage objects under the *mingei* label, and a shop/hotel also sold works of famous *mingei* artists. If the initiative to promote Tamba Sasayama as a place full of the creative vibe of craftspeople was an idea that was developing during my fieldwork, it seemed that there was no longer the need to explicitly spell out *sōzō nōson*. The newcomer craftspeople had started a new local festival called the Craft Village (*kurafuto birejji*) in 2021. The organisation of the event was distinctive from the one in Tachikui. Instead of an established working group or an assembly to run the event, it was organised under loose ties of friends and neighbours. The event attracted the attention of the local media, and a modest number of tourists. I could not help but compare it to the new initiative led by the native craftspeople, the Tamba potters, that I had heard the day before.

I was warmly invited to stay one night at B-san's home in Tachikui during my visit. The village landscape seemed unchanged, with the familiar white trucks, piles of firewood, gas tanks, and pottery shards. The new shops that had opened during my fieldwork had aged gracefully, decorated with a few shaded paintings. Throughout the pandemic, orders had increased as people showed more interest in household goods, including tableware and planters, and he seemed busier than before. When I mentioned my book project, he initially waved his hand, saying that he was getting a headache just hearing

DOI: 10.4324/9781003326540-13

about it. But when I was about to leave, he briefly handed me a file of reports on *kumiai* activities.The document was a 16-page report outlining the medium-to-long-term plan for revitalising the Tamba pottery industry. It highlighted the potter's recent concerns, particularly the declining number of visitors to Sue no sato. Interestingly, they compared this with the increasing number of visitors to MCART (The Museum of Ceramic Art, Hyogo), which is right next door. Perhaps due to his increased responsibility in the *kumiai* activities over the past four years, many of the concerns seemed to resonate with those he shared with me during my fieldwork. One aspect of the report that stood out was the title: 'Creative Valley' (*Kurieichiibu bare*). The title itself seemed to imply a certain point of view shared among the potters about the future of the Tamba pottery industry.

The simultaneous emergence of the Craft Village, inaugurated by the newcomer craftspeople, and the Creative Valley, initiated by the native Tamba potters, seemed to indicate their different experiences and visions in recent years. It is important to clarify here that the juxtaposition of these two initiatives is entirely my idea, as there was no trace of connection or tension between them. The reason for comparing them immediately stems from the lingering question posed in the book about the social implications of the notion of *sōzō nōson* on the everyday lives of the local ruralites.

On the third day, B-san, C-san, and I had a chance to sit down and talk about trivial things that had happened in our lives over the pandemic. At one point, C-san asked B-san how the *kumiai* was going. B-san replied that the potters were having the best time in terms of sales since the pandemic had increased the consumption of tableware. However, he also anticipated that this might be the peak period and that from now on there might be a decline in sales and in the number of practising potters. It was inevitable that a large number of older potters would retire in the near future.

Perhaps to assuage his concerns, C-san mentioned about the increasing number of newcomers in the central Sasayama area, a significant number of whom were craftspeople, including potters. B-san responded with an excited voice, confirming that he had heard this and thought it was good news. However, he also pointed out the different perspectives of the young urban-to-rural migrants and those born and raised in the region. While the former saw the positive aspects of rural life, such as the good air and beautiful nature, the latter did not share this view and wanted to leave as soon as they graduate high school. He emphasised that we should think more critically about the intersection points of the rising curve of newcomers and falling curve of the natives.

To expand on his point, the positive aspects of rural life that the young migrants valued in Tamba Sasayama seemed to overlap with the very elements that the young locals wanted to move away from. The former saw new possibilities in the rusticity of the rural lifestyle: the natural environment, local tradition, and the small size of the neighbourhoods. If offered them a fresh perspective, coming from urban areas. This can be seen, for example, in the recent boom in rural art festivals, which have become increasingly popular (see Kirchberg and Kagan 2013; Qu and Zollet 2023; Zollet and Qu 2023). In this context, the title of the local craft fair, Craft Village, created by the newcomer craftspeople, seemed to reflect the image they wanted to promote of themselves and the value they placed on rural life. However, the merit that they saw and voluntarily adopted was an innate reference to the identity of the locals: rurality was never really a choice, but something they were born with, just like the green landscapes they (have to) see every day. While for newcomers rurality is perceived as a bounded idea, implying certain values such as a preference for nature, the slow life, or anything reminiscent of an ideal rural life (whatever that may be), which they used to recalibrate their lifestyle or rebrand themselves, it was rarely a matter of choice for the natives.

In this context, the Creative Valley initiative announced by the Tamba potters was an exciting revelation. The title seemed to contrast how the concept of creativity itself was a challenge for them four years ago. The aim, as denoted in the report, was to create "a kiln town that creates values of hand skills with nature" (*shizen to tomoni teshigoto no kachi o sōzōshi tsuzukeru kama sato*). One might ask whether the pottery community had already sufficiently promoted itself as a creative village through the years of the *sōzō nōson* campaign, as evidenced by its designation as a UNESCO Creative City of Crafts and Folk Arts. However, these activities were primarily driven by the local government in its attempt to rebrand the region based on a concept that was abstract and distant from the locals' everyday lives. The Creative Valley was an initiative led by the *kumiai* with the goal of achieving independence from the local government subsidy. Some of the proposed ideas were to increase social media promotion, to renovate Sue no sato (with a space-specific plan to redecorate it), and to create a stronger link with MCART. The potters were now willing to describe their own lives as creative. They had come up with new visions of Tamba pottery. A new sense of rurality seemed to be springing from *within*.

Bibliography

Abma, Tineke A. 2000. "Responding to ambiguity, responding to change the value of a responsive approach to evaluation." *Evaluation and Program Planning* 23 (4): 461–470.

Adamson, Glenn. 2010. *The Craft Reader*. Berg Publishers.

Allison, Anne. 2014. *Precarious Japan*. Duke University Press.

Allison, Anne. 2015. "Precarity and Hope: Social Connectedness in Postcapitalist Japan." In *Japan: The Precarious Future*, edited by Frank Baldwin and Anne Allison, 36–57. Social Science Research Council, New York University Press.

Allison, Anne. 2023. *Being Dead Otherwise*. Durham and London: Duke University Press.

Aoki, Shigeo. 1976. *Hyōgo no yakimono* [*Ceramics of Hyōgo*]. Kōbe shinbun shuppan senta.

Aoyama, Reijiro. 2015. "Global Journeymen: Re-Inventing Japanese Craftsman Spirit in Hong Kong." *Asian Anthropology* 14 (3): 265–282.

Appadurai, Arjun. 1990. "Disjuncture and Difference in the Global Cultural Economy." *Theory, Culture and Society*, 7: 295–310.

Ardener, Edwin. 2012. "Remote Areas." *HAU: Journal of Ethnographic Theory* 2 (1): 519–533.

Banks, Mark. 2010. "Craft Labour and Creative Industries." *International Journal of Cultural Policy* 16 (3): 305–321.

Banks, Mark, and Justin O'Connor. 2017. "Inside the whale (and how to get out of there): Moving on from two decades of creative industries research." *European Journal of Cultural Studies*, 20 (6): 637–654.

Befu, Harumi. 1963. "Patrilineal descent and personal kindred in Japan". *American Anthropologist* 65 (6): 1328–1341.

Befu, Harumi. 1984. "Civilization and Culture: Japan in Search of Identity." *Senri Ethnological Studies* 16: 59075.

Befu, Harumi. 1992. "Symbols of Nationalism and 'Nihonjinron'." In *Ideology and Practice in Modem Japan.*, edited by Roger Goodman and Kirsten Refsing, 26–46. London: Routledge.

Befu, Harumi. 2001. *Hegemony of Homogeneity: An Anthropological Analysis of "Nihonjinron"*. Melbourne: Trans Pacific Press.

Bell, David, and Mark Jayne. 2010. "The Creative Countryside: Policy and Practice in the UK Rural Cultural Economy." *Journal of Rural Studies* 26 (3): 209–218.

Bernstein, Anya, and Elizabeth Mertz. 2011. "Introduction: Bureaucracy: Ethnography of the State in Everyday Life." *Political and Legal Anthropology Review* 34 (1): 6–11.

Best, Jacqueline. 2012a. "Bureaucratic ambiguity." *Economy and Society* 41 (1), 84–106.

Best, Jacqueline. 2012b. "Ambiguity and uncertainty in international organizations: A history of debating IMF conditionality." *International Studies Quarterly*, 56 (4): 674–688.

Bestor, Theodore. 1989. *Neighborhood Tokyo*. Stanford, CA: Stanford University Press.
Bestor, Theodore. 2004. *Tsukiji: The Fish Market at the Center of the World*. Berkeley and Los Angeles: University of California Press.
Billaud, Julie. 2020. "Masters of disorder: Rituals of communication and monitoring at the international committee of the red cross." *Social Anthropology* 28 (1): 96–111.
Bortolotto, Chiara, Philipp Demgenski, Panas Karampampas, and Simone Toji. 2020. "Proving participation: Vocational bureaucrats and bureaucratic creativity in the implementation of the UNESCO convention for the safeguarding of the intangible cultural heritage." *Social Anthropology* 28 (1): 66–82.
Brachet, Julien, and Judith Scheele. 2019. "Remoteness Is Power: Disconnection as a Relation in Northern Chad." *Social Anthropology* 27 (2): 156–171.
Brandt, Lisbeth. 2007. *Kingdom of Beauty Mingei and the Politics of Folk Art in Imperial Japan*. Duke University Press.
Brumann, Christoph, and Rupert Cox. 2009. *Making Japanese Heritage*. London: Routledge.
Campbell, Peter. 2014. "Imaginary success? - The contentious ascendance of creativity." *European Planning Studies* 22 (5): 995–1009.
Cant, Alanna. 2019. *The Value of Aesthetics: Oaxacan Woodcarvers in Global Economies of Culture*. Austin: University of Texas Press.
Carolan, Michael S. 2008. "More-than-representational knowledge/s of the countryside: How we think as bodies." *Sociologia Ruralis* 48 (4): 408–422.
Carter, Thomas F. 2006. "Introduction: The sport of cities spectacle and the economy of appearances." *City & Society* 18 (2): 151–158.
Caves, Richard. 2002. *Creative Industries: Contracts Between Art and Commerce*. Harvard University Press.
Chang, Sang-un. 2007. "*Myeongmyeonge gwanhan yeongu: Hangukgwa ilbonui seongssiwa gachingmyeongui unyong* [A study on naming practice: management of surname and pseudonym in Korea and Japan]." *The Japanese Language and Literature Society of Korea* 36: 391–408.
Chiavacci, David. 2008. "From class struggle to general middle-class society to divided society: Societal models of inequality in Postwar Japan." *Social Science Japan Journal* 11 (1): 5–27.
Chiavacci, David, Simona Grano, and Julia Obinger. 2020. *Civil Society and the State in Democratic East Asia Between Entanglement And Contention in Post High Growth*. Amsterdam: University of Amsterdam Press.
Chiavacci, David, and Carola Hommerich. 2017. *Social Inequality in Post-Growth Japan: Transformation during Economic and Demographic Stagnation*. London: Routledge.
Chio, Jenny. 2017a. "Introduction: Rural as space and sociality." *Critique of Anthropology* 37 (4): 361–363.
Chio, Jenny. 2017b. "Rendering Rural Modernity: Spectacle and Power in a Chinese Ethnic Tourism Village." *Critique of Anthropology* 37 (4): 418–439.
Choi, Wooyong. 2014. "*ilbon jibanghaengjeongchejeui gaepyeongwa tonghapsiui jaejeonge gwanhan gochal: hyogohyeon sasayamasireul daesangeuro hayeo* [A study of revision of regional administrative system and financial condition of merged cities: a case of Sasayama, Hyōgo Prefecture]." *Public Law Journal* 15 (1): 329–355.
Cloke, Paul. 2006. "Conceptualizing Rurality." In *The Handbook of Rural Studies*, edited by P. Cloke, Terry Marsden, and Patrick Mooney, 18–28. Thousand Oaks CA: Sage Publications.
Cody, Sacha. 2018. "Borrowing from the Rural to Help the Urban: Organic Farming Exemplars in Postsocialist China." *Asia Pacific Journal of Anthropology* 19 (1): 72–89.
Cohen, Anthony. 2000. *The Symbolic Construction of Community*. London: Routledge.
Cort, Louise Allison. 2001. *Shigaraki: Potter's Valley*. Bangkok: Orchid Press.

Cowan, Jane. 2020. "'The Feeling of Pursuing an Ideal': A League of Nations Civil Servant Reflects on His Work." *Social Anthropology* 28 (1): 17–34.

Creative Village. n.d. *Project 5: Hyōgo-ken Tamba Sasayama*. https://creative-village.jp/project/project05.html. (accessed 16 March 2020).

Creed, Gerald, and Barbara Ching. 1997. "Recognizing Rusticity: Identity and the Power of Place." In *Knowing Your Place: Rural Identity and Cultural Hierarchy*, 1–38. Routledge.

Creighton, Millie. 1995. "Japanese craft tourism: Liberating the crane wife." *Annals of Tourism Research* 22 (2): 463–478.

Creighton, Millie. 1997. "Consuming Rural Japan: The Marketing of Tradition and Nostalgia in the Japanese Travel Industry." *Ethnology* 36 (3): 239–254.

Cunningham, Stuart. 2011. "Creative industries, its critics, and some answers." *Ekonomiaz* 78 (3): 47–60.

Daniels, Inge Maria. 2001. "The Fame of Miyajima: Spirituality, Commodification and the Tourist Trade of Souvenirs in Japan." PhD diss., University College London.

de Genova, Nicholas. 2002. "Migrant "Illegality" and Deportability in Everyday Life." *Annual Review of Anthropology* 31 (1): 419–447.

Dilley, Luke, Menelaos Gkartzios, and Tokumi Odagiri. 2022. "Developing Counterurbanisation: Making Sense of Rural Mobility and Governance in Japan." *Habitat International* 125: 1–10.

Dilley, Luke, Shinzato Sae, and Ando Mitsuyoshi. 2017. "Revitalising the rural in Japan: Working through the power of place." *Electronic Journal of Contemporary Japanese Studies* 17 (3).

Ding, Dang, Pingyang Liu, and Neil Ravenscroft. 2018. "The new urban agricultural geography of Shanghai." *Geoforum* 90: 74–83. https://doi.org/10.1016/j.geoforum.2018.02.010

Dusinberre, Martin. 2013. "Searching for Furusato in Kaminoseki." In *Japan since 1945: From Postwar to Post-Bubble*, edited by Christopher Gerteis and Timothy S. George, 47–65. London: Bloomsbury.

Edensor, Tim. 2006. "Performing rurality." In *The Handbook of Rural Studies*, edited by P. Cloke, Terry Marsden, and Patrick Mooney, 484–495. SAGE Publications.

Ehrentraut, Adolf. 1993. "Heritage Authenticity and Domestic Tourism in Japan." *Annals of Tourism Research* 20 (2): 262–278.

Ehrentraut, Adolf. 1995. "Cultural Nationalism, Corporate Interests and the Production of Architectural Heritage in Japan." *Canadian Review of Sociology & Anthropology* 32 (2): 215–242.

Elis, Volker. 2011. "The Impact of the Trinity Reforms and the Heisei Mergers on Processes of Peripherisation in Japan's Mountain Villages." *Japanese Journal of Human Geography* 63 (6): 44–56.

Ertl, John. 2007. "Revisiting Village Japan." PhD diss., University of California, Berkeley.

Fielding, Toni, and Yoshitaka Ishikawa. (2021). "COVID-19 and migration: A research note on the effects of COVID-19 on internal migration rates and patterns in Japan." *Population, Space and Place* 27 (6): 1–11. https://doi.org/10.1002/psp.2499

Florida, Richard. 2003. "Cities and the Creative Class." *Cities and the Creative Class* 2 (1): 3–19.

Fois, Francesca, Michael Woods, Yuanyuan Yang, and Xiaoyu Zheng. 2019. "Recovering tradition in globalizing rural China: Handicraft birdcages in Da'ou village." *Sociologia Ruralis* 59 (4): 661–684.

Foster, Michael Dylan. 2011. "The UNESCO Effect: Confidence, Defamiliarization, and a New Element in the Discourse on a Japanese Island." *Journal of Folklore Research* 48 (1): 63–107.

Furuichi, Noritoshi. 2017. *The Happy Youth of a Desperate Country: The disconnect between Japan's malaise and its millennials*. Japan Publishing Industry Foundation for Culture.

Gagné, Nana Okura. 2020. "Neoliberalism at work: Corporate reforms, subjectivity, and post-Toyotist affect in Japan." *Anthropological Theory* 20 (4): 455–483.

Ganseforth, Sonya, and Hanno Jentzsch. 2022. *Rethinking Locality in Japan*. London and New York: Routledge.

Garnham, Nicholas. 2005. "From Cultural to Creative Industries: An Analysis of the Implications of the 'Creative Industries' Approach to Arts and Media Policy Making in the United Kingdom." *International Journal of Cultural Policy* 11 (1): 15–29.

Genda, Yuji. 2017. "Hope and Society in Japan." In *The Economy of Hope*, edited by Hirokazu Miyazaki and Richard Swedberg, 97–125. Philadelphia: University of Pennsylvania Press.

Gough, Katherine, and Jonathan Rigg. 2012. "Reterritorialising rural handicrafts in Thailand and Vietnam: A view from the margins of the miracle." *Environment and Planning* 44 (1): 169–186.

Graeber, David. 2015. "Radical Alterity Is Just Another Way of Saying 'Reality': A Reply to Eduardo Viveiros de Castro." *HAU: Journal of Ethnographic Theory* 5 (2): 1–41.

Guth, Christine. 2021. *Craft Culture in Early Modern Japan: Materials, Makers, and Mastery*. Oakland: University of California Press.

Halfacree, Keith. 2006. "Rural Space: Constructing a Three-Fold Architecture." In *The Handbook of Rural Studies*, edited by P. Cloke, Terry Marsden, and Patrick Mooney, 44–62. SAGE Publications.

Han, Seungmi. 1995. "From regional craft to national art: Politics and identity in a Japanese regional industry." PhD diss., Harvard University.

Hannerz, Ulf. 1980. *Exploring the City: Inquiries toward an Urban Anthropology*. Columbia University Press.

Hansen, Paul and Susan Klien. 2022. "Special issue: Exploring rural Japan as heterotopia." *Asian Anthropology* 21 (1): 1–9.

Hansen, Thomas and Oskar Verkaaik. 2009. "Introduction - Urban charisma: On everyday mythologies in the city." *Critique of Anthropology* 29 (1): 5–26.

Harootunian, Harry. 2000. *Overcome by modernity*. Princeton University Press.

Harootunian, Harry. 2008. "Figuring the Folk: History, Poetics, and Representation." In *Mirror of Modernity: Invented Traditions of Modern Japan*, edited by Stephen Vlastos, 144–159. University of California Press.

Harvey, David. 1990. *The Condition of Postmodernity*. Oxford: Blackwell.

Harvey, David. 2012. *Rebel Cities: From the Right to the City to the Urban Revolution*. Verso.

Herzfeld, Michael. 2004. *The Body Impolitic: Artisans and Artifice in The Global Hierarchy of Value*. Chicago: University of Chicago Press.

Hong, Seong Heup. 2009. "Local Revitalization Movement through Revival of Traditional Ceramic Industry in Japan - A Case of Mashiko-Cho in Tochigi-Ken." *Journal of the Economic Geographical Society of Korea* 12 (4): 597–612.

Hull, Matthews S. 2012. *Documents and Bureaucracy*. *Annual Review of Anthropology* 41 (1): 251–267.

Hwang, Dal Kee. 2015. "Sustainability of 'Syokunin' Culture in Japan" *Journal of the society of Japanese Language and Literature, Japanology* 69: 419–438.

Hwang, Dal Kee. 2016. "Meaning and Function of the Invention of Japanese Traditional Crafts - The Case of Arita Porcelain of the Saga Prefecture." *The Association of Japanology in East Asia* 4: 351–370.

Hyōgo ken kōgyō shōrei kan. 1968. *Kōgyō shiken kenkyūjo kikan gojyūnen rekishi* [The 50 years history of Industrial Testing Laboratory]. Kōbe shuppan insatsu kabushikigaisha.

Idegawa, Naoki. 1988. *Mingei: Riron no hōkai to yōshiki no tanjō* [Mingei: The Collapse of Theory and the Birth of a Style]. Tokyo: Shinchōsha.
Ingold, Tim. 1993. "The temporality of landscape." *World Archeology* 25 (2): 152–174.
Ingold, Tim. 2000. *The Perception of the Environment: Essays on Livelihood, Dwelling and Skill*. London and New York: Routledge.
Ingold, Tim. 2004. "Culture on the Ground: The World Perceived through the Feet." *Journal of Material Culture* 9 (3): 315–340.
Ivy, Marylin. 1995. *Discourses of the vanishing: Modernity, Phantasm, Japan*. University of Chicago Press.
Jones, Meghen M. 2014. *Tomimoto Kenkichi and the discourse of modern Japanese ceramics*. PhD diss., University of Boston.
Jørgensen, Helle. 2011. "Remoteness and Development: Transnational Constructions of Heritage in a Former Danish Trading Colony in South India." *History and Anthropology* 22 (2): 169–186.
Kakiuchi, Emiko. 2016. "Culturally Creative Cities in Japan: Reality and Prospects." *City, Culture and Society* 7 (2): 101–108.
Kakiuchi, Emiko, and Kiyoshi Takeuchi. 2014. "Creative industries: Reality and potential in Japan." *GRIPS Discussion* (April).
Kalab, Kathleen A. 1992. "Playing Gateball: A Game of the Japanese Elderly." *Journal of Aging Studies* 6 (1): 23–40.
Kato, Hikari. 2015. "*Sōzō nōson no ryōgise*. [The ambiguity of creative village]." *Hokkai-Gakuen University, the Journal of Economics* 62 (4): 1–11.
Kavedžija, Iza. 2016. "Introduction: reorienting hopes." *Contemporary Japan* 28 (1): 1–11.
Kawamoto, Kenichi. 2020. "1960 nendai kara gendai nikakete no Nippon no dentōteki na sue sanchi no hatten Tanbayaki to bizen'yaki o jirei ni. [The development of traditional Japanese ceramic production areas from the 1960s to the present day - a case study of Tanba and Bizen ware]." *Journal of Political Science* 60: 169–194.
Kawashima, Kumiko. 2021. "Why migrate to earn less? Changing tertiary education, skilled migration and class slippage in an economic downturn." *Journal of Ethnic and Migration Studies* 47 (13): 3131–3149.
Kelly, William. 1990. "Regional Japan: The price of prosperity and the benefits of dependency." *Daedalus* 119 (3): 209–227.
Kikuchi, Yuko. 1994. "The myth of Yanagi's originality: The formation of mingei theory in its social and historical context." *Journal of Design History* 7 (4): 247–266.
Kikuchi, Yuko. 1997. "A Japanese William Morris: Yanagi Soetsu and Mingei Theory." *Journal of William Morris Studies (JWMS)* 12: 39–45.
Kikuchi, Yuko. 2004. *Japanese modernisation and mingei theory: Cultural nationalism and oriental orientalism*. London and New York: Routledge Curzon.
Kim, Hyesuk. 2016. "jiyeokjaesaengeuroseo sasayamasi seonggongyoin bunseok: jimnangmaruyama modereul jungsimeuro [An analysis of Sasayama City's success in regional revitalization: based on the case of Maruyama Village model]." *Korea Association of Japanology* 8: 364–370.
Kingsbury, Aaron J. 2019. "Running Ethnography: Engaging the Culture and Landscapes of Rural Japan." *Asian Anthropology* 18 (1): 56–68.
Kirchberg, Volker, and Sacha Kagan. 2013. "The Roles of Artists in the Emergence of Creative Sustainable Cities: Theoretical Clues and Empirical Illustrations." *City, Culture and Society* 4 (3): 137–152.
Klein, Jakob. 2009. "Creating Ethical Food Consumers? Promoting Organic Foods in Urban Southwest China." *Social Anthropology* 17 (1): 74–89.
Kleinberg, Jill. 1979. "Kinship and economic growth: Pottery production in Japan village." PhD diss., The University of Michigan.
Kleist, Nauja, and Stef Jansen. 2016. "Introduction: Hope over Time—Crisis, Immobility and Future-Making." *History and Anthropology* 27 (4): 373–392.

Klien, Susanne. 2016. "Shinto Ritual Practice in Miyagi Prefecture after the Great East Japan Earthquake: The Case of the Ogatsu Hōin Kagura." *Asian Ethnology* 75 (2): 359–376.

Klien, Susanne. 2019. Entrepreneurial Selves, Governmentality and Lifestyle Migrants in Rural Japan. *Asian Anthropology* 18 (2): 75–90.

Klien, Susanne. 2020. *Urban Migrants in Rural Japan: Between Agency and Anomie in a Post-Growth Society*. New York: SUNY Press.

Klien, Susanne. 2022. "'The Young, the Stupid, and the Outsiders': Urban Migrants as Heterotopic Selves in Post-Growth Japan." *Asian Anthropology* 21 (1): 10–23.

Knight, John. 1994. "Rural Revitalization in Japan: Spirit of the Village and Taste of the Country." *Asian Survey* 34 (7): 634–646.

Koh, Vanessa, Paul Burow, Lav Kanoi, and Michael Dove. 2021. "Locating the 'Rural' in Anthropology." In *The SAGE Handbook of Cultural Anthropology*, edited by Lene Pedersen and Lisa Cliggett, 296–310. Thousand Oaks: Sage Publishers.

Koike, Osamu. 2009. "Local Government Amalgamation in Japan: Creating a New Local Governance or New Crisis of Governance?" *Yokohama Journal of Social Sciences* 15 (4): 375–383.

Kondo, Dorinne. 1990. *Crafting Selves: Power, Gender, and Discourses of Identity in a Japanese Workplace*. Chicago and London: The University of Chicago Press.

Kong, Lily. 2014. "From Cultural Industries to Creative Industries and Back? Towards Clarifying Theory and Rethinking Policy." *Inter-Asia Cultural Studies* 15 (4): 593–607.

Kuwayama, Takami. 2001. "The Discourse of *Ie* (Family) in Japan's Cultural Identity and Nationalism: A Critique." *Japanese Review of Cultural Anthropology* 2: 3–37.

Kweon, Sukin. 2011. "'Sotokomori': Escaping from the Blockage of Japanese Modernity or Scapegoats of Neoliberalism." *Korean Journal of Japanese Studies* 5: 22–49.

Leheny, David. 2018. *Empire of Hope: The Sentimental Politics of Japanese Decline*. Cornell University Press.

Lewerich, Ludgera. 2020. "Nai Mono Wa Nai - Challenging and Subverting Rural Peripheralization? Decline and Revival in a Remote Island Town." In *Japan's New Ruralities: Coping with Decline in the Periphery*, edited by Wolfram Manzenreiter, Ralph Lützeler, and Sebastian Polak-Rottman, 212–229. New York and London: Routledge.

Love, Bridget. 2007. "Fraught Fieldsites: Studying Community Decline and Heritage Food Revival in Rural Japan." *Critical Asian Studies* 39 (4): 541–559.

Love, Bridget. 2010. "Mountain Vegetables and the Politics of Local Flavor in Regional Japan." In *Japanese Foodways, Past and Present*, edited by Eric Rath, and Stephanie Assman. University of Illinois Press.

Love, Bridget. 2013. "Treasure hunts in rural Japan: Place making at the limits of sustainability." *American Anthropologist* 115 (1): 112–124.

Love, Bridget. 2014. "Sustainability at dead-ends: The future of hope in rural Japan." *RCC Perspectives* 3: 95–100.

Luckman, Susan. 2012. *Locating cultural work: The politics and poetics of rural, regional and remote creativity*. London: Palgrave Macmillan.

Luckman, Susan. 2015. *Craft and the creative economy*. London: Palgrave Macmillan.

Luo, Yu, Tim Oakes, and Louisa Schein. 2019. "Resourcing Remoteness and the 'Post-Alteric' Imaginary in China." *Social Anthropology* 27 (2): 270–285.

Lützeler, Ralph. 2020. "The Urban-Rural Divide in Japan: A Matter of Social Inequality?" In *Social Inequality in Post-Growth Japan: Transformation during Economic and Demographic Stagnation*, edited by David Chiavacci and Carola Hommerich, 187–200. London: Routledge.

Lützeler, Ralph, Wolfram Manzenreiter, and Sebastian Polak-Rottman. 2020. Introduction. In *Japan's new ruralities: Coping with decline in the periphery*, edited by Wolfram Manzenreiter, Ralph Lützeler, and Sebastian Polak-Rottman, 1–24. London and New York: Routledge.

Mabuchi, Masaru. 2001. "Municipal Amalgamation in Japan." *WBI Working Paper* 1.

MacClancy, Jeremy. 2015. Alternative countryside: anthropology and rural West Europe today. In *Alternative countryside: anthropology and rural West Europe today*, edited by Jeremy MacClancy, 1–28. Manchester: Manchester University Press.

Maekawa, Youhei, Shigeyuki Miyabashi, and Haruo Sekioka. 2013. "Effects and problems of the 'Law for the Promotion of Traditional Crafts Industries." *Journal of Agriculture Science* 58 (2): 85–91.

Manzenreiter, Wolfram, Ralph Lützeler, and Sebastian Polak-Rottman. 2020. *Japan's New Ruralities: Coping with Decline in the Periphery*. London and New York: Routledge.

Marchand, Trevor. 2008. "Muscles, morals and mind: Craft apprenticeship and the formation of person." *British Journal of Educational Studies* 56 (3): 245–271.

Marcus, George. 1995. "Ethnography in/of the World System: The Emergence of Multi-Sited Ethnography." *Annual Review of Anthropology* 24: 95–117.

Matanle, Peter. 2007. "Organic Sources for the Revitalization of Rural Japan: The Craft Potters of Sado." *Japanstudien* 18 (1): 149–180.

Matanle, Peter. 2020. "Understanding the Dynamics of Regional Growth and Shrinkage in 21st Century Japan: Towards the Achievement of an Asia-Pacific 'Depopulation Dividend'." In *Social Inequality in Post-Growth Japan: Transformation during Economic and Demographic Stagnation*, edited by Ralph Lützeler and Carola Hommerich, 213–230. London: Routledge.

Mathews, Gordon. 2017. "Happiness in Neoliberal Japan." In *Happiness and the Good Life in Japan*, edited by Wolfram Manzenreiter and Barbara Holthus, 227–242. Taylor & Francis Books.

Mathur, Nayanika. 2017. "Bureaucracy". In *The Open Encyclopedia of Anthropology*, edited by Felix Stein. Facsimile of the first edition in *The Cambridge Encyclopedia of Anthropology*. Online: https://doi.org/10.29164/17bureaucracy

MCART. 2015. *Sai tanba (fuyu): Tanba nobori kama to sono jidai*. Hyogo: The Museum of Ceramic Arts.

McMorran, Chris. 2008. "Understanding the 'heritage' in Heritage Tourism: Ideological Tool or Economic Tool for a Japanese Hot Springs Resort?" *Tourism Geographies* 10 (3): 334–354.

McMorran, Chris. 2014. "A Landscape of 'Undesigned Design' in Rural Japan." *Landscape Journal* 33 (1): 1–15.

McRobbie, Angela. 2012. "A Good Job Well Done: Richard Sennett and the Politics of Creative Labour." In *Futures of Modernity: Challenges for Cosmopolitical Thought and Practice*, 155–174. Bielefeld: Transcript-Verlag.

Mead, Margaret. 1960. "Work, Leisure and Creativity." *Daedalus* 89 (1): 13–23.

Miller, Chloe Fox. 2017. "The contemporary geographies of craft-based manufacturing." *Geography Compass* 11 (4): 1–13.

Mitsubishi UFJ Research and Consulting. 2017. *Dentōteki kōgeihin sangyōno jiritsukani muketa gaido buku* [Guidebook for the autonomy of traditional crafts industry].

Miyazaki, Hirokazu. 2004. *The Method of Hope: Anthropology, Philosophy and Fijian Knowledge*. Stanford, CA: Stanford University Press.

Moeran, Brian. 1989. "Bernard Leach and the Japanese folk craft movement: the formative years." *Journal of Design History* 2 (2–3): 139–144.

Moeran, Brian. 1990. "Japanese ceramics and the discourse of 'tradition'." *Journal of Design History* 3 (4): 213–225.

Moeran, Brian. 1997. *Folk art potters of Japan: Beyond an anthropology of aesthetics*. University of Hawaii Press.

Moon, Okpyo. 1986. "Is Ie Disappearing in Rural Japan? The Impact of Tourism on a Traditional Japanese Village." In *Interpreting Japanese Society: Anthropological Approaches*, edited by Joy Hendry, 117–130. London: Routledge.

Moon, Okpyo. 2002. "The Countryside Reinvented for Urban Tourists: Rural Transformation in the Japanese Muraokoshi Movement." *In Japan at play: The ludic and the logic of power*, edited by Joy Hendry and Massimo Raveri, 228–244. London: Routledge.

Moon, Okpyo. 2011. "Traditional Craft as Cultural Heritage: The Case of Nishijin Weaving in Kyoto, Japan." *Korean Society for Cultural Anthropology* 44 (3): 3–35.

Morais, Liliana G. P. 2019. *Western Potters in Japan: Identities, Traditions and Histories from a Cosmopolitan Perspective*. PhD diss., Tokyo Metropolitan University.

Moriwaki, Toshimasa. 2008. "Heisei Grand Amalgamation and Local Council Members: An Analysis of Empirical Research." *Japanese Journal of Electoral Studies* 23: 82–90.

Mormont, Marc. 1987. "Rural Nature and Urban Natures." *Sociologia Ruralis* 27 (1): 3–20.

Mould, Oli. 2018. *Against Creativity*. London: Verso.

Murdoch, Jonathan, and Andy Pratt. 1993. "Rural Studies: Modernism, Postmodernism and the 'Post-Rural'." *Journal of Rural Studies* 9 (4): 411–427.

Nagatomo, Jun. 2016. "Cultural Practices of Traditional Performing Arts by Lifestyle Migrants in Ama-Chō, Oki Islands, Japan: Identity Politics and Cultural Practices of I-Turn Migrants as 'Middlemen'." *Kwansei Gakuin Daigaku Kokusaigaku Kenkyū* 5 (1): 5–17.

Nakane, Chie. 1967. "Kinship and economic organization in rural Japan." *Monographs on Social Anthropology*. London School of Economics.

Nakanishi, Tōru. 1971. *Kōtamba [Old Tamba Pottery]*. Hyōgoken: Tanba Kotōkan.

Nakano, Takashi, and Keith Brown. 1970. "Changing Rural Japan." *Rice University Studies* 56 (4): 195–206.

Nielsen, Bjarke. 2011. UNESCO and the 'Right' Kind of Culture: Bureaucratic Production and Articulation. *Critique of Anthropology* 31 (4): 273–292.

Niezen, Ronald and Maria Sapignoli. 2017. *Introduction*. Palaces of Hope: The Anthropology of Global Organizations. 1–32. Cambridge University Press.

O'Connor, Erin. 2005. "Embodied Knowledge: The Experience of Meaning and the Struggle towards Proficiency in Glassblowing." *Ethnography* 6 (2): 183–204.

Obikwelu, Faith, Koichi Ikegami, and Tadasu Tsuruta. 2017. "Factors of Urban-Rural Migration and Socio-Economic Condition of I-Turn Migrants in Rural Japan." *Journal of Asian Rural Studies* 1 (1): 70–80.

Ochiai, Emiko. 2000. "Debates Over the *Ie* and the Stem Family: Orientalism East and West." *Japan Review* 12: 105–127.

OECD Country Note. 2020. *Rural well-being: geography of opportunities*.

Ogawa, Osamu. 2016. "*Chiiki kasseika to chihō sōsei* [Regional revitalization and chihō sōsei]." *Onomichi City University Journal of Economics, Management & Information Science* 16 (2): 17–37.

Onitsuka, Kenichiro, and Satoshi Hoshino. 2018. "Inter-community networks of rural leaders and key people: Case study on a rural revitalization program in Kyoto Prefecture, Japan." *Journal of Rural Studies*, 61: 123–136.

Ono, Mayumi. 2015. "Descending from Japan: Lifestyle Mobility of Japanese Male Youth to Thailand." *Asian Anthropology* 14 (3): 249–264.

Otani, Shinsuke. 1998. "Personal Community Networks in Contemporary Japan." In *Networks in the Global Village: Life in Contemporary Communities*, 279–297. Routledge.

Paredes, Alyssa. 2017. "The Problem of Mechanization: Craft, Machines, and 'Centering' in a Japanese Mingei Pottery Village." *Journal of Material Culture* 23 (2): 133–150.

Park, Choong Hwan. 2014. "Nongjiale Tourism and Contested Space in Rural China." *Modern China* 40 (5): 519–548.

Partner, Simon. 2009. *The Mayor of Aihara: A Japanese Villager and His Community, 1865–1925*. University of California Press.

Peck, Jamie. 2005. "Struggling with the Rise of the Creative Class." *International Journal of Urban and Regional Research* 29 (4): 740–770.

Pinker, Annabel. 2015. Papering over the gaps: Documents, infrastructure and political experimentation in Highland Peru. *The Cambridge Journal of Anthropology* 33 (1): 97–112.

Pratt, Andy. 2008. "Creative Cities: The Cultural Industries and the Creative Class." *Geografiska Annaler, Series B: Human Geography* 90 (2): 107–117.

Qu, Meng, and Simona Zollet. 2023. "Neo-Endogenous Revitalisation: Enhancing Community Resilience through Art Tourism and Rural Entrepreneurship." *Journal of Rural Studies* 97: 105–114.

Rausch, Anthony. 2008. "Japanese rural revitalization: The reality and potential of cultural commodities as local brands." In *Cultural commodities in Japanese rural revitalization: Tsugaru Nuri Lacquerware and Tsugaru Shamisen*, 223–245. Brill Academic Pub.

Rausch, Anthony. 2009. "Capitalizing on Creativity in Rural Areas: National and Local Branding in Japan." *Journal of Rural and Community Development* 4 (2): 65–79.

Rausch, Anthony. 2016. Tensions in Chihō Sōsei, 2015: Local realities, national policies and international agreements. *Journal of Regional Education and Culture*, 4.

Reiher, Cornelia. 2020. "Embracing the Periphery: Urbanites' Motivations for Relocating to Rural Japan." In *Japan's New Ruralities: Coping with Decline in the Periphery*, edited by Wolfram Manzenreiter, Ralph Lützeler, and Sebastian Polak-Rottman, 230–244. London and New York: Routledge.

Rhodes, Daniel. 1972. *Marks of Fire on Old Tamba Pottery*. International Symposium on Japanese Ceramics, Seattle Art Museum.

Robertson, Jennifer. 1987. "A Dialectic of Native and Newcomer: The Kodaira Citizens' Festival in Suburban Tokyo." *Anthropological Quarterly* 60 (3): 124.

Robertson, Jennifer. 1988. "Furusato Japan: The Culture and Politics of Nostalgia" *International Journal of Politics, Culture, and Society* 1 (4): 494–518.

Robertson, Jennifer. 1998. "It takes a village: internationalization and nostalgia in postwar Japan." In *mirror of modernity: Invented traditions of modern Japan*, edited by Stephen Vlastos, 110–129. University of California Press.

Rosaldo, Renato, and Kirin Narayan. 1993. "Introduction: Creativity in anthropology." In *Creativity/Anthropology*, edited by Smadar Lavie, Kirin Narayan, and Renato Rosaldo, 1–8. Ithaca, NY: Cornell University Press.

Rosenberger, Nancy. 2017. "Young Organic Farmers in Japan: Betting on Lifestyle, Locality, and Livelihood." *Contemporary Japan* 29 (1): 14–30.

Rosenberger, Nancy, and Ayumi Sugimoto. 2022. "Agriculture Corporations in Rural Japan: Fractured Mirrors of Past, Present and Future." *Asian Anthropology* 21 (1): 24–38.

Ryang, Sonia. 2004. *Japan and National Anthropology: A Critique*. London and New York: Routledge Curzon.

Sasajima, Hideaki. 2012. "Creative Cities and Neo-Liberalism: The Idea of 'Entrepreneurial City' by David Harvey." *The Annual Reports of the Tohoku Sociological Society* 41: 79–89.

Sasaki, Masayuki. 1997. "*Sōzō toshi no keizaigaku*. [The Economy of Creative City]." Keisō Shobō.

Sasaki, Masayuki. 2006. "*Nihon niokeru sōzō toshi no riron to seisakuteki kadai* [The theory of Creative City and its political issues in Japan]." Osaka City University Urban Research Plaza

Sasaki, Masayuki, Sachiko Kawaida, and Hagihara Mawaya. 2014. "*Sōzō nōson: kaso wo kuriētibu ni ikiru senryaku* [Creative Farming Villages: Strategies to Live Depopulation Creatively]." Kyoto: Gakuei Shuppansha.

Sasaki, Masayuki, Sachiko Kawaida, and Hagihara Mawaya. 2015. "*Changjonongchoneul dijainhara: nongchoneul doesallineun changjojeollyak* [Design creative village: Creative Strategies to revitalize villages]." Misewoom Publisher.

Sasaki, Nobuo. 2015. "Regional Revitalization: Another Perspective." *The News Japan*: Chuo Online, February 23, 2015. http://www.yomiuri.co.jp/adv/chuo/dy/opinion/20150223.html. (accessed 28 August 2020).

Sasayama City Hall. 2016. *Sasayama shi sōgō senryaku* [Sasayama General Strategy]. Sōzō toshi ka.

Sasayama City Hall. 2018. *Dai ikkai Nihon isan sōzō toshi suishin iinkai kaigiroku* [The Report of the first Japan Heritage Creative City Promotion Assembly]. Sōzō toshi ka.

Sasayama City Hall. 2019a. *Kōhō Tamba Sasayama* [Tamba Sasayama Public Relations]. Tamba sasayama shi kikaku sōmubu sōmuka.

Sasayama City Hall. 2019b. *Tamba Sasayama: City of Crafts and Folk Arts Monitoring Report*. Sōzō toshi ka.

Sasayama City Hall. 2021. *Kōhō Tamba Sasayama* [Tamba Sasayama Public Relations]. Tamba sasayama shi kikaku sōmubu sōmuka.

Sayre, Robert, and Michael Löwy. 2019. *Romantic anti-capitalism and nature: The enchanted garden*. Abingdon and New York: Routledge.

Schrade, Anna. 2019. "Depopulation, Abandoned Houses and Entrepreneurship: How Rural Communities in Hyogo Prefecture Try to Revitalise Their Locality." *Sanken ronshu. The review of economics and business management* 46: 13–23.

Sennett, Richard. 2008. *The Craftsman*. London: Penguin Books.

Sennett, Richard. 2018. *Building and Dwelling: Ethics for the City*. Allen Lane.

Shimoda, Hikaru. 2013. "Memorializing the Spirit of Wit and Grit." In *Japan since 1945: From Postwar to Post-Bubble*, edited by Christopher Gerteis and Timothy George, 242–256. London and New York: Bloomsbury.

Singleton, John. 1989. "Japanese folkcraft pottery apprenticeship: Cultural patterns of an educational institution." In *Apprenticeship*, edited by Michael William Coy, 14–30.

Solomon, Joshua Lee. 2017. *The Stink of the Earth: Reorienting Discourses of Tsugaru, Furusato, and Place*. PhD diss., The University of Chicago.

Song, Jiyeoun. 2015. "Japan's Regional Inequality in Hard Times." *Pacific Focus* 30 (1): 126–149.

Soper, Kate. 2020. *Post-Growth Living: For an Alternative Hedonism*. Verso.

Sorge, Antonio, and Jonathan Padwe. 2015. "The Abandoned Village? Introduction to the Special Issue." *Critique of Anthropology* 35 (3): 235–247.

Stasch, Rupert. 2010. "The Category of 'village' in Melanesian Social Worlds: Some Theoretical and Methodological Possibilities." *Paideuma* 56: 41–62.

Stasch, Rupert. 2017. "Afterword: Village space and the experience of difference and hierarchy between normative orders." *Critique of Anthropology* 37 (4): 440–456.

Sugimoto, Katsuo. 1969. *Tamba no kōgama*. [Ancient Tamba Kilns]. Kōbe, Japan: Hyōgoken Tōgeikan.

Sugimoto, Yoshio. 1999. "Making Sense of Nihonjinron." *Thesis Eleven* 57: 81–96.

Sugiyama, Takeshi. 2015. "Conceptual Examination of 'Creative Villages': A Geographical Approach." *Human Geography* 67 (1): 20–40.

Sugiyama, Takeshi. 2020. *Jisedai ni tsunagu komyunithiron no seishin to chirigaku*. [The Ethos and Geography of the Next Generation of Community Theory]." Bookway.

Suzuki, Ayako. 2015. "Young Japanese men's transnational mobility: A case study in Dublin." *Asian Anthropology* 14 (3): 235–248.

Tachibana, Akira. 2022. "Consideration on Regional Resilience Centered on Pottery Associations in Ceramic Cities in Covid19-Crisis: From a Survey of the Tamba-Sasayama Model and the Tokoname Model." *Journal of the Faculty of Sociology at the Yamato University Veride* 1: 9–23.

Takaharu, K. (2007). The Great Heisei Consolidation: A Critical Review. *Social Science Japan* September: 7–11.

Takahashi, Yasuo, Hiroyuki Kubota, Sawako Shigeto, Takahiro Yoshida, and Yoshiki Yamagata. 2021. "Diverse values of urban-to-rural migration: A case study of Hokuto City, Japan." *Journal of Rural Studies* 87: 292–299.

Takeda, Shunsuke. 2020. "Fluidity in Rural Japan: How Lifestyle Migration and Social Movements Contribute to the Preservation of Traditional Ways of Life on Iwashima." In *Japan's New Ruralities: Coping with Decline in the Periphery*, edited by Wolfram Manzenreiter, Ralph Lützeler, and Sebastian Polak-Rottman, 196–211. London and New York: Routledge.

Takeyasu, Hideko. 2007. "*'Sue no sato' Tachikui no genjō to kasseika: chiiki shakai no shiten kara*. [The current state and revitalization of 'Sue no sato' Tachikui: from the perspective of the local society]." *Humanities and Sciences* 22: 58–63.

Tanikawa, Chiho, and Masaya Nakatsuka. 2020. "Geographical Location Pattern of Immigrants' Entrepreneurship in Rural Area: A Case Study on Tambasasayama City, Hyogo Prefecture." *Papers on Environmental Information Science* 34: 127–132.

Thompson, Christopher. 2004. "You are your house: The construction and continuity of family and identity using yagō in a Japanese suburban farming community." *Social Science Japan Journal* 7 (1): 61–81.

Traphagan, John. 1998. "Reasons for gateball participation among older Japanese." *Journal of Cross-Cultural Gerontology* 13 (2): 159–175.

Traphagan, John. 2017. "Entrepreneurs in Rural Japan: Gender, Blockage, and the Pursuit of Existential Meaning." *Asian Anthropology* 16 (2): 77–94.

Traphagan, John. 2018. "Empty Houses, Abandoned Graves: Negative Population Growth and New Ideas in Neorural Japan." *Brown Journal of World Affairs*, xxiv(2): 161–174.

Traphagan, John. 2020. *Cosmopolitan Rurality, Depopulation, and Entrepreneurial Ecosystems in 21st-Century Japan*. Amherst, New York: Cambria Press.

Troy Chen, Zhen. 2018. "Policy, Locality and Networks in a Cultural and Creative Countryside: The Case of Jingdezhen, China." In *Crafting Economies: Contemporary Cultural Economies of the Handmade*, edited by Susan Luckman and Nicola Thomas, 150–161. Bloomsbury Publishing.

Tsing, Anna Lowenhaupt. 2000. "Inside the Economy of Appearances." *Public Culture* 12 (1): 115–144.

Tuckett, Anna. 2015. "Strategies of Navigation: migrants' everyday encounters with Italian immigration bureaucracy." *The Cambridge Journal of Anthropology* 33 (1): 113–128.

UNCTAD. 2010. *Creative Economy: A Feasible Development Option*.

Vasantkumar, Chris. 2017. "From World Cities to World Sites: Strategic Ruralism and the Case for an Anthropology of Actually Existing Connectivity." *Critique of Anthropology* 37 (4): 364–382.

Weber, Max. 1978 (1968). *Economy and Society*. University of California Press.

Wilf, Eitan. 2020. "To go with the free information flow: problems and contradictions in macro-level neoliberal theories and their translation to micro-level business innovation strategies." *Social Anthropology* 28 (1): 10–13.

Wilson, Geoff. 2001. "There and Back Again? Exploring the (Un) Changed Natural and Mental Landscapes of European Agriculture." *Transactions of the Institute of British Geographers* 26 (1): 77–102.

Woods, Michael. 2007. "Engaging the Global Countryside: Globalization, Hybridity and the Reconstitution of Rural Place." *Progress in Human Geography* 31 (4): 485–507.

Woods, Michael. 2010. "Performing Rurality and Practising Rural Geography." *Progress in Human Geography* 34 (6): 835–846.

Woods, Michael. 2011. *Rural*. Routledge.

Woods, Michael. 2012. "Creative Ruralities." Presented at the Creativity on the Edge Symposium, National University of Ireland Galway, June 2012. https://www.global-rural.org/wp-content/uploads/2018/11/Creative-Ruralities.pdf

Yabūchi, Kiyoshi. 1955. "*Tachikui kama no kenkyū: gijutsu, seikatsu, ningen*. [A study of Tachikui kiln: technology, livelihood, human]." Tōkyō: Kōseisha kōseikaku.

Yamamoto, Midori. 1992. "Place names and the rediscovery of former landscapes in Izumo city and Hikawa town, Japan." MA diss., The University of British Columbia.

Yanagi, Muneyoshi. 1956. *Tamba no kotō* [The old ceramics of Tamba]. Tōkyō: Nihonmingeikan.

Yoshimi, Shun'ya. 2009. *The Postwar Society [Posuto sengo shakai]*. Tokyo: Iwanami shoten.

Zollet, Simona, and Meng Qu. 2023. Urban-to-rural lifestyle migrants in peripheral Japanese island communities: Balancing quality of life expectations with reality in *Rural quality of life*, edited by Pia Heike Johansen, Anne Tietjen, Evald Bundgård Iversen, Henrik Lauridsen Lolle, and Jens Kaae Fisker, 74–93. Manchester University Press.

Index

Pages in *italics* refer to figures, pages in **bold** refer to tables, and pages followed by "n" refer to notes.